TWENTIETH CENTURY VIEWS

The aim of this series is to present the best in
contemporary critical opinion on major authors,
providing a twentieth century perspective on
their changing status in an era of profound
revaluation.

Maynard Mack, *Series Editor*
Yale University

CHEKHOV

A COLLECTION OF CRITICAL ESSAYS

Edited by

Robert Louis Jackson

Prentice-Hall, Inc.   A SPECTRUM BOOK *Englewood Cliffs, N.J.*

To my wife Leslie

Contents

Reflections on Chekhov

—O frati—dissi—che per cento milia
    perigli siete giunti all'occidente,
    a questa tanto picciola vigilia
de' vostri sensi ch'è del rimanente
    non vogliate negar l'esperienza,
    di retro al sol, del mondo senza gente!
Considerate la vostra semenza:
    fatti non foste a viver come bruti,
    ma per seguir virtute e conoscenza.

                Dante Alighieri: *Inferno*, Canto XXVI

Introduction:
Perspectives on Chekhov

by Robert Louis Jackson

There is a striking disjunction between the image we have of Chekhov the man and the image we obtain of him, at least on first glance, through his stories and plays; between the ebullient, gregarious, and strong-willed man of action (who erected a monument to Peter the Great in Taganrog), driven by an insatiable need for movement and championing everywhere the free spirit of man, and the creator of a dreary world without exit, a subculture drained of vitality and inhabited by pseudo-tragic, sometimes ridiculous, but always pathetic and sad people.

The notion here of two Chekhovs, of course, is an arbitrary one. Chekhov, for all his cheerfulness, was of a skeptical, perhaps even of an innately melancholy nature,[1] while Chekhov the writer hardly can be identified with his weak-willed, whining characters. "His world view is entirely his own, firmly formed, humane, but without sentimentality, free of all tendencies," wrote his publisher A. S. Suvorin as early as 1889. "In him there is none of that pessimism and 'world anguish' which distinguish the majority of young talents." Chekhov does not like "either phrases or whining or despair." Yet there are contrasts, contradictions, paradoxes in the total portrait of Chekhov, and they deserve emphasis if only because they have evoked in the past, and continue to evoke, conflicting images.

We speak of Chekhov as the creator of a dreary, sad, often mediocre human type. There is no question, of course, that such people as we find in Chekhov's works really existed, that, indeed, the Chekhovian type is not too different from his real, though watered-down counterpart in the relatively quiescent period of the 1880s and early 1890s. Yet what

---

[1] The writer I. Bunin, while emphasizing in his memoirs Chekhov's love of life, his vitality and thirst for joy, speaks nonetheless of his "innate melancholia," the "sad, hopeless foundation of his character." For a portrait of Chekhov which stresses his positive, energetic, fun-loving nature, see Kornei Chukovsky's engaging study, *Chekhov the Man.* Translated by Pauline Rose. London, 1945.

Dostoevsky told his young friend, E. N. Opochinin, is entirely true of Chekhov: "The writer (the poet) creates life, a life in such full amplitude as did not exist before him." Chekhov's works live because of this enlargement of life, that is, because of that poetic generalization which transforms the individual and contemporary into the typical and universal. The Chekhovian type is superior to his prototype; he represents a profound statement on certain aspects of the human condition. The often perceptive writer and critic D. S. Merezhkovsky (1865-1941) was simply wrong when he wrote in an essay on Chekhov and Gorky[2] that Chekhov was "in the highest degree national, but not universal, in the highest degree contemporary, but not historical," that the Chekhovian environment was but "a congealed moment, a dead point of Russian contemporaneity without any connection with world history and world culture."

The inner meaning of the underlying Chekhovian theme, Kornei Chukovsky suggests, centers on fated clashes between strong-willed and weak-willed people. One might give a slightly different emphasis to this thought and say that a fundamental philosophical interest of Chekhov is the relationship, most often tragic, between will and environment, freedom and necessity, man's character and his fate. Chekhov's illumination of this central theme in Western literature is sufficient alone to give him a permanent place in the first ranks of writers. He explores this theme, moreover, through images not of heroic or unusual people, but of minor, pedestrian personalities, people who have failed to realize themselves.

Without doubt it is in Chekhov's philosophical resolution of this theme of man's character and his fate (something quite different, of course, from the unhappy endings of his heroes' endeavors) that we must seek the unity of our two initial impressions or images of Chekhov: the positive and voluntaristic Chekhov, holding to a faith in human potentiality and progress (the man with the little gavel in "Gooseberries," 1898), and the realist Chekhov, lucidly disclosing man's tragic actuality. The much-sought "point of view" of Chekhov is certainly to be found at the intersection of these two lines.

Since the appearance of Chekhov's early stories, criticism has been preoccupied with the question: Where is Chekhov in his works? What is his point of view and how does he stand in relation to his heroes, their moods and ideas? Much of Soviet Russian criticism since World

[2] Cf. D. S. Merezhkovskij, "Chekhov i Gor'kij," *Polnoe sobranie sochinenij* (St. Petersburg, 1911), XI, 39-92.

War II finds Chekhov's locus in the positive ideas and ideals which may be deduced from his works, in the "teaching" of Chekhov's art. Russian criticism as a whole, however, has never subscribed to the image of an optimistic or didactic Chekhov.

We may ignore those early critics whose mediocrity was offended by Chekhov and who believed that he wrote "nonsense," "rubbish," "a vile fiction about life and people."

Most discussions of early criticism of Chekhov contain a reference to N. K. Mikhailovsky (1842-1904), a prominent populist writer and thinker who saw in the Russian intelligentsia a "light in the night" and who insisted that "in addition to the need for knowledge there was a need for moral judgment." In an article, "About Fathers and Children and about Mr. Chekhov," published in 1890,[3] the critic recognized Chekhov's singular talent, but was distressed over its lack of tendency, its "cold-blooded," empirical approach to reality. Chekhov, he wrote, is "about the only really talented belles-lettrist in the literary generation [the 1880s] which can say of itself that for it 'only that reality exists in which it is condemned to live' and that 'the ideals of the fathers and grand-fathers have no power over us.'" And Mikhailovsky finds nothing more pathetic than "this talent which is being lost in vain." Almost nostalgically, he cites the talented writers who were shaped morally and intellectually in the idealistic and radical ethos of the 1840s and 1860s (Saltykov-Shchedrin, Ostrovsky, Dostoevsky, Turgenev) and notes with satisfaction their "definite, finished physiognomies" and their defined "mutual relations with the reader." These writers had a "constant link" with the reader. Not so Chekhov. He himself does not live in his works, but seems to stroll past life picking out at random now this and now that. "But just why this and not that? Why that and not something else?" Mikhailovsky is particularly pleased by Chekhov's "A Boring Story" (1889)[4] wherein the main character, a professor, frankly confesses that "a general idea" is lacking to his life. He sees in this admission of the hero a crucial confession, also, of Chekhov, and one which illuminates the weakness of his artistic method. "For all his talent Mr. Chekhov is not a writer who independently analyzes his material and selects from the point of view of some general idea, but from some kind of almost mechanical apparatus." Still, "A Boring Story" is evidence of the birth of an "anguish for 'that which is called a general idea or a god of a living man'"; it contains the author's pain, and even if the author can-

---

[3] Cf. N. K. Mikhailovskij, "Ob otsakh i detjakh i o g. Chekhove," in *Literaturno-kriticheskie stat'i* (Moscow, 1957), pp. 594-607.

[4] Also translated as "A Dreary Story."

not recognize the general ideas of the fathers and grandfathers as his own, or work out his own general idea, Mikhailovsky concludes, "then let him at least be a poet of anguish for the general idea and of torment-ing consciousness of its need. In this case he will not have lived in vain and will leave his mark in literature." Mikhailovsky strikes what will remain a central note in Russian criticism. More than thirty years later the cultural commissar of the Bolsheviks, A. V. Lunacharsky, will posit "anguish" as the central element in Chekhov's art. "In Chekhov him-self, unquestionably, this anguish lived consciously."

Mikhailovsky's own anguish over Chekhov's talent of course evokes a smile today. His criticism, in the final analysis, is social: it is the expres-sion of an intensely civic-minded generation which is moving off the stage of history and is frantically, but vainly, seeking a successor in the generation of the 1880s. Yet it must be said that Mikhailovsky touches upon fundamental aspects of Chekhov's art and talent. His reference to Chekhov's seemingly random choice of material and details from reality points to his distinctive impressionistic style (noted by Merezhkovsky, Tolstoy, and others at the time). The notion of Chekhov as an "impres-sionist," though it has received little emphasis in Soviet criticism, is an established idea of Russian critics.

While Mikhailovsky and other early critics were in error when they accused Chekhov of social apathy or indifference, Chekhov was indeed not "living in" his works in the same way as a Tolstoy or Dostoevsky; he reveals, unquestionably, a certain aloofness, a kind of principled ob-jectivity, a deliberate restraint in setting forth his own point of view. Chekhov's remark to Ivan Bunin that one had to be ice cold before sitting down to write is indicative of his writer's stance. Though in Chekhov there is deep conviction and a firm moral pivot, there is none of the unsettling emotionality, the sometimes uncontrollable didacticism and moral passion, the striving to play the social historian or critic, the enjoyment of the fray, or the tendency toward radical solutions which in one measure or another strongly mark the art of Dostoevsky, Tolstoy, Nekrasov, Saltykov-Shchedrin, or even of Turgenev.

Chekhov did not wish to be enmeshed in the party programs and con-flicts of his time; he sought freedom from sterile and binding ideologies. He writes A. N. Pleshcheev, October 4, 1888:

> I fear those who seek tendencies between the lines and who without fail wish to see me as a liberal or a conservative. I am not a liberal, not a con-servative, not a gradualist, not a monk, and not an indifferentist. I would like to be a free artist—and that's all, and the only thing I regret is that

God has not given me the forces to be one. I hate lies and violence in all their forms. . . . Pharisaism, stupidity, and arbitrariness dwell not only in the houses of merchants and in lockups; I see them in science, in literature, among the youth. . . . I regard trademarks and labels as prejudices. My holy of holies is the human body, health, mind, talent, inspiration, love, and absolute freedom—freedom from violence and lies, and in whatever forms these last two may be expressed. Here you have the program to which I would adhere if I were a great artist.

More than fifty years ago the Russian critic and cultural historian D. N. Ovsyaniko-Kulikovsky noted in an extended essay on Chekhov[5] that the writer's featuring of *mind, talent* and *inspiration, health* and the *human body,* as a "program," as things important in themselves, as cultural values which have a social as well as a personal significance, gave expression to something vital that was ripening in Russian social consciousness. Whereas, he noted, people in the 1870s examined these values and asked: "What cause, what ideas and ideals do they serve?" in the 1880s one found a recognition of everything that goes under the notion of "cultural well-being." This turn toward the problem of general culture was accompanied by a renewed interest in science.

"Culture with all its great values," N. Berdyaev observed, "is middle of the road [*seredina*]; there is no end in it, no limit for its achievements." On the other hand, he continues, the apocalyptic striving—present in Nietzsche and, in the highest degree, in Dostoevsky—inheres in the crisis of culture. Russian antipathy to middle-of-the-road culture, according to Berdyaev, finds its expression in Dostoevsky.[6] Whether or not Berdyaev is correct in regarding hostility to middle-of-the-road culture as a "Russian trait," there is no question that Chekhov's art and outlook is deeply antipathetic to the apocalyptic mood and represents a radical reaffirmation of the values of middle-of-the-road culture. In Chekhov this reaffirmation does not represent a compromise with reactionary culture or milieu, nor does it imply an impoverished sense of the ideal or a lowering of moral criteria. Rather it represents a turn toward the practical tasks of culture in the immediate life and needs of man and society. Dostoevsky's suggestion that without achievement of the religious ideal there can be no just society, that brotherhood must precede bread, while an expression of ultimate truth, nonetheless conceals elements of sociological sterility and reaction. Chekhov—in whom (as in Dostoevsky) "aesthetic pleasure . . . is harnessed precisely with

[5] Cf. D. N. Ovsjaniko-Kulikovskij, "Chekhov," in *Istorija russkoj intelligentsii,* III, *Sobranie sochinenij* (St. Petersburg, 1911), IX, 45-128.

[6] N. Berdjaev, *Mirosozertsanie Dostoevskogo* (Prague, 1923), pp. 233-34.

the perception of pain and sadness" [7]—also has a vision of the ideal, but he is deeply concerned with the real personal and social avenues toward the achievement of the ideal. It is not surprising that moral and religious teachings, which stand in the foreground of the art of Tolstoy and Dostoevsky, take a second place in Chekhov, giving way to a pronounced rational and scientific outlook. Though neither a radical nor a revolutionary in temperament or ideology, Chekhov is receptive to radical social change.

In retrospect one may recognize that one of the central actions of Chekhov's art in Russian literature and culture was to provide an antidote to the moral and spiritual extremism which is felt so strongly in Dostoevsky and Tolstoy, to reassert (entirely, of course, in his own idiom and form) the strong Pushkin elements of rationality, economy, measure, and sobriety. Pushkin and Chekhov: in both, objectivity and classical restraint are tense with ideas and broad social and philosophical implication. Both, essentially rationalists and of a skeptical turn of mind, react strongly to an overemotional, excited romantic ethos (whether that of a sentimental Karamzin or a late romantic Dostoevsky). Neither Chekhov nor Pushkin makes excessive demands upon man. Man as we find him in Pushkin or Chekhov is revealed in a light that is free of romantic distortion. Lucid realism always blends with a rich but not sentimental or prettifying compassion.

Chekhov's art may be seen, finally, as representing implicitly an arbitration of the gigantic conflicts that split the Russian literary and cultural world into two entities—that of the radical democrats, the revolutionary activists, with their strongly rationalist, materialist, and fundamentally antiaesthetic program, and that of such writers as Turgenev, Tolstoy, Dostoevsky, Leskov, and others who (for all the intensity and diversity in their social and political viewpoints) remain faithful to the artistic vision; in the final analysis, these writers chose to give expression to the entire complex human, social, and historical dilemma imposed upon nineteenth century Russian man. In Chekhov the scientific and rationalist view is reasserted, but freed from that moral utopianism and "rational egoism" which Dostoevsky criticized so sharply in his *Notes from the Underground*. Chekhov is typically himself when he observes, in connection with his early interest in Tolstoyanism, that he had been impressed "not by the basic propositions, which I had been familiar with even before, but the Tolstoyan manner of expressing himself, the rationality and, probably, a kind of hypnotism. But now something protests in

[7] N. Nevedomskij, "Bez kryl'ev," in *Chekhovskij jubilejnyj sbornik* (Moscow, 1910), p. 112.

me: rationality and truth tell me that in electricity and steam there is more love for man than in chastity and vegetarianism."

Yet faith in science and reason never led Chekhov to view reality smugly or in any way to simplify the complexity of man. He wrote Pleshcheev April 9, 1889, apropos of work on a story, that he wanted "truthfully to depict life and in passing to show how much this life deviates from a norm." He then added: "This norm is not known to me, as it is not known to any of us. We all know what is a dishonorable act, but what is honor—we do not know." For Dostoevsky the norm is known: it finds embodiment first of all in the image of Christ; life is meaningful to the extent that man strives to imitate the perfection of this image. For Chekhov, too, the norm is something that is sought, but as Ovsyaniko-Kulikovsky noted, it is not something that is given beforehand, not something established *a priori* by philosophical or theological means. Chekhov's vision of man's striving is nonreligious, almost bleak. Man is alone. Chekhov wrote S. P. Diaghilev on December 30, 1902:

> Contemporary culture is the beginning of work in the name of a great future, work which will continue, perhaps for tens of thousands of years more, so that in the distant future mankind will know the truth of the real God, i.e., not guess at it, not seek it in Dostoevsky, but know clearly, as one knows that twice two is four. Contemporary culture is the beginning of the work, while the religious movement of which we were speaking is a carry-over, already almost the end of something that is spent, or is near-spent.

Apropos of these lines Merezhkovsky sadly affirmed in his essay on Chekhov and Gorky cited earlier that Chekhov here signs "the death warrant not only of the contemporary religious movement in Russia, but of all Christianity, of the whole religious life of mankind," that he "breaks the living link between the past and future world culture" and in essence turns Christianity and contemporary culture into enemies. Merezhkovsky points to Chekhov's story "The Student" (1894) as evidence that Chekhov did not in fact draw such conclusions. Yet it is true that these lines reveal a stress sharply antithetical to that of a Dostoevsky or Vladimir Soloviev. One is inclined to agree with the editor and historian F. D. Batyushkov, who noted shortly after Chekhov's death in connection with Chekhov's letter to Diaghilev: "These lines eloquently testify to Chekhov's unlimited faith in the power of knowledge, in the infinitude of science, and he did not conceive of any other religion, any other 'real God' except that which confronts an unprejudiced reason, one enriched by knowledge." [8] Later on in the 1920s the noted French

[8] F. D. Batjushkov, "A. P. Chekhov po vospominanijam o nem i pis'mam," in *Na pamjatnik Chekhovu* (St. Petersburg, 1906), p. 28.

critic Charles du Bos clearly perceived Chekhov's philosophical temperament when he wrote in his journal that he wanted to show in his
book on Chekhov "what man can achieve without religion and, more
subtly still, without any spiritual heroics."

The view of Chekhov as a pessimist is deeply rooted in Chekhov
criticism. It stems in part, at least, from the tendency to identify Chekhov
closely with the moods and heroes of his works. The very descriptions
of Chekhov in prerevolutionary and early Soviet Russian criticism invoke
an image of a gloomy writer: "a singer of twilight moods," "a poet of
superfluous people," "a sick talent," "a poet of anguish" (Mikhailovsky),
an expresser of "world sorrow" (Yu. Aleksandrovich), an "optimopessi-
mist" (S. Bulgakov), "a poet of the stagnant years" (P. D. Boborykin),
"a poet of our ruin" (S. Andreevich), a writer of disintegration (Merezhkovsky compares *The Three Sisters* and *The Cherry Orchard* to Dostoevsky's grotesque tale "Bobok"), "the last singer of disintegrating trifles"
(Zinaida Gippius), a writer characterized by a "heroic pessimism" (V.
Volzhsky), "a writer who takes the ulcers of society from his own soul
and depicts them extraordinarily beautifully" (A. V. Lunacharsky), a
writer who in his mature work "steadily distills a sweet and comforting
decoction of despair which will produce a happy and 'drowsy numb-
ness' " (D. S. Mirsky).

Perhaps the most impressive exponent of the view of Chekhov as a
melancholy and destructive writer is the Russian philosopher Shestov
(1866-1938). In a remarkably provocative, though one-sided essay written
immediately following Chekhov's death, entitled "Creation from the
Void," [9] Shestov flatly declares of the writer whom he places far ahead
of Maupassant and at the peak of European literature: "Chekhov was
a singer of hopelessness. Stubbornly, dolefully, monotonously, in the
course of his literary career of almost twenty-five years Chekhov did only
one thing: in one way or another he smashed human hopes. Herein, in
my view, is the essence of his creative work." All that Chekhov touched,
Shestov believed, withered and died: art, science, love, inspiration,
ideals. Significantly, Shestov is not concerned with Chekhov as he emerges
in his letters or in the memoirs of many of those who knew him. Like
Mikhailovsky, he concentrates his analysis upon the play *Ivanov* (1887-
1889) and "A Boring Story" (1889); and like the populist critic he views
these works as "strongly autobiographical in character."

[9] Cf. Leon Shestov, *Chekhov and Other Essays.* New Introduction by Sidney Monas
(Ann Arbor: University of Michigan Press, 1966), pp. 3-60. All citations in my discussion are from the Russian.

He compares Chekhov to Ivanov as one who has "overstrained himself": from his former mood, "cheerful and joyful," Chekhov turned into a "gloomy, somber person, a 'criminal' frightening with his words even experienced and tried people." In "A Boring Story," according to Shestov, Chekhov turns his back on all ideas and world views, metaphysical and positivist. In the end, he "completely emancipated himself from all kinds of ideas and even lost a sense of connection between living events." Shestov believes that *The Seagull* (1896) is a significant example of this phenomenon. "The only real hero of Chekhov is the despairing man." The element of destruction is all-conquering in Chekhov and in the end "the Chekhovian hero is left to himself. He has nothing, he must create all himself. And thus 'creation from the void,' or more correctly the possibility of creation from the void, is the only problem with which Chekhov is capable of occupying and inspiring himself."

We may note that Shestov limits himself to a close analysis of only three or four of Chekhov's works—an unsettling fact in the face of his bold generalizations. Even apart from this, however, much of his thinking is questionable. The view of a "cheerful and joyful" early Chekhov is difficult to accept. As Dmitri Chizhevsky observes, a reading of Chekhov's early humoresques is suited more to the "evocation of a melancholy than of a humorous mood." On the other hand, precisely in the decade and a half following "A Boring Story" and *Ivanov*, strongly affirmative notes may be heard in many of Chekhov's works. Certainly one of the weakest links in Shestov's approach is his almost complete identification of Chekhov with the Chekhovian hero and mood. Despite the fact that the professor undoubtedly gives expression to Chekhov's own yearning for a "general idea" and voices Chekhov's opinions on many subjects (the theater, need for reforms in the education of women, faith in science), he is not Chekhov any more than Dostoevsky is Ivan or Alyosha Karamazov. In the representation of the professor's bankruptcy and in the analysis of its causes Chekhov maintains his aesthetic distance.

Yet though Shestov dramatically overstates his case (wherein lies its special appeal), he indirectly calls attention to a decisive feature in Chekhov's developing world view when he notes that "the Chekhovian hero is left to himself. He has nothing, he must create everything himself." It would be misreading Chekhov's artistic philosophy to view his heroes, retroactively, as existential types (though Uncle Vanya, without any prodding by the author or ratiocination, is brought to the threshold of a consciousness of the absurd). Yet it is certainly true that we may perceive in many of Chekhov's characterizations of his heroes—in his rejection of religious, metaphysical, political, or purely ethical teachings as foundations for a world view—a search for a philosophy whereby man can exist *on his own,* in lucid and creative confrontation with the harsh realities of his fate. It may have been this aspect of Chekhov's world view, this alarming perspective, which caused even so fervent an admirer of Chekhov as Charles du Bos ultimately to draw back, to stake out "a solitary area of self-examination"—the problem of God—in which Chekhov failed to satisfy him, and to suggest that nowadays (1927) Chekhov "would no longer maintain just any kind of scientific approach." Shestov, then, touches on something central to Chekhov's world view: man must create everything himself, must seek out—in the words of the professor in "A Boring Story"—the "general idea or god of a living man." This may be a bleak, even tragic perspective, but it is for Chekhov the path of the free man.

A concept that comes to mind in connection with Chekhov's illumination of man is certainly that of tragedy. M. Kurdyumov, the author of an interesting study on the religious element in Chekhov's art,[10] is entirely correct in affirming that Chekhov's "chief theme was the tragic fate of man in the world." But in her conception of man's tragic fate Kurdyumov's point of departure is similar to that of Shestov. The most original and significant feature of Chekhov's work, Shestov believed, related to Chekhov's loss of a sense of the connections among life's happenings. The basis of action in *The Seagull* is not the logical development of passions, not inevitable connections between the preceding and the following, but "naked ostentatiously unconcealed chance. . . . In everything and everywhere autocratic chance reigns, this time boldly issuing a challenge to all world views."

In Kurdyumov's interpretation of the Chekhovian universe, the life of man is tragic because life is given and taken regardless of his will and because "blind chance" reigns to a great extent over his life. The thread of personal fate is complexly interwoven with the threads of environment, education, heredity, and the thousands of "trivial incidents" (the phrase is from Chekhov's story, "A Trivial Incident," 1886) which determine the life of man, together with one's own and others' sins and mistakes. ("The infinite insurmountable identity of existence," wrote D. S. Mirsky in reference to what he considered the "unqualified determinism" that reigns in Chekhov's world.[11]) Chekhovian tragedy, then, in Kurdyumov's view, bears witness to a senseless universe in which

[10] M. Kurdjumov, *Serdtse smjatennoe* (Paris, 1934).

[11] D. S. Mirsky, "Chekhov and the English," *The Monthly Criterion* (1927), No. 6, pp. 296, 298.

godlessness deprives human existence of all meaning and justification.

Kurdyumov argues from the standpoint of a Christian believer. The tragedy of the Chekhovian hero is for the writer an extension of Chekhov's own tragedy: the fact that he stands only on the threshold of a Christian outlook. "The humanistic world view of Chekhov did not reconcile itself with his intuitive Christian apprehension of the world."

There is no doubt that Chekhov deeply empathized with—and could give embodiment to—the Christian ethos (to have an un-Christian outlook, after all, does not imply one that is anti-Christian). But to posit a conflict between humanism and a Christian intuitive world view in Chekhov, to conceive of the tragedy of the Chekhovian hero in a Christian perspective, violates both the maturity and the integrity of Chekhov's humanistic outlook; above all, it obscures the conscious and heroic content of Chekhov's humanistic world view. Chekhov's world view, it cannot be overemphasized, is free of the problem which transfixes so many of Dostoevsky's heroes: if there is no God, there is no virtue and, consequently, no meaning in the universe.

Chekhov's story "Typhus" (1887) provides evidence of his deep awareness of, and troubled preoccupation with, the element of accident and chance in human fate. Yet in his work at large, Chekhov's view of tragedy extends far beyond the notion of man as the victim of blind chance. The notion of determinism, of course, is inherent in all forms of scientific work; and certainly Chekhov's own involvement in a scientific discipline, as well as the influence of such contemporaries as Darwin, Claude Bernard, and Zola deepened his sense of the limits of human will in interaction with the *given*—the multiple and complex elements of reality. Chekhov unquestionably shares the view—expressed by Orlov in "An Anonymous Story" (1893)—that "in nature, in man's environment, nothing happens indifferently. Everything has reason and is necessary." Yet this is only half of the truth. Chekhov also recognizes (as Orlov does not) man's involvement in his own fate, his "guilt," his responsibility for his condition, and, therefore, his responsibility before the present which he is preparing for the future. This is the essential other half of the truth. "I believe both in the innate purposefulness and in the necessity of all that is going on around us," the narrator declares in "An Anonymous Story" in response to Orlov, to his attempt to seek some "objective," even "biological" rationale for the feebleness of his generation; "but what do I care for this necessity. . . . One wants to live independently of future generations. . . . Life is given but once and one would like to live it boldly, intelligently, beautifully. One would like to play a prominent, independent, generous role, one would like to make history so that those same generations will not have the right to say of each of us: they were an insignificant lot, or even something worse than that." Man's tragedy, for Chekhov, lies primarily not in any absolute helplessness before his fate, but in the fact that he is continually affirming fate's autonomy through abdication of his own responsibility.

In his later works Chekhov comes to grips with the notion of blind chance or "fate" as a rationale for passivity and inaction. In such works as "The Duel," "The Lady with the Pet Dog," "The Betrothed," and especially in *The Seagull,* he views man's interaction with reality as one which contains a creative potential. Chekhov stands with Sophocles, Shakespeare, and Dostoevsky in his mature view of man's fate, in his affirmation of the freedom as well as the limits of man confronting reality and himself.[12]

A great literary work (or body of works), like a Gothic cathedral, reveals different emphases according to the perspective from which it is viewed. The whole dynamics of a cathedral can be comprehended only in the abstract, that is, in movement through multiple perspectives. Yet the work of art is concrete; it is satisfying only when viewed from a single perspective. The history of Chekhov criticism is a history of "perspectives." Contemporaries of Chekhov were too close to him and to the Chekhovian environment. They tended to view Chekhov on the naturalistic level of life where his art *begins,* but where his heroes floundered and failed. There was no aesthetic distance between actor and audience, character and reader. Chekhov's *fin de siècle* theater audience was "onstage," and its critical reaction to Chekhov was often nervous and subjective. The spectator could empathize deeply with the elements of lyric despondency and nostalgic dream in Chekhov's art, or (even while empathizing) could criticize him for his "pessimism," his preoccupation with the depiction of a gray, toneless, hopeless life. Chekhov does not "dispel, but deepens the social gloom," wrote one conservative critic in 1901 who was distressed over what he considered Chekhov's one-sided depiction of reality in *The Three Sisters.* "Chekhov is so objective, so objective!" the

---

[12] Of course, as Richard B. Sewall has remarked in *The Vision of Tragedy* (New Haven and London: Yale University Press, 1962, p. 106), it is only "ideally" that tragedy reveals "simultaneously, in one complete action, man's total possibilities and his most grievous limitations—all that he should and can do as a creator of good, all that he does or fails to do or cannot do as a creature of fate, chance, or his own evil nature . . . the stress on one side or the other of the paradox of man differs from one tragedy to another." Chekhov's various stories and plays, insofar as they touch on the problem of man's fate, express different aspects of the paradox. A full assessment of the nature of Chekhov's "tragic vision," then, would have to rest on a thorough examination of the whole body of Chekhov's work.

radical A. V. Luncharsky wrote despairingly apropos of the same play at that time. "It is so clear that there is no place to break out into—so crushing, so stagnant is the milieu in which all sorts of slave-people are floundering about or lying inertly, that one is overcome by a frightful feeling. . . . We are awaiting impatiently for Chekhov . . . to show us man who *can* pierce the slime and emerge from the slough into fresh air, to show us the seeds of a new life."

Yet despite a certain nearsighted quality in prerevolutionary (and early postrevolutionary) criticism which stresses the somber colors in Chekhov, one cannot deny its contribution to an understanding of him. It is painfully sensitive to the poetry of grief in Chekhov's art; it is not at all inclined to underplay its elements of skepticism and despair. Despite a somewhat moodily obscure image of Chekhov, there is sometimes more of a sense of a whole, complex, struggling artistic consciousness in the prerevolutionary image of Chekhov than in the more polished image of the poet that we find in some of Soviet criticism since World War II.

Prerevolutionary Chekhov criticism and commentary, moreover, constitute a broad spectrum. The view of Chekhov as a pessimist or destroyer of values did not go unchallenged. The memoirs of writers who knew Chekhov (Gorky, Bunin, Korolenko, and others), as well as the publication of his letters, did much to dispel the notion of a gloomy Chekhov. A. S. Suvorin, as we have noted, early recognized that Chekhov's independence of thought and objectivity were "far from pessimism." Cultural historians and critics such as D. N. Ovsyaniko-Kulikovsky, F. D. Batyushkov, A. Izmailov, and others perceived the positive content of Chekhov's art and disputed the notion of pessimism in the writer. Leonid Grossman grasps the creative dialectic of Chekhov the man and poet in the final pages of his essay, "The Naturalism of Chekhov." In all his creative work, Grossman concludes, Chekhov confirms "the remarkable words of Beethoven—that the only heroism in the world is to see the world as it is, and still to love it."

"What Meaning Can Chekhov Have for Us?" is the title of an article written by A. V. Lunacharsky in 1924.[18] The very title suggests the problem which the "singer of the twilight" presented to the self-confident and optimistic ethos of the revolution. Lunacharsky himself offered no revolutionary outlook on Chekhov. Indeed, his view of Chekhov's art as a kind of "aesthetic sublimation" of the horrors of Russian reality did not open up perspectives for a radical revaluation of Chekhov. But his article

[18] A. V. Lunacharskij, "Chem mozhet byt' A. P. Chekhov dlja nas?" *Pechat' i revoljutsija* (1924), IV, 19-34.

was among a number which helped bring about a reexamination of the image of Chekhov inherited from the past.

The evolution of this image in the Soviet Union has proceeded under the impact of two forces. On the one hand, Soviet Chekhov criticism has represented a forceful elaboration and intensification of critical approaches already present or indicated in much prerevolutionary Russian criticism and commentary. On the other hand, the dramatic emphasis (particularly in post-World War II criticism) upon the positive ideas and content of Chekhov's thought and art has reflected the voluntaristic and activist ethos of Soviet culture. Such critics and scholars as S. D. Balukhaty, Yu. Sobolev, and A. Derman in the first decades of Soviet society, as well as A. Roskin, V. Yermilov, A. Skaftymov, and others more recently, have made outstanding contributions to Chekhov research, scholarship, and criticism. Their work directly and indirectly has stimulated much fresh thinking on Chekhov in the West.

This revaluation has emphasized the positive, life-affirming, idealistic elements in Chekhov's art. In analyses of Chekhov's prose and drama, Soviet criticism certainly has eradicated the view of Chekhov as an artist who simply gave expression to the aimless anguish of his epoch. It has insisted that a distinction be made between the point of view of Chekhov the artist and "Chekhovism," the moods and miasmas of his heroes, and has given much-needed emphasis to the critical and cognitive content of Chekhov's art. In this emphasis, however, content or meaning at times appears to reside in the didactic intentions of the artist (or in the words of this or that character) rather than to emerge from the poetic ensemble, whereas, in fact, poetry in a Chekhov work *is* meaning. The significance of the final episode in *The Three Sisters* lies not alone in the words of hope, but also in the music of despair; not just in the final line of the play (Olga's), "If we only knew, if we only knew," but in the painful dialectic which this line forms with the preceding line (Chebutykin's), "Ta-ra-ra-boom-de-ay. Sit on a curb I may. . . . It's all the same! It's all the same!" [14]

The "main content" of Chekhov's art, writes B. I. Aleksandrov in an essay, "Chekhov in Russian Criticism," is found not in his passive reflection of reality, but in the "active and destructive element (in respect to

---

[14] Chekhov's stage direction for the final scene of *The Three Sisters* in its original version—the removal of the dead body of Tusenbach, the bustle of the crowd about him, Kulygin "happy, smiling" etc.—points in its bitter (almost Brechtian) irony to the dialectic which is the core of Chekhov's poetic idea. Stanislavsky's reasons for ignoring this stage direction—with Chekhov's approval—are set forth in M. N. Stroeva's essay on the Moscow Art Theater's production of *The Three Sisters*. See pp. 121-135 in this collection.

the old world). Therefore, Chekhov belongs to us, to the people of the revolution, and not to the old bourgeois society overthrown by its forces." [15] V. Yermilov concludes his informative analysis of *The Three Sisters* with words that sum up the "activist" emphasis of Soviet Chekhov criticism since World War II. He cites an article by Lunacharsky in 1928 in which the latter recalls his despairing response to *The Three Sisters* in 1901, as well as a letter in that year from a student who had criticized him for it. "No, Anatoly Vasilevich," the student had written, "this play is instructive and calls for struggle." Yermilov remarks:

> Chekhov, too, wanted *The Three Sisters* to have an active impact upon the audience. Precisely for this reason, therefore, while grieving over the sad fate of his heroes, he condemned their weakness. Precisely for this reason he was terribly afraid of sentimentality, impotent tears, sighs, and so energetically insisted that he had "written a vaudeville." His whole play affirms the arrival in life of the kind of people who know no break between word and deed, who are alien to everything vain and petty and are capable of realizing the dream of universal happiness.[16]

But does the play in any sense affirm the arrival in Russian life of a new, ideal man? And is the "active" element of the play (for all Chekhov's ruthless exposé of a life based upon illusion, of weakness and vulgarity) *poetically* the predominant one? The content of Chekhov's art, of course, cannot be broken down into static entities—"passive" and "active"—without violating the organic artistic integrity of the play.

The appropriation of Chekhov in the name of the revolution, then, has not been without its negative aspects. Elements of utilitarianism and utopianism have tended to simplify and sentimentalize Chekhov's image. He sometimes emerges more as a didacticist than as an artist affirming the complexity and contradictory character of human experience. His moods of doubt and anguish, on the other hand, have been ascribed to a faulty historical perspective, a failure to perceive the precise (Bolshevik) paths to a "bright future." But Chekhov's "message," as Ilya Ehrenburg has observed, does not lie in any teaching but in his art.[17] And art, while always imbued with the elements of the social moment, recognizes the permanence of man in the permutations and combinations of history and culture. Certainly Chekhov, as we have seen, viewed as a lengthy evolution man's movement toward the "truth of the real God."

Finally, the element of contradiction or fracture in the artist's view of

---

[15] Cf. B. I. Aleksandrov, *Seminarij po Chekhovu* (Moscow, 1957), p. 76.
[16] V. Ermilov, *Dramaturgija Chekhova* (Moscow, 1948), p. 222.
[17] I. Ehrenburg, *Chekhov, Stendhal and Other Essays* (London, 1962), p. 13.

society is frequently the element which provides an angle for maximum vision. Turgenev undoubtedly had a saner, more balanced, and more understanding view of Russian society and its evolution than did Dostoevsky or Tolstoy, but in his social novels he does not reach the depths of perception of *Anna Karenina* or *The Brothers Karamazov*—though the purely political and social views of the authors of these novels are often weak and even uninformed. The great revolutionary activist and socialist thinker, N. G. Chernyshevsky (1828-1889), unlike Dostoevsky, anticipated the broad avenues of Russian social development, but he did not envisage (as did the artist Dostoevsky) the elements of human and social tragedy that belonged to Russian historical development. Here, undoubtedly, a useful distinction might be made between a view of what man *can accomplish* and a view of what man *is*.

"The truth about life, to which the writer should be in duty bound," observed Thomas Mann in an essay on Chekhov, "devalues his ideas and opinions." But against this tragic view one must set Lessing's audacious assertion (as Nietzsche expressed it) that the search for truth is more important than the truth itself. Even more, the search for truth and the belief in an ideal—as Dostoevsky so clearly realized—is itself part of reality, part of the truth. Mann himself recognizes the centrality of the voluntaristic element, of striving, in Chekhov's art and consciousness: the " 'honorable sleeplessness,' " the constant "search for the right, redeeming word in answer to the question: 'What are we to do?' " [18] Yet it is finally the lyrical element in Chekhov's art—that poetry which structures disfigured human reality and gives it beauty and harmony—even more than the positive ideas and ideals we may deduce from his art, that serves as the conveyer of his idealism, that dynamic striving whereby man overcomes reality.

A Note on the Essays

A twofold idea has governed the selection of essays for this volume: to introduce the reader to the prose and drama of Chekhov and to bring to the foreground central, provocative questions about Chekhov's art and outlook.

Much has been written on Chekhov in English. A fair sampling of the work of Russian scholars, critics, and theatrical producers has been translated into English. The reader who wishes to reach some of this material may turn to the bibliography at the end of this volume or con-

---

[18] Thomas Mann, *Last Essays* (New York, 1959), pp. 191, 197.

sult the English bibliographies referred to there. In editing this collection I have drawn upon some pieces that have already appeared in English, but the majority of the essays have been translated from the Russian, German, or French, or have been prepared specifically for this collection.

The emphasis of the selection is upon essays of broad theoretical and practical scope, analyses which turn up basic features and problems of Chekhov's art. At the same time, I have sought to make the collection representative of different critical approaches and points of view, as well as of different periods in twentieth century criticism.

A wide range of problems confronts the Chekhov scholar, critic, or reader. In this introductory essay, I have tried to bring some of these problems into focus: the problem of the "image" of Chekhov in Russian criticism—the view of him as a pessimist, a negator of values, or as an active affirmer of positive ideals and ideas; the nature of Chekhov's tragic vision; the concept of Chekhov as an adherent of middle-of-the-road culture; the question of his place in Russian literature, and so forth. I have given specific attention in this essay to critics and scholars who for reasons of space were not represented in the collection.

The opening essay, "Chekhov at Large," by Boris Eichenbaum, one of the most distinguished Soviet scholars, has always seemed to me one of the more substantial and perceptive introductions to Chekhov in Russian. Of particular interest is his discussion of the literary origins of Chekhov in Russian literature (in this connection he singles out the names of the writers N. S. Leskov and A. T. Pisemsky).

The next two essays, by Grossman and Chizhevsky, introduce the reader to sharply differing views on the nature of Chekhov's art. Leonid Grossman's essay, written before the October Revolution, is a monograph on the impact upon Chekhov of Maupassant, Zola, and Flaubert. The question of influence, unquestionably, is here too narrowly conceived. Insufficient attention is given to those features of Chekhov which distinguish him from Maupassant or Zola (he does not, for example, share Maupassant's moral cynicism). Yet Grossman awakens the reader to crucial characteristics of Chekhov's literary milieu. At the same time, his view of Chekhov as a writer despairingly preoccupied with the tragedy of man's nature offers a stimulating contrast to the modern view which tends to emphasize the soft and optimistic tonalities in Chekhov.

The essay by the distinguished Ukrainian scholar Dmitri Chizhevsky is, at its core, a creative elaboration of a long-established view of Chekhov as an "impressionist." Unlike contemporary Soviet critics, Chizhevsky emphasizes elements of *break* in Chekhov's relation to an earlier Russian realistic tradition—one which sought a connection between man's experiences and the events of his life. Chekhov's impressionistic style, according to Chizhevsky, is an expression of this perceived disjunction between man's inner experience and "outer cause." Chizhevsky's approach to Chekhov is especially noteworthy, then, for its attempt to pose the question of Chekhov's style in the context of the writer's world view. Whether Chekhov can indeed definitively be identified with the view that "decisive changes of human life and fate are either unmotivated or dependent upon minor causes" is, I believe, debatable. In any case, the whole question is forcefully posed by Chizhevsky.

Chekhov's plays have many dimensions that emerge in the reading— the locus of all their meanings and dramatic potentialities is here—but their true organic life begins on the stage. The range of various producers' interpretations, with their many truths, bear witness to this vitality. The section on Chekhov's theater opens with an early essay (1906) on the Chekhovian theater of "mood" by the brilliant Russian actor and director Vsevolod Meyerhold. The Russian theater director K. S. Stanislavsky, writing in the 1920s, alluded to the "mysticism and Maeterlinckism" of the early Meyerhold. Indeed, Meyerhold's approach to Chekhovian theater is intuitive, almost mystical; poetic mood for Meyerhold provides the structural dynamics of Chekhovian theater, and he perceives that mood as a poet.

A. Skaftymov's fine discussion (1948) of the principles of structure of Chekhov's plays seeks to correlate the new Chekhovian dramatic forms with the author's "new attitude toward reality." He emphasizes that for Chekhov the "peaceful flow of life, as it is lived" is not simply a setting, an exposition serving as a transition to events, "but the central area of life's dramas, that is, the direct and fundamental object of his creative act of representation."

A very different approach to Chekhov's drama—to many, perhaps, an unsympathetic one—will be found in S. D. Balukhaty's discussion of *The Cherry Orchard*. Rigorously descriptive in method, rather than deductive, Balukhaty—one of the theoreticians and practitioners of the "formalist" school of literary analysis in the 1920s—seeks to determine the dramatic principle underlying Chekhov's works through a systematic characterization of the peculiarities of his dramatic form and its functions. His stylistic and structural analysis of *The Cherry Orchard*, with its view of the work of art as an autonomous, self-sufficient interaction of parts, was a far cry from the earlier nineteenth century criticism which stressed "social significance" and "message," or from the ideology-laden Marxist criticism which was already beginning to bear down in the 1920s.

Balukhaty's analysis of *The Cherry Orchard* has much to recommend it (at root he perceives the poetic—the *musical* principle organizing the structure in a Chekhov play); yet at the same time it is illustrative of the limits of a formal method which divorces analysis of structure and device from poetic ideas and meaning. As Skaftymov notes in his essay in this collection, the vital question of unity of form and content is ignored by Balukhaty. Francis Fergusson's sensitive analysis of poetic structure and device in *The Cherry Orchard,* it may be remarked here, appears almost as a living thing beside Balukhaty's hard algebra of criticism.

The main focus in the section on the theater of Chekhov is upon general analyses of the major plays.

G. Berdnikov's succinct analysis of *Ivanov* lifts the discussion of this early play of Chekhov above the critical void in which it is sometimes found in Western criticism. In my own essay on *The Seagull,* I am concerned, among other things, with the allegorical function of Konstantin Treplev's myth-play (in Act I) in Chekhov's development of Konstantin's character; with Chekhov's conception of the essential unity of man's character and fate; and with Plato's myth of the cave as a suggestive device for revealing the mythopoetic base of the dramas of Konstantin and Nina Zarechnaya. V. Yermilov's essay, *"Uncle Vanya:* The Play's Movement"—abstracted from a more extensive discussion of the play —skillfully brings before the reader some of the larger problems of the play.

K. S. Stanislavsky's commentary on *The Three Sisters* in his prompt book—in M. N. Stroeva's essay on the Moscow Art Theater's production of that play—not only provides a view of the director's art, but offers a coherent interpretation of the play. A differing interpretation by the well-known Russian director V. I. Nemirovich-Danchenko is noted by Stroeva. Her observation, in this connection, that Stanislavsky's position was "more progressive" since it "better reflected the progressive moods of the epoch" is a fairly good example of how ideology can produce naïve results in criticism. On the whole, however, Stroeva's discussion of Stanislavsky is conscientious and productive.

Francis Fergusson's essay, *"The Cherry Orchard:* A Theater-Poem of the Suffering of Change," is certainly one of the most satisfying pieces of Chekhov criticism in its grasp of the organic unity of Chekhovian poetry and technique, dramatic ideas and materials. The word *poetry* is at the core of Fergusson's analysis, which is in many respects an interweaving of the strands of diverse critical traditions. Fergusson reveals Chekhovian drama in its striking originality, yet at the same time views it as an organic part of literary tradition and sensibility, both past and present.

Nils Åke Nilsson posits rhythm and intonation in Chekhov's dramaturgy as basic elements which may carry as much significance as the words themselves. In general, he cautions against too persistent attempts to find exact—and hidden—meanings in so-called "indifferent" lines in a Chekhov play. For Nilsson, as for Fergusson, Chekhovian poetry does not yield readily to the rationalizing mind.

The final group of essays approaches Chekhov more generally. We are concerned here more with direct, personal responses to Chekhov— to the man and his art—than with tightly organized or disciplined analysis. In a ranging essay, John Gassner distinguishes between different pulls in Chekhov's personality and world view. "His health of spirit was hard-won and heroically maintained." Gassner's Chekhov, like that of Du Bos or Gorky, never is without a tragic sense of life. The pages from the *Journal* of Charles du Bos (taken from the years 1922-1927) provide some very perceptive insights into Chekhov. Through the prism of his own very personal literary and philosophical sensibility, Du Bos reveals the genius of Chekhov's apprehension of life and (in his concluding observations on Chekhov, almost fearfully, hesitantly) its limits. The notes on Chekhov represent a happy conjunction of subjective disposition and objective literary insight. Du Bos's view of Chekhov as essentially free of the moods of his characters anticipates a main tendency of Soviet Chekhov criticism—though without the heavy didactic or ideological emphasis of the latter.

Gorky's reminiscences of Chekhov, with which this collection terminates, are of particular interest. Gorky, unlike Du Bos in his journal, withdraws almost entirely from the scene and allows Chekhov to dominate the stage. Yet the presence of Gorky is surely felt in the selection of Chekhov features, in the creation of an eminently positive, constructive, but perhaps too tender-sweet Chekhov. At the same time, a curious melancholy of Chekhov finely emerges from Gorky's reminiscences; as the memoirist proceeds, the image of Chekhov clouds over with a skepticism, and one has a vague sense of the dissonances in Chekhov which he (and perhaps Gorky, too) succeeded in reconciling.

Any collection of essays—and ours is no exception—has its limits. But it is essential that such a collection induce the reader to stray beyond those limits. This is certainly possible with Chekhov.

Chekhov at Large

by Boris Eichenbaum

It was inevitable that the 1880s should appear to contemporaries a period of literary impoverishment and decline. Indeed—Turgenev was dead, Dostoevsky was dead, Ostrovsky was dead, and Saltykov-Shchedrin was dying. The mighty generation which had made its debut as early as the 1840s was disappearing from the scene, and there was no worthy replacement. Pomyalovsky, Reshetnikov, Levitov, Sleptsov, Garshin— one after another the young "plebeian" writers perished in the unequal struggle for existence. The greatest of these "men of the sixties," Gleb Uspensky, was also on the threshold of death. Leo Tolstoy alone was alive and was "working for everyone," as Chekhov put it; but the solitary, cracking voice of the old man only heightened the sensation of a gathering void.

It might have seemed that the forces of Russian literature were already exhausted. The interlude that followed was filled haphazardly with all sorts of humorous "fragments," as well as with the works of the unwearying Boborykin, who, in his own words, wrote "quickly and well."

The situation, however, was not as hopeless as it seemed. History had its own plan and its own reserves. Literature is an affair of the people and the people were alive and wanted to go on living. Not Russian literature, but the populist intelligentsia was going through a crisis. A new literature was needed, free from populist illusions and from many already played-out traditions—and it appeared.

Chekhov had his immediate teachers and predecessors. Alongside the literature which concentrated exclusively on acute questions of social and political struggle, there also existed another literature which was developing outside the narrow circle of the intelligentsia's traditions. It lived by its close ties with provincial, backwater Russia, with a world which many writers avoided. It preached nothing openly, taught nothing

"Chekhov at Large" by Boris Eichenbaum. From *Zvezda* (1944), No. 5-6, 75-79. Translated from the Russian by Elizabeth Henderson.

directly, but only told vividly and in detail about Russian life, about
people of every class and profession, engaged in their daily affairs. Here
there were no Rudins, nor Bazarovs, nor Raskolnikovs, nor Rakhmetovs.
Here there were not even any sharply stated social questions. This literature seemed to lack a definite direction, lofty ideas, and rooted "principles." Because of this people often censured it and even slighted it,
relegated it to a "second-rate" position. Sometimes it tried to come forward in self-defense, but without success. Nevertheless, this literature
had its own unquestionable organic rights to existence and development.
It was necessary to show Russia not only in depth, but in breadth as
well, with all the features of her national life, her daily existence and
nature. It was necessary not only to resolve questions, but to collect
materials for their correct statement as well; it was necessary to study
Russia comprehensively in all her originality, in all the variety of her
class, professional, and intellectual existence. This "second-rate" literature was represented by the names of Pisemsky and Leskov. In what is
most basic and essential, Chekhov's literary origins come from them.
Not without reason he constantly delighted in Pisemsky and called
Leskov his favorite writer.

Chekhov entered literature from a by-path—not from the ranks of
the greater intelligentsia, not from that milieu out of which his contemporaries expected a new writer to emerge. For a long time he did
not even have any connections with that milieu, as though he had little
interest in it. It is characteristic that even subsequently he spoke in an
unfriendly and irritable way of the Russian intelligentsia of his time,
reproaching its members with laziness and apathy and ignorance and
chatter. For the first few years he was satisfied with minor humor magazines. At first, literature was something like a second profession for him:
he was occupied more with medicine, and even respected it more as a
real, serious, and unquestionably useful concern. He wrote his first
stories, scenes, and feuilletons lightly, gaily, and carelessly, as though he
were not intending to go into major literature.

This lightness, however, was not simply the fruit of a writer's levity
or cynicism. The nature of this lightness was different: Chekhov discovered a whole broad realm of life which had been unexploited by
literature, a realm of everyday trifles and occurrences which seem insignificant and funny or strange at first glance, but which really are characteristic and worthy of concentrated attention. It turned out that literature was showing out of every window, every crack; all that was necessary
was to have time to jot down in a notebook this colossal material from
observations. Subjects sprang up at every step. It was not yet major

literature, but was already a confrontation with it and its traditions. It was not accidental that many of Antosha Chekhonte's first jokes and trifles had the obvious character of parody: not only life with its confusion and disorder was ridiculed; the tradition of the great literary heroes, of enigmatic natures, of complex passions, and of tragic questions was ridiculed as well.

Korolenko recalls how Chekhov said to him: " 'Do you know how I write my little stories? This is how.' He glanced over the table, picked up the first thing that met his eye (it turned out to be an ashtray), placed it before me, and said: 'Would you like there to be a story entitled "The Ashtray" tomorrow?' " In its own way this was a polemic. Chekhov demonstratively was introducing into literature trifles of life—"the first things to meet the eye"—which formerly seemed to lie outside of literature. Thus far he meant to bring in these trifles merely as a joke, as laughter, behind which could be sensed neither anger, nor grief, nor indignation, and only sometimes, perhaps, perplexity: how strangely, how awkwardly and absurdly people live!

After Turgenev, Dostoevsky, Tolstoy, Saltykov-Shchedrin, and Gleb Uspensky, Chekhov's stories seemed to many critics an expression of social indifference and apathy. They began to speak of the "fortuitous" character of Chekhovian themes, of the indifferent collection of facts and incidents, of the absence of a world view. They were amazed that Chekhov only recounted various trifles and explained nothing. "Can it be that all Russia has become so emptied of content," Shelgunov, for example, wrote in astonishment, "that for a thinking man there is nothing in her which he would like to understand and explain?"

This, of course, was a profound error. What seemed a "fortuitous collection of facts" was in fact the realization of one of the basic principles of Chekhov's artistic work—the endeavor to embrace all of Russian life in its various manifestations, and not to describe selected spheres, as was customary before him. The Chekhovian grasp of Russian life is staggering; in this respect, as in many others, he cannot be compared with anyone (partially perhaps only with Leskov). It would seem that there is no profession, no class, no corner of Russian life into which Chekhov has not peered. He set himself the task of giving a picture of all of Russia, because he thought of her and loved her as a whole. A postal official, a district doctor's assistant, and a sexton were just as necessary to him as an engineer, a professor, or an artist. It was important to him to understand the correlation of all that made up Russian life—to understand the very essence of its national character and its possibilities. It was not without reason that he had in mind using the form of *Dead Souls:* putting his narrator in Chichikov's position as a traveler through Russia. Traces of such a scheme remain in several pieces ("Man in a Shell," "Gooseberries," "About Love"—all of 1898). Reproaching Korolenko for never parting from his convicts, Chekhov said: "I have a whole army of people in my head, begging to come out and awaiting the command." If one were to gather together all the people Chekhov portrayed, it almost would turn out to be an army.

His contemporaries did not understand that the reason Chekhov wrote about life's trifles was not because he did not see or did not want to see anything of major importance. This was not the point at all. The Chekhovian method removed the differences and contradictions between the social and the personal, the historic and the intimate, the general and the particular, the large and the small—those very contradictions with which Russian literature had struggled so agonizingly and so fruitlessly in the search for a renewal of life. Indeed, Tolstoyanism, so dubious to Tolstoy himself, arose precisely as a result of these contradictions. It is characteristic that for a time Chekhov too submitted to the influence of this doctrine (in the stories "The Beggar," "Good People," and especially "The Meeting" of 1887): and it could not have been otherwise, for the problem of moral self-consciousness lay at the center of his observations and work. But several years passed—and Chekhov himself declared: "Tolstoyan morality has ceased to move me, in the depths of my soul I regard it with hostility. . . . Peasant blood flows in my veins and you won't astonish me with peasant virtues. . . . For me Tolstoy has passed away already, he is not in my soul, and he has left me, saying: 'Behold, I leave your house empty.' I am free from billeting." In the story "Gooseberries," Chekhov answers Tolstoy directly and sharply: "To leave the city, the struggle, worldly noises, to leave and hide oneself on one's estate—this is not life, it is egotism, laziness; it is a sort of monasticism, but monasticism without good works. Man needs not six feet of earth, nor an estate, but the entire globe, all of nature where he can have scope to develop all the characteristics and features of his free spirit."

It was just this consciousness that man is created for great things that forced Chekhov to deal with the everyday, petty side of life—not in order to expose or to express indignation directly, but in order to show how incompatible this life is with people's inherent possibilites. He appealed to reason, to will—sometimes with laughter, sometimes with sadness. He saw that people themselves feel burdened by disorder—this "tangle of trifles," this everyday "slime." He sensed in the Russian a deep intellect,

broad scope, and love of freedom, subtlety of feeling, and a lively conscience—all bestowed upon him so as to make life significant. Precisely
for this reason he worked with such zeal and such passion to show the
Russian reader all of Russia—her strivings, dreams, impulses, and good
works, as well as her degradation, idleness, and boredom. It is especially
significant that his characters themselves feel this "tragedy of trifles";
they themselves speak of "logical absurdity" and "misunderstandings."
They are like sick people, stricken with an ailment and dreaming of
health, but powerless themselves to cope with the sickness.

In an article on Chekhov, directed against the criticism of that time
(1900), Gorky pronounced these remarkable words: "Chekhov has something more than a world view—he has mastered his conception of life
and thus stood above life. He illuminates its tedium, its absurdity, its
strivings, all of its chaos from a higher point of view. And although this
point of view is elusive, resists definition—perhaps because it is high—
it always can be sensed in his stories and pierces through them ever more
vividly." These words can be applied not only to Chekhov, but also to
any great artist, including Gorky himself. But in relation to Chekhov
they have a particular significance—both because they were uttered by
Gorky and because Chekhov was long reproached with not having a
"world view." In the same article Gorky defines world view as "a man's
personal conception of the world and of his role in it." Since in this
sense it is personal, it is not obligatory for everyone and cannot be the
only source for creative work. Artistic creation is born from a consciousness of life's complexities, its contradictions, the insufficiency and incompleteness of its achievements; from the striving to influence reality,
to change it. Only with this condition can a writer's work gain the necessary features for literature of ineluctable meaningfulness for all, cogency,
and genuine veracity—features which make it equal with science. Gorky
found just this in Chekhov: "He says nothing new, but what he does say
comes out overwhelmingly convincing and simple, terribly simple and
clear, irrefutably right."

Chekhov was a doctor and it was not without reason that precisely
a doctor should have turned to literature in the 1880s. Medicine was
precious to him both as a true method for obtaining knowledge of man
and society, and as a scientific support for artistic observation and analysis of material. A writer who thinks about life seriously needs such
scientific support—just so as not to fall into subjectivism, not to yield
to personal conceptions, not to lose a sense of the whole, not to leave
the *circle* of life. For Pushkin history was such a support; for Tolstoy,

pedagogy. Chekhov himself said: "I have no doubt that my study of medicine had a serious influence on my literary activity; it extended the area of my observations considerably, enriched me with knowledge whose true value for me as a writer can be understood only by someone who is himself a doctor." And further on in the same letter (to G. Rossolimo, 1899): "My acquaintance with the natural sciences, with scientific method, always kept me on my guard, and, where it was possible, I tried to conform to scientific facts, and where it was impossible, I preferred not to write at all. . . . I do not belong to those literary men who disapprove of science; and I would not want to belong to those who approach everything with their intellect." Chekhov praised Paul Bourget because "he is as completely familiar with the method of the natural sciences as if he had good training in the natural sciences or medicine." He said: "In Goethe the naturalist got along wonderfully with the poet." Chekhov's ideological link with the 1860s ("the holy time," as he once put it) and with materialism was evident in this interest in the natural sciences and particularly in their method.

Medicine begins with the problem of diagnosis and ends with the problem of treatment; Chekhov did the same: he began with diagnosis and then went on to treatment. At the beginning he emphatically affirmed many times that what can and must be demanded of an artist are not the solutions to problems (for that there are other specialists), but only their "correct statement," that is, a diagnosis. He said: "Not a single problem is solved in *Anna Karenina* and *Eugene Onegin*; but they satisfy you completely, simply because all problems are stated correctly in them." He might have referred as well to Lermontov, who, in the preface to *A Hero of Our Time* (as though he foresaw the future appearance of Chekhov), defined his position in medical terms: "Let it be enough that the disease is indicated, but how to cure it, God alone knows!" After Lermontov this question became fundamental for Russian literature; it ended with Tolstoy's renunciation of art and "Tolstoyanism."

What did Chekhov mean by the *correct* statement of a question? The same thing that he tried to achieve in his work: the transcending of contradictions between the social and the personal, the large and the small. With Tolstoy, to the end of his days, "real life" (as he said as early as in *War and Peace*), that is, private life, was opposed to historical life; with Chekhov this contradiction was removed. For him "the correct statement of a problem" meant just that in each event, even the most intimate and insignificant, the life of Russia should come to light in its entirety, an important social-historical theme should be heard. He never gives advice, instructions, or explanations, but all the same, he makes the unhappiness of Russian life felt with all its force. It is through trifles that he makes this unhappiness convincing to the reader and precisely through them that his picture of it becomes all the more striking.

Chekhov found Russia on the eve of a historical crisis; and just for this reason, he understood that the problem of her treatment was extraordinarily complex and beyond the strength of literature alone. He concerned himself with what was most immediate and necessary—the formulation of a diagnosis. The genius of his diagnoses lay not only in that they were accurate, brilliant, and convincing, but also in that he made them on the basis of the most imperceptible, minute symptoms. He discovered the traces and after-effects of disease in trifles of daily life and behavior, in gait and intonation, where another eye would find everything perfectly all right or unworthy of attention.

Of course, Chekhov's artistic method conceals a distrust for the social and political theories and prescriptions of his time, and therefore, as an artist, he avoided open, emphatic, direct tendentiousness in his work and disliked it in the work of others. He found, for example, that Korolenko was "a little conservative" and that he thought "like a forty-five-year-old journalist"—precisely because he was just too bluntly tendentious. For the 1880s, infected with liberal and populist tendencies, this position, progressive and very necessary, of course, made it possible for Chekhov to overcome a whole series of played-out traditions, and to lead Russian literature on a new path.

Always modest in evaluations of his own work, Chekhov nevertheless recognized himself as an innovator. "Everything I have written," he said, "will be forgotten in five or ten years; but the paths I have cut out will be safe and sound—my only service lies in this." Tolstoy immediately noticed Chekhov's originality. He saw a serious rival only in Chekhov among all the young writers—one absolutely new and permanently significant. "Chekhov is an incomparable artist," he said, "yes, yes: just incomparable. . . . An artist of life . . . Chekhov created new forms of writing, completely new, in my opinion, to the entire world, the like of which I have encountered nowhere. . . . And already it is impossible to compare Chekhov, as an artist, with earlier Russian writers—with Turgenev, with Dostoevsky, or with me. Chekhov has his own special form, like the impressionists." [1]

The point is not only that Chekhov introduced the short story to Russian literature, but that this brevity was a matter of principle and

[1] P. Sergeenko, *Tolstoj i ego sovremenniki* (St. Petersburg, 1911), pp. 226-228.

stood in opposition to the traditional genres, the novel and the novella, as a new and more perfect method for the depiction of reality. Just for this reason, everything written before Chekhov began to seem somewhat old-fashioned—not in theme or plot, but in method. Chekhov himself said: "It's a strange thing; nowadays I have a mania for everything short. Whatever I read—of my own or others'—nothing seems short enough to me." Or: "I can speak briefly on long subjects." So it is remarkable that Chekhov's stories bear no resemblance to what it is customary to call novelle; rather they are scenes in which the characters' conversations or thoughts are far more important than the plot. Often nothing special happens in these stories: a man gets sick with spotted fever, and then gets well ("Typhus," 1887); a miller sits in a doorway and scolds some monks, and then his mother comes to him and asks for money for her other son ("At the Mill," 1886); Vanka Zhukov writes a plaintive letter which he sends "to the village to grandpa" ("Vanka," 1886). Instead of a plot, a situation characterizing a custom or a man was enough for Chekhov. He said to Kuprin: "Why write that someone boards a submarine and sails to the North Pole to seek some sort of reconciliation with people, and at the same time his beloved, with a dramatic wail, throws herself from a belfry? All that is false, and does not happen in reality. One must write simply: about how Peter Semenovich married Maria Ivanovna. That is all." Seeing how Chekhov crossed out anything that was superfluous in trying to achieve the utmost brevity, his friends said: "It is necessary to take the manuscript away from him; otherwise he will leave in his story only that they were young, fell in love, and then got married and were unhappy." Chekhov replied to this: "But listen, after all, that's the way it really is."

Another feature of the Chekhovian method also is important and new in literature. Chekhov compressed the author's remarks to the limit, sometimes reducing them to the importance of scenic directions. Sometimes his characters speak a great deal; he himself, very little. Usually the theme and the situation in his works are revealed not by the author, but by the actors themselves (often they do more talking than acting). It is as if the author stepped aside and allowed his characters to say and do just what they were accustomed to and what they considered necessary. Chekhov maintained: "It is best of all to avoid describing the spiritual state of one's heroes; one must enable the reader to understand what is happening from the course of the story, from the characters' conversations, from their actions, without explanations by the author." This seemingly slight adjustment of tradition had, in fact, the significance of a revolution and exerted a powerful influence not only on

Russian literature, but also on the literature of the world. Freed from the author's interference, people became more talkative and frank, and the reader had a chance to come closer to them and to understand them more deeply. The importance of trivial details and trifles was revealed here: they were given a new and sometimes complex lyrical meaning.

It is completely natural that from stories Chekhov went on, not to novels (as many people had expected and as he himself often dreamed), but to plays, to the theater. Chekhov's entire system was based on the lyrical element—on laughter and sadness; the epic element in no way accorded with his method. This profound lyricism was revealed precisely when Chekhovian characters came onstage and began to speak of just such "trifles" before an auditorium. People began to call Chekhov's theater a theater of mood. What long lay unnoticed in the stories was revealed: the author's lyric was concealed in the subtext, in "the undercurrent." A second meaning came to light in the characters' conversations which lent the most commonplace everyday words an important, vital meaning. The result was that human life entered literature in all its fullness. Chekhov transcended the hierarchy of objects, transcended the difference between the "prose of life" and its "poetry," and became, in Tolstoy's words, a true and incomparable "artist of life."

Chekhov was by no means the despondent, mild dreamer that criticism usually depicted him as being. He was a man who made lofty demands on life, a man of labor and heroics, a man with great scope, great vitality, and great strength of will. Not for nothing did he write with such pathos of the traveler N. M. Przhevalsky and people like him. "I do infinitely love people like Przhevalsky," he wrote to Suvorin, "Their personality is a living document which shows society that beside the people who argue about optimism and pessimism, who, out of boredom, write trivial stories, unnecessary projects, and cheap dissertations, who lead a depraved existence in the name of denial of life, and who lie for the sake of a hunk of bread—beside the skeptics, mystics, psychopaths, Jesuits, philosophers, liberals, and conservatives—there are still people of another order, people of heroic action, of faith and a clear, conscious goal." How much bile and disdain is here—and yet at the same time how much nobility and respect for life! This was written in 1888, and in 1890 Chekhov fled from these skeptics, mystics, and philosophers to the end of the world, to Sakhalin Island—a remarkable act which throws an unexpected light on his entire life and work. Before the trip he wrote to Suvorin: "No longer than twenty-five or thirty years ago our own Russian people, in exploring Sakhalin, accomplished amazing feats for which one might idolize man, but this does not interest us; we do not know what kind of people they were, and just sit within four walls and complain that God created man badly."

Gorky was right when in opposition to the run-of-the-mill critics he wrote: "Chekhov's every new story constantly intensified a note profoundly valuable and necessary for us—a note of courage and love of life." Then he quoted from the story "In the Ravine": "Life is long—there will yet be both good and bad, there will be some of everything! Great is Mother Russia!" Even in Siberia, on the banks of the Yenisei, Chekhov looks to the future and sees: "On the Volga man began with daring, but ended with a moan, which is called a song; his bright golden hopes were replaced by an infirmity which is customarily called Russian pessimism; on the Yenisei life began with a moan, but will end with a daring such as we have not even dreamed of. I stood, and thought: What a full, intelligent, and courageous life will light up these shores in time!"

Yes, Chekhov was not at all as "skeptics, mystics, philosophers," or people who wrote "unimportant stories" and "cheap dissertations" depicted him. Here is his true portrait, also sketched by Gorky: "A delicate mockery always played about his melancholy gray eyes, but at times these eyes would grow, cold, piercing and hard; at such moments his melodious sincere voice sounded harsher and then it seemed to me that this unpretentious, gentle man, if he had to, could stand up strongly and firmly against a hostile force and not give before it."

This also told in his work. With the years, Chekhov's artistic diagnoses became more accurate and more profound. Under his pen, the sickness of Russian life acquired ever sharper and more vivid outlines. And the clearer this sickness became to Chekhov himself, the more frequently and definitely his heroes began to talk about it. From diagnoses Chekhov began to turn to problems of treatment. This stood out with particular force in the story "Gooseberries" (1898)—where the veterinarian Ivan Ivanich tells about a trip to his brother's estate:

I was thinking: basically how many satisfied, happy people there are! You look this life over: the insolence and idleness of the strong, the ignorance and brutishness of the weak, everywhere impossible poverty, crowdedness, degeneracy, drunkenness, hypocrisy, lying. Nevertheless, in all the houses and in the streets all is quiet, peace; out of the fifty thousand living in this city there is not one who would shout out, rebel loudly. . . . Someone with a gavel should stand outside the door of each satisfied, happy person and by constantly knocking remind him that misfortune exists, that however happy he may be, sooner or later life will show him its claws. . . . But there is no man with a gavel, the happy man lives away, and petty, every-day problems disturb him only slightly, as a breeze does an aspen tree—and everything is fine. . . . But what are we waiting for, I ask you? In the name of what considerations?

It is noteworthy that Chekhov himself does not say all this, but his hero—an ordinary provincial veterinarian. Chekhov never invented—he heard these words in real life and rejoiced at them because he himself was the *man with a gavel*. He knocked at the very heart of Russia—and his knock was answered.

Chekhov died on the eve of the revolution of 1905. People no longer appeared with gavels, but with workers' hammers. To Chekhov's question: "What are we waiting for?" they answered: "We will wait no longer."

Forty years have passed.[2] Chekhovian Russia has receded into the past. An era of wars and revolutions has fallen between Chekhov and us. And one might possibly think that now his words would come true: "Everything I have written will be forgotten." But in fact it has turned out differently: his heroes have passed away, but he himself, as a man and a writer, has become closer and dearer than he was. We have understood both his laughter and his sorrow, we have felt his faith in Russia and her future, his thirst for good deeds and work, his dream of a "full, wise, and courageous life," and his confidence that this life would come even to Siberia. Restored to health and strength, the new Russia finds moral support for the future struggle in Chekhov's work.

[2] [Eichenbaum's essay was published in 1944—the fortieth anniversary of Chekhov's death. Ed.]

The Naturalism of Chekhov

by Leonid Grossman

"In Goethe the naturalist got along wonderfully with the poet," Chekhov wrote in one of his letters. And did he not in this brief sentence express with his usual compactness his view of the perfect artist while at the same time he neatly characterized his own art?

* * *

In Chekhov, as in Goethe, the poet wonderfully harmonized with the naturalist. His medical training and practice unquestionably played a decisive role in his creative work. They laid guidelines for his artistic method, introduced to him extraordinarily rich, living material for literary processing, structured his world view, deepened and to a great extent clarified his philosophy of life. It is no wonder that he took such pride in his medical profession, repeatedly called medicine his legal wife, and often turned from literature to the practical work of the physician. . . .

The impact of medical school appears first of all in his working methods. We are not surprised that he speaks with such reverence of those to whom God gave the rare gift of thinking scientifically. In his letters he expresses delight over a literary article because it is written in the matter-of-fact style of a report, because it interprets elementary things coldly and simply and, like a good textbook, tries to be precise. As a diligent intern would, he likes to individualize each separate case in every description, carefully to examine all its little details and bring to light all its particularities and peculiarities. . . . Scientific precision in poetic creation was for him an indispensable element. Goethe was not the only person in whom he discovered his favorite type of poet-naturalist. He praises Paul Bourget—perhaps excessively—because he was so thoroughly familiar with the methods of the natural sciences; and he castigates Edouard Rod for renouncing naturalism. He repeatedly

"The Naturalism of Chekhov" by Leonid Grossman. From *Vestnik Evropy* (1914), **No. 7**, 218-247, in abridged form. Translated from the Russian by Robert Louis Jackson.

comments in his own work upon the advantage of medical school training.

"As a doctor I feel that I correctly diagnosed the psychic ailment according to all the rules of the science of psychiatry," he writes in connection with "An Attack of Nerves" (1888). An exacting artist, positively obsessed by a mania for the concise, he decides to insert like a wedge a special scientific conversation into the story in order to give it greater verisimilitude. "I am a physician," he writes in answer to reproaches, "and for this reason—if I am not to be shamed—I must provide motivation for incidents related to medicine in my stories." Chekhov takes it as the highest praise when women confirm the correctness of his description of childbirth in "The Nameday Party" (1888). "You know, it's not so bad to be a physician and to understand what it is you are writing about." And even in letters to young writers, as he indulgently and gently examines their purely artistic shortcomings, Chekhov mercilessly chides them for the slightest defect in medical matters in their stories. "Leave it to us, the doctors, the physicians, to depict cripples and black monks," he writes in one letter. "You have not seen corpses," he notes with reproach in another.

Chekhov makes the same demands upon his great teacher, Tolstoy. He is "full of admiration for 'The Kreutzer Sonata' from an artistic point of view." But as for the medical side of the story, he indicts the author as an "ignorant man who has not troubled in the course of his long life to read two or three books written by specialists." He is carried away by *War and Peace*, but he does not let pass the opportunity to note here, too, the possibility of the same type of defect. At the first occasion the physician awakes in the delighted reader, and with his skepticism spoils all aesthetic pleasure. "It is strange to read that the wound of the prince, a rich man who spent days and nights with a doctor and enjoyed the care of Natasha and Sonya, gave off a smell of putrefaction. If I had been around Prince Andrei, I would have cured him," the medical expert calmly concludes in the wake of the aesthetic response of the literary critic.

The school of Darwin and Claude Bernard planted strictly materialistic principles in the methodology of Chekhov's literary work.[1] He carries them over even into his mystical searches with amazing consistency. He demands of the enemies of positivism that they point out to him in the heavens an incorporeal God that he can see, and in the middle of the

[1] [For a discussion of the impact upon Chekhov's artistic method of the work of the French physiologist Claude Bernard (1813-1878)—particularly his *Introduction à l'étude de la médicine expérimentale*—see A. Roskin's "Notes on Chekhov's Realism" (in Russian) in *Literaturnyj kritik* (1939), No. 7, pp. 58-77—ED.]

1890s he predicts with joyous hope that Russian society will once again take up the natural sciences. Like a faithful pupil of Bazarov in *Fathers and Sons*, he calls the 1860s a sacred time, and affirms that thinking people can find truth only where microscopes, probes, and scalpels are useful. . . .

Medical practice brought home to Chekhov with remarkable fullness the horror of life, the cruelty of nature, and the impotence of man. Incidents from his medical practice found in his stories and letters create such a painful picture of life's absurdity that they are enough in themselves to make a pessimist of the observer. . . . Chekhov saw man first of all as a *sick animal*, and from then on, he looked at the world with a deep and at times even scornful sadness; from then on, despair shrouded all his dreams of a future golden age. Here and there in his letters you find the Shakespearean image of the wounded deer that suffers so horribly:

> The wretched animal heav'd forth such groans
> That their discharge did stretch his leathern coat
> Almost to bursting, and the big round tears
> Cours'd one another down his innocent nose
> In piteous chase . . . (*As You Like It*)

This image of a hunted animal merges in Chekhov's consciousness with the spectacle of a half-crushed human being to which he is so accustomed. It is worth rereading in his letters the story of the spring migration in Melikhovo when Isaac Levitan shot down a young woodcock, and Chekhov had to finish him off with a rifle butt; Chekhov's usual identification of man with a wounded animal is strikingly evident here. In this slight tale of a beautiful and enchanting bird, senselessly crushed by indifferent murderers—by a famous painter and a famous writer—the author of *The Seagull* makes his usual reflection on blind cruelty in the fate of all living creatures. The wounded woodcock with its bloodied wing and madly astonished eyes rose before him as an eternally sad symbol of human fate. The heroes of his stories unambiguously draw these philosophical parallels. "When I lie in the grass," one of them says, "and spend a long time watching an insect that was born just yesterday and understands nothing, it seems to me that its life consists of nothing but horror, and I see myself in it."

*   *   *

One of Chekhov's heroes (in "An Attack of Nerves"), who like the author has a delicate sensitivity to the pain of others, lands in a place where there is the most intense suffering, shame, and humiliation of the free human personality. But he does not pity either the tortured prostitutes or the musicians or the lackeys. "All of them resemble animals more than they do people," concludes this fanatical lover of humanity. And while a complex protest wells up in him, he continues to distinguish in every woman the insolent, obtuse, or abased animal.

It is not only prostitutes who are seen in this light. Among the sensitive idealists of Chekhov's world who speak glowingly about women, one meets cold philosophers who frankly declare that in our times the urban woman of the intelligentsia is returning to her primitive condition and has already been half transformed into an animal. "Little by little woman is disappearing and her place is being taken by the female," says Shamokhin ("Ariadne," 1895). And even Gurov ("The Lady with the Pet Dog," 1899), capable of generous and deep feeling, recalls with hate those beautiful frigid women with rapacious, venal expressions passing across their faces. "And the lace on their lingerie seemed to him to resemble scales."

These women-sirens are not only to be found in urban situations. Chekhov notes the very same serpentine attributes in the village beauty, Aksinya ("In the Ravine," 1900). Like a reptile emerging from fresh rye she looks at those about her and, at the right moment, strikes at them like a snake with her poisonous fangs.

At the very best, woman resembles a wounded bird gazing with silent amazement at the cruel tortures of life. Nina Zarechnaya (*The Seagull*, 1896) is a wounded seagull; Maria Dolzhikova ("My Life," 1896) a lonely, homeless wanderer, a green parrot who has flown out of the cage and now flutters about lazily from garden to garden; Anna Sergeevna ("The Lady with the Pet Dog") a charming bird that has been snared, a female separated from its mate. Even the best human features—suffering, anguish, hopelessness—evoke first of all in this keen poet of spiritual misfortune the usual zoological parallels of the naturalist. Even the meek and enraptured girl reverently following the work of a man she loves, the charming and clever Vera Lyadovskaya, recalls to Chekhov a sick animal warming itself in the sun.

Nothing much can be said of the men here, of course. A nice worldly man produces the unpleasant impression of some kind of crab; an unhappy schoolboy just before committing suicide is represented as a pitiful and disgusting duckling; a lonely, embittered old man, a huge toad.

The heroes see themselves as worn-out beasts. "They caress me in this house the way one would a sick, unhappy dog who has been driven away by his master," reflects Poloznev ("My Life"). And to Yakov Ivan-

ovich ("The Murder," 1895) life seems terrible, insane, and as cheerless
as it seems to a dog. When he wanders about at night in the snow,
lashed by a cruel wind, it seems to him that it is not he, but some kind
of beast that is walking, "a huge, fearful beast and that, if he should
cry out, his voice would sound with a roar across the fields and forests
and frighten everybody."

"In what way are they better than animals?" the hero of "My Life"
asks about his fellow citizens. And all his reflections on people are
haunted by recollections of tortured dogs who have been driven mad,
of live sparrows plucked bare by little boys and then tossed into the
water.

"Man is still the most predatory and most unclean animal," remarks
even his beloved artist in "The House with a Mezzanine" (1896), sum-
ming up in this brief remark all of Chekhov's tremendous work:

> The cold observations of the mind
> The bitter insights of the heart.[2]

Of course, a man needed great strength of creative love not to despair
in this huge menagerie of reality and to maintain inviolable in it all
the liberating dreams of snowy white cherry orchards.

*   *   *

The range of Chekhov's reading was unusually extensive: novels and
dramas side by side with reference books and medical almanacs, ancient
literature with modern, foreign writers with Russian. But in this broad
literary school the French moderns play almost the dominating role.
It is significant, therefore, that Chekhov's old professor has a special
liking for French books whose authors invariably have a strong feeling
for personal freedom.

According to Ivan Bunin, Chekhov took particular pleasure in Maupassant, Flaubert, and Tolstoy. These three writers, along with Zola,
must be recognized as his principal teachers. Chekhov was a convinced
adherent of modern French naturalism. His first teacher, Darwin, had
prepared him for the literary theories of Zola.

Darwin without doubt played a major role in the education of Chekhov's talent by helping him work out precise literary methods and a
strict materialistic world view; he developed in Chekhov the ability to
distinguish the animal element in man. The teacher of Chekhov the
doctor must to a certain extent be considered also the educator of Che-

[2] The lines are from the dedication of Pushkin's *Eugene Onegin:* "Uma kholodnykh
nabljudenij/I serdtse gorestnykh zamet." [ED.]

khov the writer. Chekhov's early letters give evidence of a strong interest in Darwin. "I'm frightfully fond of his methods," he writes to his brother. "I am reading Darwin," he notes three years later, "what a wealth of material! I am terribly fond of him." And in some of his later letters he defends the English naturalist from attacks in the press. . . . Darwin . . . introduced one of the main planks into Chekhov's joyless philosophy with his basic theory of the animal origins of man. Chekhov's constant habit of seeing maimed birds or wounded animals in his heroes may be explained in part by a Darwinian element in his world view. . . .

It is interesting to note that just at the time of Chekhov's literary debut, the journal *Vestnik Evropy* was publishing Zola's articles on the experimental novel. These manifestos of naturalism led to the broad dissemination in Russian society—a society always inclined toward a positivistic world view—of ideas about a scientific literature, about writer–physiologists, about the death of metaphysical man and the triumphant dominion of observation and experiment in art. The name of Zola gained a popularity among us that continued to grow until his very death.

Zola, too, occupies a prominent place in the literary schooling of Chekhov. His correspondence indicates that he never ceased to follow Zola's new work. He considers *Le Docteur Pascal* a very good novel and devotes whole pages to an analysis of it in his letters. He regards *Thérèse Raquin* as a fairly good play and even recommends to Suvorin that Zola be produced in his theater. *Lourdes* is mentioned in his letters and *Nana* several times.

Chekhov's strong attraction to Zola is understandable. A naturalist by education, a poet by temperament, a novelist by profession, Zola is a remarkable unity of those spiritual elements which, in Chekhov's view, go to make up the perfect writer. The demand that scientific method be applied to literature, the systematic introduction of physiology into the novel, the whole complex of precise methods of observation, of detailed reports about life, of abundant gathering of the infinitesimal facts of reality—the experimental method was just as congenial to Chekhov the writer as was the whole humanitarian utopianism of Zola: his dreams of how in the future happiness would replace the cheerless present for mankind.

We may exclude from the field of our comparison those differences of artistic temperament which determine the special character of literary form: Zola's need for grandiose frescoes and Chekhov's eternal craving for the miniature as an art form. Despite these differences, we find in these writers extraordinarily kindred natures. Both of them recognized that the writer must approach his literary material like a scholar; he must deal with human passions and the everyday phenomena of life the way a chemist does with inorganic bodies or a physiologist with living things.

"The writer," Chekhov writes in a letter, as though continuing to develop Zola's theory, "is not a pastry cook, a beautician, or an entertainer. However unpleasant it may be to him, he must conquer his squeamishness, must soil his imagination with the grime of life. He is the same as an ordinary reporter. For chemists there is nothing unclean on the earth. The writer also must be objective, like the chemist; he must renounce everyday subjectivity and know that dungheaps in a landscape play a very respectable role and evil passions are just as much part of life as good ones."

These lines seem to echo the epigraph to *Thérèse Raquin:* "Virtue and vice are just as much products as sugar and sulfuric acid."

But when the object under observation has been studied in all its tiny facets and the schema of investigation is precisely sketched . . . the physician and naturalist give way to the poet . . . and the calm anatomist drops all his precise tools in order to speak of the horror, the beauty, or the eternal enigma of life. . . . Zola and Chekhov seem to have shared this method of creation and to have been completely conscious of it.

Their differences, at first glance, may be seen in the artistic development of their themes. Zola strikes us usually as consciously crude, as if he cynically depicted the vilenesses of everyday life as a matter of principle. And in this respect, of course, he cannot be juxtaposed with the chastely restrained Chekhov. But this difference appears significant only at first glance. There are far too many poetically tender, sometimes even idyllic scenes in Zola's work to allow him to be regarded as the antipode of Chekhov. Even in the most crude, sodden, and cumbersome novels of Zola, scenes of unbridled passion will alternate with the most lyrically dreamlike pages, and stormy descriptions of modern crowds and machines with twilight pastels. Whole pages in Zola's cycle of experimental novels are imbued with this typically Chekhovian mood. It is no wonder that in the preface to *Une page d'amour* he defines this novel as an intimate creation written in half tones.

But Zola's influence on Chekhov is felt chiefly in his philosophy of man. It seems as though nobody in world literature can compare with the author of *Bête humaine* in the unremitting, stubborn way he exposes human animality. At root, the chronicle *Rougon-Macquart* is a document most humiliating to man. Out of the multivolume history of wild, unbridled passions, savage struggles for booty, mad thirst for pleasures, and endless search for them in women, money, power, alcohol, crimes, and incest—out of this emerges in all its cynical ugliness the beast in man which civilization cannot eradicate. . . .

To reveal this man-animal most clearly, Zola turned to the milieu in which culture has the least softening and moderating influence. He exposed in the peasant world such unrestrained explosiveness of passion, monstrous greed, savage cruelty, and rapaciousness that all the refined crimes of the worldly Rougon-Macquarts pale before these primitive forces.

Perhaps it was Zola's direct example that made Chekhov turn to the peasant world to develop more fully that theme of the human menagerie which always intrigued him. There is no doubt, however, that the picture of savage avarice, cruelty, and uncontrolled passion in "The Peasants" (1897) and "In the Ravine" were not created independently of Zola's painful peasant epic.

It is interesting here to compare the manners and morals of Kholuevka or Ukleevo with the everyday order of life of the French Beauce. Greed and self-seeking, the struggle for money, land, or women, the readiness to commit any crime in order to get at the booty, cruelty to the sick and infirm, to everyone who has lost the capacity to work, who has ceased to be a "plunderer" (to use a term of Chekhov's peasants), unbridled sensuality, the eternal narcotic of vice, the eternal power of darkness—this is the peasant world as we find it in Zola and in Chekhov. The story "In the Ravine" appears to repeat on a small scale Zola's *La Terre*. The elements of description here are identical; the representation of day-to-day existence basically the same. . . .

* * *

But first of all among Chekhov's teachers is the powerful representative of French naturalism, Guy de Maupassant. . . . The titles of the major works of Maupassant turn up throughout his correspondence. He mentions *Bel-Ami* and considers *Mont-Oriol* to be an excellent novel. In conversations with young writers he recognizes Maupassant as the head of a new school in European literature. "Maupassant, as a literary artist, made such tremendous demands, that it became impossible to write in the old fashion any longer," he says to Bunin and to Kuprin.

To begin with, Maupassant's realistic style had a very great impact on Chekhov. It is this special method of depicting life in all its colorlessness, formlessness, and disorder which was equally typical of two other literary models of Chekhov—Tolstoy and Flaubert. But in these writers the art

of putting down on paper authentic, everyday life was usually conditioned by the broad dimensions of their works. . . . Rapidly and
deftly manipulating his small mirror fragments, Maupassant was able
in each of them clearly to reflect a new side of life; he was able to reveal
behind the torn lines of the tiny design the broad spaces of receding
horizons. . . .

So Maupassant first of all responded to a basic need of Chekhov's
temperament as a writer—his love for the miniature. We shall return
to Maupassant's role in the creation of the external form of Chekhov's
short story. But his role in forming Chekhov's world view was far more
significant and important. On this point, the creative works of the two
writers are firmly linked. Maupassant suggested to Chekhov, or rather
reinforced his convictions about the colorlessness of life, the horror of
death, the animal nature of man. Life in its basic nature is much
simpler, shallower, and more insignificant than we are accustomed to
think it—here is the hard core of Maupassant's work. Our existence is
so plain and ordinary that we unquestionably do great honor to that
miserable story called life when we expect from it some kind of dazzling
joy or quail before its difficult dramas. The first never comes, the second
are almost always lived through. Unrealized desires humble themselves
before necessity, heavy blows are forgotten with the passing of pain, and
the deepest wounds are healed by time. The real horror of life is its
colorlessness and insignificance, the dullness of its most festive sensations,
the drabness of its most vivid colors, the poverty of its most fanciful
forms. "Life is never so frightful, never so beautiful as it seems to us,"
one of Maupassant's heroines says—and these words might herald all of
Chekhov's work. . . .

"I should like to describe everyday love and family life," Chekhov
observes in one of his letters, "without villains and angels, without
lawyers and female devils; I should take as a subject life as it is in fact—
even, smooth, ordinary." Chekhov unquestionably gives expression here
to a method which is that of Maupassant. . . . It is as if both of them
wanted to show that the design of ordinary human existence, no matter
how fanciful, elegant, and brilliant it appears from a distance, always
on closer inspection turns out to be infinitely simple, flat, without luster
or color.

The story "Three Years" (1895) strikingly illustrates this method.
According to Chekhov's original idea it was supposed to develop into a
major novel. Chekhov clearly wanted to give a comprehensive account
of a woman with all her maiden hopes, marital disillusionments, and
maternal joys. In other words, Chekhov took up the theme of Maupas-

sant's *Une Vie.* The basic threads of this novel are to be found also in Chekhov's story. A hasty and unnecessary marriage without understanding, bitter disillusionment in marriage, the consolation of motherhood, acute sufferings over the loss of children, followed by inevitable resignation in the fact of the most terrible misfortunes—here you have three years in the life of Chekhov's Yulia, repeating on a smaller scale the story of the life of Maupassant's Jeanne. . . . The quiet, toneless moan of Chebutykin: "It's all the same; it's all the same!" (*The Three Sisters,* 1901) echoes through the Chekhovian world like a heavy, tired, hopeless sigh.

But however colorless and senseless life may be, nonbeing is still more terrible. The sharp terror of death which grips the last works of Maupassant, who is slowly losing his sanity, is felt distinctly also in the later works of the tubercular Chekhov.

The famous old poet Norbert de Varin senses the approaching end. The slow process of physical disintegration of the body deprives him of all the attributes of his former youthful vigor—lithe muscles, firm skin, hair, teeth, eyesight, excellence of memory, and keenness of thought; all he has left for the time that remains is a soul shaken with despair.

The famous old professor Nikolai Stepanovich ("A Boring Story," 1889) knows his days are numbered. During his last days he assiduously makes notes on the signs of his approaching end. His hands tremble with feebleness, his mouth is twisted, his face is creased with the wrinkles of death; his memory and his talent as a spellbinder begin to fade, and he observes with horror that he is no longer able to finish the most ordinary lecture.

In this condition all the foundations of life crumble and in the place of his former inspiration, of intellectual engagement, of creative excitement, of intense curiosity, there is only one devastating feeling of despair. Maupassant's old poet senses the imminence of death so strongly that sometimes he wants to scream with his hands outstretched so as to repel this enemy who is creeping up on him. . . . The indifference of the world around to his tragic end strikes him as a monstrous cruelty, and with a scream he is ready to curse even the silence of the walls.

"I want to cry out in a loud voice," says Chekhov's professor, "that I, a famous man, have been condemned to death by fate. I want to cry out that I am poisoned; new thoughts, that I did not know before, have poisoned my last days and continue to stab at my brain like mosquitoes. Then my position seems so dreadful that I would like my whole audience to be filled with horror, to leap from their seats in terrified panic, and rush to the exits with cries of despair." . . .

The half-mad author of *Le Horla* communicated to his Russian disciple all this cheerless philosophy about life and death, about the world and people. Possibly, of course, he was only reinforcing in Chekhov a world view which had already taken root in him independently. Medical school, a mass of personal experience, the development of a mortal illness—all these circumstances of his own life directly instilled in Chekhov those views of the world and people which he had already found brilliantly developed in the work of his literary mentor. . . .

Flaubert's name crops up both in Chekhov's letters and in his conversations with young writers. There can be no doubt that Flaubert was his teacher in the creation of the faultless literary form of his short story.

The influence of this first naturalist mingled with those cheerless impressions of humanity which Chekhov drew from the books of Maupassant and Zola. Flaubert's hatred for the eternal philistine and his unconquerable contempt for the female laid the groundwork for nascent naturalism's epic of the man–animal, and was distantly reflected in the world view of Chekhov.

One might imagine that the talent of the author of *The Three Sisters* had been created by nature itself to give ideal creative embodiment to the eternal-feminine element. The capacity for spirituality and love, the quiet and sad melodiousness of woman's spirit pining with anguish and love, the lofty embraciveness of the Desdemonas of all times; finally, a keen understanding of all the oppressive pains of the troubled and melancholy masculine spirit—all this could scarcely have been conveyed with a softer and more delicate brush than that of Chekhov's art.

And yet, in the gallery of his radiant female figures, of these sad dreamers and pensive mourners, there appear some other un-Chekhovian images of predatory females. These exceptions in the Chekhovian world of maimed seagulls serve us as one further reminder of that school of French naturalism through which Chekhov passed. His Ariadne, his Susanna, his Anna Petrovna ("Anna on the Neck," 1895) or Natasha Prozorova (*The Three Sisters*) unquestionably are closely related to Emma Bovary. . . .

"She imagined herself in the future in no other state than that of a very rich and distinguished person," Chekhov writes in description of the typical *"Bovarysme"* of one of his heroines, "she dreamed of balls, races, servants, an elegant drawing room, her own salon, and a whole train of counts, princes, ambassadors, famous writers and artists, all of whom danced attendance on her and were thrilled by her beauty and her finery. She dreamed about a title, about glory."

Two very opposite qualities develop simultaneously in a woman of this type. On the one hand, a refined sensuality cultivates in her a delicate aesthetic taste and creates an invincible need for elegance and glamour in everything around her—in her surroundings and finery, in sights and conversation. But on the other hand, the thirst for pleasures which dominates everything seriously lowers the level of her spiritual life, endows her inevitably with cynicism, brutality, and heartlessness. With amazing insight Flaubert united in his immortal heroine these diverse elements when he endowed her with all the charms of an aristocratic attraction to the beautiful as well as the typical attributes of the female odalisque. Emma Bovary's refined aestheticism does not save her from crude sensuality, restrained ferocity, cruelty to people around her, and even cutting indifference to her own child.

Chekhov combines in his heroines the same contrasting qualities. His charming Ariadne "was perfectly capable, even in a moment of good spirits, of offending a servant, squashing an insect. She loved bullfights, liked to read about murders, and would get angry when the defendants were acquitted."

One device in the characterization of these Chekhovian heroines is typical of Flaubert and Maupassant. The central fissure in their psychology, the decisive moment when their fundamental nature is disclosed, often turns out to be a chance visit to some place of unusual elegance and splendor. Some elegant ball or festive occasion once and for all poisons their existence, reveals to them in all its fullness the philistinism of their daily life, the poverty of their circumstances, the humdrum character of the people around them, the unattractiveness of their husbands.

Chekhov used this typical theme of Flaubert and Maupassant for one of his stories ("Anna on the Neck"). A product of poverty and squalor, oppressed by a despotic husband, the humble and almost crushed Anna on landing at a brilliant ball instantly is transformed. The slumbering woman in her awakens through the combined action of all the currents of the electric atmosphere of the ball—the thunderous music, the bright lights, the ecstatic faces of the crowd, and the tantalizing proximity of the dancers. Unexpectedly and in a flash she realizes that she has been created just for this tumultuous, brilliant, gay life with its music, dances, admirers, and flattery. As she first becomes conscious of the great power in her feminine charm, a profound contempt awakens in her for everyday life, for her husband and her domestic surroundings. The once miserable sufferer returns from the ball with the awakened instincts of a spend-thrift and adulterer. . . .

The usual references to the transition period of the 1880s are not enough to explain the sources of Chekhov's pessimism. Among the personal, social, and literary factors which go to make up his cheerless world view, the influence of French naturalism must be taken into account. Its final conclusions never ceased to act upon Chekhov; their inner meaning frightened him, aroused him to unrelenting protest, but compelled him despotically all the same to acknowledge their terrible truth. . . .

Reading Flaubert and his disciple Maupassant slowly cultivated in Chekhov those rules of strict literary work which the author of *Salammbô* never ceased to expound in his letters and conversations. Flaubert's famous objectivity is of first importance here. His insistence that the author be completely absent from his creations, the campaign against lyricism in artistic prose, were fixed canons of Flaubert's art. Chekhov, for his part, gives expression to these same principles from the very beginning of his literary career; undoubtedly many of them were wholly his own and only subsequently found support in the high authority of Flaubert. "In everything cast yourself overboard; don't thrust yourself upon the heroes of your novel; renounce yourself for at least a half hour"—such are the literary principles of the young Chekhov. "Subjectivity is a terrible thing," he writes in one of his early letters.

He formulates in his correspondence a literary code and advances as one of its first points the demand for a complete objectivity which will always remain his guiding principle. "The more objective, the stronger the impression will be," he writes even in 1892. And a principle he formulates in a letter to Suvorin is purely Flaubertian: "The artist must not be a judge of his characters, but only a dispassionate witness."

This demand for strict objectivity consciously banishes from literature the whole element of lyrical sensibility. Flaubert considered a certain measure of coldness to be the highest quality of a writer's temperament. In his letters to young authors Chekhov never ceases to repeat these same precepts. He constantly warns them against the sentimental or maudlin. "When you depict some poor luckless wretch and you want to move the reader to pity, try to remain quite cold—this will provide a kind of background, against which the stranger's misery will stand out in bold relief. Otherwise your heroes will be crying and you will be sighing. Yes, be cold." Such is the purely Flaubertian principle with which Chekhov ends one of his letters on the technique of writing.

Finally, Chekhov fully accepted Flaubert's principle of intense fidelity to life in descriptions. Flaubert's famous precept—when you describe a sunset, the page must seem ensanguined; when you depict a meadow, green—always seems to have remained a guiding principle for Chekhov. When he writes "The Steppe" (1888), he wants the story to smell of hay; when he finishes the story he reports with satisfaction that his pages have an aroma of the summer and the steppe. "I have given such an account of the climate that you will feel cold when you read about it," he observes of his *Island of Sakhalin*.

His advice to other writers is similar. "Women must be described in such a way that the reader feels that your jacket is unbuttoned and your tie is off," he advises one of his literary correspondents. In his letters he praises Sienkiewicz and Zola for being able to give such vivid descriptions that the reader wants to have lunch in Ploshovo, marry Anielka, or embrace Klotylda.

But Maupassant always remained Chekhov's direct and principal teacher of literary form. Maupassant seemed to Chekhov an incomparable artist in his love of brevity and his passion for the short story. He set before Chekhov perfect examples of vivid literary landscapes in three lines and finished human characterizations in several strokes. He convinced Chekhov that brevity is the sister of talent, and taught him to compress his images and thought to the utmost degree of concentration. He revealed to Chekhov the artistic secret of those short stories that are without entanglement or denouement, without introduction or conclusion, that have a trifling title and are almost without plot, stories which strike one as a simple vignette of passing reality but are the final attainment of an extraordinarily complex and refined art.

In the realm of literary form Maupassant disclosed to Chekhov the first devices of transition from the realism of everyday life to symbolic realism. Chekhov's subtle distillation of a symbol from the simple elements of life—a feature that marks the last period of his creative work—is already distinctly visible in Maupassant. . . .

The symbolism of ordinary life is found in all Maupassant's major creations, where events are mysteriously caught in the strands woven by fate, and external happenings herald future tragedies. Olivier Berton, crushed by a bus, seems to be himself the emblem of his dying love for the countess. Scorched letters stained with floods of melting sealing wax are a mournful symbol of the end of a sad story. Christiane in *Mont-Oriol* (a novel which Chekhov is enthusiastic about in his letters), even before the onset of her unhappy love, in the first days of her arrival at the health resort, witnesses the frightful death of a small black dog. As she leaves the public ceremony she accidentally comes upon a piece of bloody flesh, covered with black hair, without recognizing in this tiny fact the terrible epigraph which reality itself is writing for her future fate.

These devices of Maupassant represent the first sources of Chekhovian symbolism. Nothing passes without leaving some trace, say the heroes of Chekhov's stories and dramas; everything is pregnant with some universal thought; our every step has significance for present and future life; all of us are part of one miraculous and rational organism, and human suffering of the distant past stirs us mysteriously down through the millennia.

The final scene of Chekhov's *The Cherry Orchard* is regarded as the high point of Chekhovian symbolism. The feeble Firs, forgotten in the boarded-up house by the owners who have departed, and quietly dying to the vigorous thud of axes, synthesizes the usual thoughts of Chekhov on the mystery of life and death, on their secret meaning, on the significance of everything transitory. "There is a far-off sound that seems to come from out of the sky—the sound of a snapped string, sad and dying away. A stillness falls, and all you can hear is the thud of an ax on a tree far away in the orchard." *The Cherry Orchard* ends with this philosophical observation.

The origin in Maupassant of Chekhovian symbolism is especially evident here. The death of Firs strongly recalls the end of Olivier Berton. When the wounded artist, pressing the hand of his lover, gives a deep sigh and expires, something ominous sweeps through his room. The fire goes out in the fireplace under the black ashes of burned letters; two candles unexpectedly go out; a sinister crack sounds from some piece of furniture; and a moment later the agitated countess senses through cold stiffening fingers that her friend already has found comfort from all woes in a great forgetting.

Chekhovian realism was much refined by the example of modern French literature. Flaubert and Maupassant did much to clarify and strengthen Chekhov's style as a writer and unquestionably play a significant role in the creation of his clean-cut, steady, lucid, and precise form. They introduced him to a whole series of new stylistic devices; they awakened him to the basic rule of all French literature—that one should see to it that every line be vital, engaging, and full of literary import.

The fundamental postulates of naturalism had a most decisive influence on Chekhov. Man's age-old incapacity to structure his life intelligently, his inability to bridle the predatory beast in himself, the complete powerlessness of his spirit before the mighty elements of instinct, the triumph of cruelty, stupidity, vice—this somber content of the human comedy was already revealed by the great precursor of naturalism, Balzac, and reiterated, after a careful review of his conclusions, by such knowledgeable masters of life as Flaubert, Zola, and Maupassant.

These authors wrote the crowning works of French literature of the past century. They could not but make a profound impression upon Chekhov—one that was wholly confirmed by his own observations and reflections. Everything that his heroes briefly sum up in the words, "Everything is vile; there is no reason for living," all his impressions about harrowing poverty, hunger, ignorance, anguish, the feeling of anger and humiliation, animality, and rapacity, all those Arakcheev thoughts[3] of Chekhov's heroes completely accord with the basic conclusions of French naturalism.

But Chekhov did not want to—or perhaps could not—reconcile himself with them. . . . And in the mood of hopelessness evoked by the personal experience of a physician and his study of the experimental novel, he turned to those hopes of salvation to which he was led by his Slavic nature and the enduring traditions of his native literature. In the sick animal, overdriven or embittered, rapacious or meek, he began with anguish and hope to seek out glimmerings of the divine element. The notion of humanity as an attribute of the highest spirituality became the hallmark of his creative work and the symbol of his faith. The question of whether the preachment of human charity in literature was in consonance with art or appropriate to the times did not exist for him. This preachment was his only means of salvation from final despair. . . .

Chekhov, in one of his last stories, acknowledges as the only meaning of life and the highest law of existence man's great capacity for active good. And as he moved toward this outlook, Chekhov introduced into Russian literature a new crowd of insulted and injured, quite different from the malicious, hysterically excited, or meekly vile outcasts of Dostoevsky. The feeling of profound injury, of undeserved affliction, of unbearable pain only heightens in Chekhovian heroes their primordial need for active love. All these martyrs and victims of life reveal in their quiet humility such a lofty spirituality that man's violent, predatory nature is redeemed in advance by this capacity for heroic renunciation.

In his revelation of these evangelical elements the atheist Chekhov is

---

[3] The allusion here is to Count Aleksey A. Arakcheev (1769-1834), a war minister in the reign of Alexander I. Because of his internal policies, his name became a symbol in Russia of reaction and despotism. [ED.]

unquestionably one of the most Christian poets of world literature. The final lines of his story "In the Ravine"—the depiction of Lipa in the field at night, submissively carrying her dead child with great maternal anguish but without the slightest feeling of enmity toward her murderer —is, of course, one of the greatest pages in the ancient legend about human meekness. Only a great force of love in the artist could create this new perfect image of the sorrowing mother.

Chekhov's chief strength lies in a love for man which overcame all revulsion. At root, he did not bring to his creations any new philosophy. An artist of extraordinary gifts, a lyrist of boundless spirituality, Chekhov was not a thinker of genius. He did not leave humanity revelations which strike one by their newness, boldness, or depth, revelations which immediately turn the broad current of human thought into a new channel. Even in the sphere of abstract wisdom, as in his purely artistic pages, he spoke the most simple words devoid of any philosophical profundity. Everything that is said in his works about the fate of the world and of people is in essence so simple that it might enter the head of any ordinary person. . . . But Chekhov expressed this simple wisdom in words so magically beautiful and, in their beauty, so comforting, that everyone was left with the impression that somehow he had been reassured about something, that he had been reconciled with something, that something had been set right. For all these sufferers of life the creations of Chekhov acted as a sudden revivifying flood of tears which are evoked by deep suffering, but which, after flowing, relieve the soul, lighten sorrow, and reconcile one with the most inconsolable misery.

Not only a poet lived in this naturalist, but also a rare genius of creative gentleness. One might say that nobody had ever probed with such precision the morbid fabric of life in all its tiny cellular structure and responded with such deep compassion for all its agonizing imperfections. This searching Darwinist with the love of Francis of Assisi for every living creature seems to confirm with all his creative work the remarkable words of Beethoven—that the only heroism in the world is to see the world as it is, and still to love it.

Chekhov in the Development
of Russian Literature

by Dmitri Chizhevsky

Chekhov still has no firm place in the history of Russian literature. Of course, one often ranks him among the "realists"; thus one is compelled for chronological reasons to place him alongside such epigones of realism as V. Korolenko and D. Mamin-Sibiryak. Or should one identify him with such representatives of the new realistic trends as Maxim Gorky? Or find a place for him in the ranks of the modernists and early symbolists? This kind of classifying of a literary artist in a definite literary group, naturally, is not the most important problem of literary history, and it is also not absolutely necessary. It is, however, by no means unimportant to determine whether Chekhov was in close relationship to one or another literary trend of his time, or whether he ran his poetic course as an independent.

As is well known, Chekhov frequently helped young and minor writers and delivered gracious and friendly judgments about them; many of these judgments now evoke our surprise and lead us to doubt either the soundness of Chekhov's literary judgments or his sincerity. In many cases, however, Chekhov, in the form of critical letters of reply, gave the nascent writers some rather sharply worded suggestions for improvement. And frequently we encounter in his correspondence a sharp and pessimistic judgment of the whole body of contemporary literature. Thus Chekhov wrote to A. Suvorin in a letter of November 25, 1892:

> In our works there is no alcohol which could make us drunk and carry us away. . . . Who among my contemporaries, i.e., men between thirty and forty-five years old, has given the world even one single drop of alcohol? Aren't Korolenko, Nadson, and all of today's playwrights simply lemonade?

. . . For people like us this time is feeble, sour, and boring, and we ourselves are sour and boring. . . . Remember that all writers whom we characterize as great or simply as good and who make us drunk have one common and very essential trait: they go in a definite direction and summon
us to go that way too. . . . We have, however, neither immediate nor distant goals, and our souls are weak and empty. We have no politics, we do
not believe in revolution, there is [for us] no God, we don't fear ghosts.
. . . He who wants nothing, hopes for nothing, has no fears, can be no
artist.

This letter contains still more; we find a more or less transparent allusion to the fact that even V. Garshin, as well as those writers who "want
to conceal their emptiness with old rags such as the ideas of the 1860s"
or D. Grigorovich and other representatives of the older generation who
are still living, cannot make the readers "drunk."

This scathing criticism of Russian literature of the time is much
sharper than that of D. S. Merezhkovsky, whose programmatic articles
appeared in the following year (1893) as a pamphlet, *The Reasons for
the Decline of Russian Literature and Its New Trends*. Merezhkovsky
has words of praise for all the writers mentioned in the pamphlet, and
therefore, one can scarcely understand today just what—except the bold
title—could have upset the literary circle of the time about so essentially
moderate a document. Chekhov, to be sure, makes no prognosis and
offers no programs. He understood only too well that the wish to become,
or to make others, drunk cannot bring forth drops of "alcohol."

Merezhkovsky's pamphlet was followed in the next year, 1894, by the
small collections of poetry, *Russian Symbolists*. These collections explained why readers and critics were so indignant (even such a one as
Vladimir Soloviev, who himself had contributed to the rise of symbolist
poetry). But Chekhov, as an innovator, and, consequently, as a dangerous
destroyer of the then accepted canon of poetics, had been for a decade
the object of attacks by nearly all recognized and established critics.
Up until almost 1900 they saw in his works a complete break with
sacred realism. This was the opinion not only of Chekhov's opponents
but also of his friends, for example, Gorky, who did not consider himself
at that time to be a "realist" at all. He wrote to Chekhov in 1900:

Do you know what you are doing? You are killing realism, and you will
soon finish it off—finally and for a long time. This form has outlived its
time—that is a fact! . . . You will wipe out realism. I am especially glad
about that. Enough! It should go to the devil! We have arrived at a time
when the heroic is necessary; everyone wants something exciting, dazzling,
something which is not like life but better and more beautiful than life

could be. Now it is absolutely necessary that the literature of today somewhat embellish life, and when it begins to do that, life too will be more beautiful, that is, men will live more buoyantly, more brightly.

The last words, to be sure, contain Gorky's own artistic program at that time. This program, however, has nothing to do with the creative work of Chekhov. One could hardly expect the author who wrote "A Boring Story" (1889) and who had entitled two collections of stories *In the Twilight* (1887) and *Gloomy People* (1890) to paint life "more beautifully," to present life in brighter colors. At that time a successful literary daredevil, Gorky could hardly imagine that the future might belong to literary ideals other than his own. He had, however, at least correctly sensed that Chekhov fundamentally differed from the realistic portrayers of "reality." In what way? Gorky, with his characteristic undeviating primitive way of thinking, could hardly formulate this question correctly—perhaps not even understand it.

It was clear to Chekhov that he was not able and was not permitted to go the old ways; it was clear to Gorky that Chekhov had begun something new and "killed" something old in Russian literature. The same was also clear to those critics who represented the poetic ideals of realism. As we have already said, these critics attacked Chekhov as a dangerous innovator who did not share their world view, and as an author who through his works was indicating to literature new paths which, for the adherents of realism, were wrong ways. The critics uttered these opinions with the same coarse frankness with which for decades they had habitually and futilely fought Dostoevsky, Leo Tolstoy, Leskov, and Fet.

* * *

It is of significance for us, however, that the critics and even the authors of negative judgments nonetheless noted and, albeit clumsily, brought into the foreground many features of Chekhov's style.

As early as the 1880s Chekhov came to the realization that he was creating "new paths" in literature. He wrote to Lazarev-Gruzinsky on October 20, 1888:

> Everything that I have written will be forgotten in five to ten years; but the paths which I am creating will remain safe and sound—therein lies my sole merit.

No one among Chekhov's early patrons and admirers, it seems, noticed the individuality of his creative work; in any case, no one spoke of it either in letters or in printed remarks. Most characteristic of all are the remarks of Leo Tolstoy who in his diary entry of March 15, 1889, called Chekhov's stories "pretty trifles" and who two days later, upon further reading, believed he could only characterize them as "poor, insignificant." Yet in 1890 Tolstoy already speaks of Chekhov as a "great talent" and, in fact, puts him on a par with Maupassant. As one can see from later known comments of Tolstoy, he was able to judge Chekhov, as he did most writers, primarily by the ideological content of his works. Thus, Tolstoy says, "Chekhov does not always know what he wants." "Chekhov often has no idea, no sense of the whole; one does not know why a particular story was written." Above all, Tolstoy rejects Chekhov's plays. *The Seagull* is, in his opinion, but "worthless nonsense." Tolstoy is "indignant" over *Uncle Vanya*, it seems, mainly because the heroes of the play are "idlers" and immoral people. While Tolstoy prized many stories of Chekhov, he could characterize "The Peasants" as "a sin against the people."

Only the old and at that time no longer active literary gourmet Dmitri Grigorovich (1822-1899) took an early interest in Chekhov. He did not limit himself to vague expressions of praise, but also frequently stressed what he found noteworthy in Chekhov's works: the excellent handling of details and the depiction of characters and landscapes precisely through these details and trivia. In the summer of 1885 Grigorovich noticed one of Chekhov's stories, "The Gamekeeper," in an otherwise completely uninteresting daily, *Peterburgskaya Gazeta;* he immediately called the young writer to the attention of the editor of *Novoe Vremya (New Times),* A. Suvorin. And in a letter of March 1886 Grigorovich warns Chekhov against further freelancing for the daily press. In that same letter Grigorovich emphasizes Chekhov's "mastery in description" with these words: "In a few lines a complete picture appears: little clouds against the background of fading twilight 'like ashes on dying coals.'" Grigorovich also repeats his warning in a letter from Nice in 1888. It was not without Grigorovich's influence that in 1888 the Petersburg Academy awarded Chekhov a part of the Pushkin Prize. Grigorovich expresses his astonishment in a letter of December 27, 1888, that at a reading of Chekhov's "An Attack of Nerves" to a group which included several writers, no one was struck by the sentence: "And how is it that the snow does not feel ashamed when it falls in this street?" (the street where the houses of pleasure were located; this is, however, an inexact quotation). A few days later the old writer sends Chekhov a letter with remarks about the stories "Dreams" and "Agafya." The figures in these stories, he writes, are barely touched [i.e., with the brush], and in spite of this nothing can be added which would make them more alive; and the same is true for the description of natural images and the impressions of them—barely touched, yet [the image] stands directly before the eyes; such mastery in the rendering of impressions we encounter only in Turgenev and Tolstoy (descriptions such as we find in *Anna Karenina*).

Tolstoy, too, could observe the meaning of "details" in Chekhov, that is, in those stories whose content was congenial to him. Unfortunately, we know of such comments by Tolstoy (1900-1901) only from the notes of his friend A. B. Goldenweizer: Chekhov is

a singular writer: he throws in words seemingly haphazardly, and nevertheless everything in him lives. And how clever! He never has superfluous details; on the contrary, each is either necessary or beautiful.

And again: Chekhov has the

mastery of a higher order. . . . Nevertheless, it is all only mosaic without a genuinely governing idea. . . . He casts in words apparently without order, but he achieves nonetheless an astounding effect, like an impressionist painter with his brush strokes.

Here we come upon the right word: *impressionist*. Unfortunately, one cannot be sure as to whether Tolstoy used this word himself or whether it was only an elucidation by Goldenweizer on Tolstoy's remarks.

Chekhov's impressionist painting is not simply the exterior form. As we shall see, it is also connected with the deeper motifs of his world view. But it should be emphasized that in this respect, Chekhov does not stand entirely outside Russian literary tradition. We may mention Chekhov's contemporaries who were impressionist poets, such as A. A. Fet (1820-1892) and K. Fofanov (1862-1911)—I. F. Annensky (1856-1909), however, was at that time hardly known as a poet. But, setting aside these writers, Leo Tolstoy is without doubt the Russian writer who first brought the impressionistic style into currency. Turgenev early took note of this, and his critical comments on Tolstoy's novels are in this respect very significant. Turgenev's comments on the great novels may be found in his letters (in which, indeed, Turgenev in no way denies the artistic achievements of these novels). "All these little fragments, skillfully observed and primly expressed, the little psychological remarks . . . how trivial that all is against the background of the historical novel," he writes P. Borisov on March 16, 1865. In his letter to Annenkov on March 26, 1868, Turgenev says that Tolstoy strives to "reproduce the oscillations, the vibrations of the same feelings and the same attitudes." In his letter to Polonsky on March 6, 1868, Turgenev offers the opinion that Tolstoy's historical portrayals "strike the eye with their fine detail," but his psychological art is only "moody, monotonous preoccupation with ever the same sensations." . . . These comments represent nothing other than an attack on Tolstoy's *impressionistic* style. . . .

If, however, we want to analyze the style of Chekhov's novelle, we should not be struck simply by the sporadic use of the impressionistic device—such as was emphasized in the above cited remarks by the pitiless critics or by those critics who appreciated Chekhov's style, such as Grigorovich and Tolstoy. No! Chekhov's short stories, like his longer novelle and his plays, bear throughout the traits of literary impressionism.

The main characteristics of literary impressionism can be briefly formulated as follows. In respect to outer form: 1) vagueness of the total picture, and 2) in opposition to this, the prominence of details and trivia. These two characteristics correspond somewhat to the technique of painting with separate brush strokes. The content of impressionistic literary works reveals these further traits: 3) the renunciation of the formulation of thoughts, above all, the renunciation of such elements of "didactic" art as the use of aphorisms and maxims which are supposed to communicate to the reader the intent, the "tendency" of the work; 4) in opposition to that, the creation of a "general mood" through which, if need be, certain "results" of the artistic presentation may be suggested to the feelings of the reader, to the capacity to feel, if not to the intellect. However, 5) certain small features, lines, particularities, details, speak to the feeling of the reader—these are the bearers of the soft and gentle shadings, the "differentials of mood." Chekhov uses all these devices of literary impressionism systematically, intentionally, and masterfully. . . .

We wish to direct our attention especially to such works of Chekhov as "The Steppe," "A Boring Story," "My Life," "Three Years," and the plays. Even now Chekhov passes as a "humorist" for the European reader; and this notion is deeply rooted among Russian readers as well, since new editions of Chekhov's works have become available. These new editions include a multitude of early stories which the author himself excluded from the original complete edition of his works; the little humorous stories fill up a good half of the volumes dedicated to Chekhov's prose fiction. No judgment will be given here on the artistic merit of these "bagatelles." However, it should be said that reading these "humoresques" is more apt to evoke a deep melancholy than a humorous mood. One sees in them, on the one hand, the extremely low intellectual and moral standards of the so-called "upper" classes; especially evident are the obtuseness, the coarseness, and the inhumanity of these rich and sated ones toward the poor and hungry. But even the "little" and "insulted" men are also often depicted in such a way that one can hardly find a human trait in them.

* * *

In short, the world of Chekhov the "humorist" is a sad, dark, uncanny world. And one can hardly conclude from it that a "cheery young writer" later turned into a melancholy pessimist. Rather, the pessimism of Chekhov's last years is much brighter and more life-affirming than the "humor" of his youthful years. In the later Chekhov we never encounter an irreconcilable condemnation of the "bad" or of the "nonconformist," a condemnation which otherwise is found so often in Russian literature. It is sufficient only to recall the harshness with which Leo Tolstoy in his "folk tales" and in *Resurrection* depicts quite harmless or even good men who, however, do not live up to his ideal of man. A comparison of Chekhov with Tolstoy in this sense would certainly be a rewarding task.

The forgiving, tolerant attitude of the later Chekhov toward human beings may be explained in part, at least, by those thoughts which came to him in connection with the development of his impressionistic style. Let us now, in conclusion, examine this style somewhat more closely. Much of importance was said about Chekhov's style in a little-known essay by N. Shapir, "Chekhov as a Realist–Innovator," [1] and Balukhaty has said much about Chekhov's dramas. The whole scope of the problem, however, should first be examined thoroughly.

Chekhov to a great extent forgoes the exhaustive *motivation*—so characteristic for realism—of the speeches and actions of the characters of his works. So much happens in his longer stories "without any reason" that we may see in him an anticipation of the basic tendency of symbolist poetry—the tendency to explain phenomena through blind chance. Perhaps this very feature drew Chekhov to Maeterlinck's dramas which, in any case, he first read with enthusiasm in 1897 (cf. Chekhov's letter to Suvorin of July 12, 1897). He read precisely those plays, *Les*

---

[1] Cf. N. Shapir, "Chekhov kak realist–novator," *Voprosy filosofii i psikhologii* (1904-1905), Vol. 79-80.

aveugles and *L'intruse,* which depict the intrusion of blind, ruthless forces into human lives; and, according to the testimony of Stanislavsky, Chekhov later took an active interest in the performances of both plays which were prepared in the spring of 1904 by the Moscow Art Theater.

While the realistic tradition searches for and presents a tight connection between the experiences and actions of a man and the events of his life, in Chekhov an abyss almost always gapes between the events and the experiences of the heroes, as well as between their experiences and their actions. Chekhov, like the realists, tends to stay close to reality in the dates, indications of setting, and other realistic details of his works. But this reality appears and operates in the experiences of the heroes only in a form that is unmotivated, one that is distorted, insufficient [to explain the reality]; between the "outer cause" and the inner experience there exists a strange incongruity.

The decisive changes of human life and fate are either unmotivated or dependent upon minor causes. Even more, the changes in life often do not correspond to the events which actually should lead to entirely different consequences. Thus, the weak, characterless idler Laevsky in "The Duel" experiences a kind of moral "rebirth" precisely at the moment of his deepest decline; and the infidelity of his girlfriend—under the most ugly of circumstances—does not lead him to a break with her but, quite the contrary, unexpectedly strengthens their relationship. This "rebirth," the change in Laevsky, is his victory over the Darwinist von Koren, a strong character who is firmly convinced of his ideological and moral principles. The process of Laevsky's transformation is not shown—probably intentionally. The entire life of the hero of "My Life" passes as a series of such strangely unmotivated changes. And also completely without motivation are the meaningful actions "by chance" not carried through to completion. Chekhov readily depicts lovers who without any reason, or almost without reason, decide to make no declaration: the series of such scenes extends from "Verochka" (1887) up to *The Cherry Orchard* (1904). A story such as "A Doctor's Visit" (1898) shows that even simple human relationships like friendship, good acquaintance, or just peaceful neighborliness often cannot come into being—and for no apparent reason, as though here, too, blind chance darkens the relations of men. Often quite minor causes determine the whole life of a man as, for example, in "The Cossack" (1887): A peasant refuses to give Easter bread to an ailing person during the Easter holidays. "With that began the destruction," Chekhov firmly states, of the spiritual balance of the peasant and the ruin of his home and of his whole life. Often Chekhov shows the reason for an action to be a certain mood, although the *im-*

mediate motive seems to be trivial. Thus, in the story "The Murder" (1895), a fratricide occurs because the victim wanted to eat vegetable oil on a fast day. Love, marriage, and friendship also can "by chance" originate, as in "An Anonymous Story," "Three Years," "At Home," "The Lady with the Pet Dog," and other stories.

Without analyzing a long series of Chekhov's stories it will be enough to point up a few further stylistic traits which we meet in almost all of Chekhov's stories from about 1890.

Reality, the "events," cannot be measured or judged in any way "objectively" for the very reason that they do not appear immediately to the person but rather in the form of a reflection in the mind of the individual in question. It would appear that Chekhov's first longer stories, where this fact is stressed, are "psychopathological portrayals" of one or another kind. Thus, the pregnancy of the heroine of "The Nameday Party" (1888), the too keen moral consciousness of the student in "An Attack of Nerves" (1888), the process of aging in the old professor in "A Boring Story" (1889) all permit the persons and events to be judged as unmotivated, often apparently falsely (as the author emphasizes) and ambiguously. From that time on Chekhov introduces the thoughts, experiences, and decisions (for the most part never executed) of the completely "normal" heroes as well as of the "sick" by means of constantly recurring formulas, such as: "it seemed to her"; "she saw in each and every person only the false"; "whereas they were all average and not bad people"; "everyone appeared to her to be untalented, pale, plain, narrow, false, heartless"; "it seemed to him that"; or, in the words of the hero, "something *strange* is happening to me," small causes such as sounds are "enough to fill me with a feeling of happiness," and so forth. The use of this formula reaches its high point in the years 1893 and following. In "A Woman's Kingdom" (1894) we read at every step: "she became happy" (for no obvious reason); "it seemed to her that"; "it seemed to her as though"; "she wanted to"; "she imagined"; "she dreamed"; "she was already convinced" (without reason); "this recollection—just why is not known—agitated her." The heroine experiences the "anguish of expectation"; "she passionately wanted the change in her life to occur immediately, at that very moment" (and after a short time this wish vanishes without a trace). We encounter the same phenomenon in the story "Teacher of Literature" (1894): "it seemed"; "he sensed in his soul an unpleasant impression"; "and in no way at all could he understand why"; "nevertheless, it was unpleasant"; "he began to get angry at the little white cat." And in the same way the hero of "Three Years" (1895) "was annoyed at himself and at the black dog";

"his mood changed suddenly. . . . It seemed to him that everything he said was nauseatingly stupid." The experiences of the heroine of this same story occur similarly. The hero of "Three Years" had the feeling that it was not he himself but "his double" who was thinking and acting; and to the murderer in "The Murder" (1895) it seemed that not he himself but some kind of beast, a monstrous and terrible beast, was walking around"—and all this before he even thought about the murder which occurs later.

The heroes of Chekhov's impressionistic stories vacillate between various moods, thoughts, and resolutions, and frequently experience opposite feelings simultaneously, without feeling their contradiction. Chekhov places special stress on the fact that sensations, experiences, are in a continual flux, in a process of change. Above all, he tried to record the fading of experiences and events. Examples of this can be found in "The Story of Mrs. N. N." (1887): "Everything for me, as for everybody, has vanished, quickly, without a trace, was not appreciated, and faded like mist. . . . Where is it all?"; in "The Wife" (1891): "How beautiful life could have been"; in "She Yawned" (1892): "I let it slip by, let it slip by"; in "A Woman's Kingdom" (1894): "It is already too late to dream." This motif operates perhaps most strongly at the end of Chekhov's last story, "The Bishop" (1902). Not only have all the experiences of the bishop passed away, vanished, with his death, but his existence now no longer appears to have been real: whenever his mother told about him "not everyone believed her." In this way "reality" recedes into the background, and the events which apparently constitute the causes or motivations of experiences have an effect only in the form which they assume, as they are broken up and reshaped in people's psyches.

When "reality" transformed in this way (which for Chekhov was not at all an "objective" reality) is brought into the flux of the individual spiritual life, the presentation of the spiritual life becomes the central, most important task of literary art. And, since the spiritual life of a man knows only isolated peaks and high points, and for the most part runs its course in the "lowlands" of the commonplace, this presentation must reckon with numerous "empty places." These "empty places," these insignificant moments—even periods—of human life, need to be touched upon only fleetingly in artistic prose; they must not, however, remain unnoticed in dramatic works—these certainly should present in full certain segments of time. The composition of the Chekovian play is determined to a large extent in this way: between the peaks of spiritual experiences and the turning points of the plot are inserted elements of "filling." This "filling" consists of witty episodes, such as those with Epikhodov and Semeonov-Pishchik in *The Cherry Orchard*, of "everyday" conversations which say nothing, such as are found in long sections of the second act of the same comedy, and even of silences. In the stories the author can dispose more freely of the "empty times" of the action, and so even the descriptions of nature and the theoretical observations of the author appear here with the function of filling these intervals. Such is the origin of the impressionistic composition which builds up characterizations of heroes and the portrayal of events (as we have said —seen through the eyes of the heroes) by means of isolated strokes and patches of color.

It is not without significance that in Chekhov's stories the characters are usually transients in the place of action, often staying on only by chance. The persons through whose eyes the reader is supposed to view the events are doctors who are visiting their patients, surveyors, examining magistrates, guests, and chance passersby. Or, should the heroes of the stories find themselves at home, then the other persons of the action are only guests who often appear in the heroes' lives for the first time. One sees the world to a certain degree from the window of a railroad train. In general, the railroad plays an unusually large role in Chekhov's works! How many of his heroes live at railroad stations or in the neighborhood of the railroad! Before them people flit by "like shooting stars." This kind of situation is just that of an impressionist observing life. In this respect "In the Cart" (1897) is a most characteristic story. A woman school teacher is traveling back to her native village in a miserable peasant's cart along a wretched highway.

> The tollgate on the railway overpass was let down: an express train departed from the station. . . . There was the train—the windows glittered with a dazzling light . . . so that it was painful to look at. In a front compartment of a first-class car stood a lady.

It seems to the school teacher that this lady bears great resemblance to her own mother, and she imagines with astounding clarity her life in Moscow thirteen years ago, when her mother was still alive.

> And she cried, not knowing why. . . . And it seemed to her that everywhere, in the windows, in the trees, her happiness, her triumph, was shining. Yes, her father and her mother had never died, she had never been a school teacher: that had been a long, difficult, strange dream, and now she had awakened. . . . And suddenly everything disappeared.

Here we find in a few lines the typical traits of the Chekhovian style: the "flitting past" of reality, the unexpected, unmotivated, and mutually

contradictory experiences ("she cried," "it seemed to her that everywhere . . . her happiness was shining") which in rapid flux replace one
another; the "sudden disappearance" of reality which induces sensations
—and, just as suddenly, the dying away of the sensations.

These main characteristics of Chekhov's style are not the only elements of his impressionism. The attention to details, which to the critics
of the time seemed so unnecessary, even nonsensical, belongs to the
author's method of presentation as well as to the manner in which the
heroes perceive reality and react to it. Reality and people are apprehended and characterized by apparently random and inessential traits.
Thus, people are characterized by their odor—"smelled of coffee
grounds," "smelled of raw meat," and so forth—or by their manner of
speech more than by the content of what they say—"The Man in the
Case" (1898), Chebutykin in *The Three Sisters,* and others. Nature is
presented through separate patches of color, as in "The Steppe"—a
device which critics correctly identified as an innovation—or through
completely indefinite pictures, as "in the imperceptible distance . . .
hazy, odd figures arose and climbed upon one another" ("The Steppe").
Finally, indeterminate sounds which above all fulfill a vital symbolic
function as a feature of the author's presentation of reality: for example,
the following section from "The Steppe." "There resounded, disturbing
the motionless air, some kind of wondrous 'Ah-ah,' and one heard the
cry of a wakeful or dreaming bird." An almost identical passage occurs
a few pages later on in this same story. One finds another example of
this kind of sound in Act II of *The Cherry Orchard*: "suddenly a distant
sound, right from the sky, the sound of a breaking string which dies
away sadly." Almost an identical sentence is repeated in the concluding
stage directions of Act IV of the same play.

Chekhov's work comes immediately before the appearance of symbolism; this is not merely a chronological fact. His impressionism, exactly
like that of V. Garshin and Fet and some other writers, in a certain
sense prepared the way for symbolism. One must not forget that fact
when one poses the question of Chekhov's place in the development of
Russian literature. There is poor documentation of Chekhov's views on
symbolism, and what there is is frequently contradictory. But one can
expect no unequivocal opinion about the new literary trends from a
writer who always stressed his antipathy toward every "bias." Chekhov's
"impartiality," moreover, was one of the reasons for the intense attacks
against this allegedly "faceless" and "viewless" writer, the author of
"meaningless trifles." However, it must be emphasized in conclusion that
Chekhov was, as we have seen, a serious and keen satirist even in his

"humoresques." And his later impressionistic style rests on a definite conception of the world and of man, a conception which deserves special attention. . . . But it is still more significant that Chekhov attempts to give his own answers to old questions posed by the great Russian writers. Thus, his story "The Duel" is an answer to Tolstoy's *Anna Karenina*; alongside that there is an argument with the Russian Darwinists and with Nietzsche—that is, with Nietzsche as he was interpreted (and wrongly) by the Russians. The investigation of such references and direct discussion of ideological problems in Chekhov is a further task for research to which I can here only allude.

Naturalistic Theater
and Theater of Mood

by *Vsevolod Meyerhold*

The Moscow Art Theater has two faces: one—naturalistic theater;[1] the other—theater of mood.[2] The naturalism of the Moscow Art Theater is borrowed from the Meininger company.[3] Its ruling principle is precision in reproduction of nature. As far as possible, everything on the stage must be real—ceilings, moldings, fireplaces, wallpaper, even doors, vents, and so on.

* * *

Naturalistic theater, obviously, denies that the audience has any ability to fill in the picture or daydream, as happens when one listens to music; but an audience does have this ability. During Act I of A. A. Yartsev's *At the Monastery*,[4] in which the *intérieur* of a monastic guest-house was shown, one heard the peaceful sound of vesper bells. There was no window in the set, but through the sound of the monastery bells the audience could picture in its imagination a yard heaped with piles of bluish snow, the spruce trees of Nesterov's paintings, worn paths from cell to cell, the golden cupolas of the church—one spectator will picture such a scene, a second thinks of another, a third of yet another. Mystery takes possession of the audience and leads it into a world of dreams. In Act II the director had already given the audience a window, show-

"Naturalistic Theater and Theater of Mood" by Vsevolod Meyerhold. From *Teatr. Kniga o novom teatre. Sbornik statej.* (St. Petersburg, 1908), pp. 136-150, in abridged form. Translated from the Russian by Joyce C. Vining. Meyerhold's essay was written in 1906.
    [1] Repertoire: A. T. Pisemsky: *The Usurpers of the Law* (*Samoupravtsy*); G. Hauptmann: *Drayman Henschel*; Naidenov [S. A. Alekseev]: *Walls* (*Steny*); M. Gorky: *Children of the Sun* (*Deti solntse*).
    [2] Repertoire: the plays of A. P. Chekhov.
    [3] The Meininger company: a German theatrical troupe, well known in Europe, which toured Russia in 1885 and 1890 and roused considerable discussion in theatrical circles. [ED.]
    [4] The play was performed in the Moscow Art Theater.

ing him the courtyard of the monastery. The trees were not the same, nor were the piles of snow, nor the color of the cupolas. The audience was not only disappointed—it was infuriated: mysteries had disappeared; fantasies were profaned.

That the theater was consistent and resolute in banishing the power of mystery from the stage is proved in the case of *The Seagull*. In the first production, one could not follow the characters' exits during Act I: running across a small bridge, they disappeared into a dark thicket, going *somewhere*. . . . During the revival of *The Seagull*, however, every corner of the stage was exposed. They built a summerhouse with a real cupola and real columns. There was a ravine on the stage, and one could see clearly how people went offstage onto it. In the first production of *The Seagull*, during Act III, there was a window to one side, so placed that no landscape was visible. When the actors entered a foyer in galoshes, plaids, and shawls, shaking rain from their hats, one pictured autumn, drizzle, and puddles in the yard with small planks squelching down on them. But in the revival, on a technically improved stage, a window has been cut through opposite the audience. A landscape can be seen. Your imagination is reduced to silence, and no matter what the characters say about the landscape, you do not believe them. It could never be what they describe; it is shown—you can see it. According to the first production plan, the departure on horses with bells was only intimated offstage, and was distinctly etched in the audience's imagination. In the second production, the audience expects these horses with bells, once it can see the veranda from which the characters depart.

"A work of art can influence man only through his imagination. Thus, art must constantly arouse it." (Schopenhauer). Precisely that—arouse, and "not leave in a state of inertia" by trying to spell out everything. . . . Voltaire wrote somewhere: *"Le secret d'être ennuyeux, c'est de tout dire."* Conversely, when the imagination of the audience is not lulled to sleep, it can be cultivated. Art can then be even more subtle. How was medieval theater able to manage without any stage equipment? Because of the lively imagination of its audience.

*   *   *

In his didactic poem, "Essay on Criticism" (1711), Alexander Pope enumerates the factors which hinder criticism from pronouncing reliable judgments. Among other things, he points out the habit of concentrating on details, when the primary object of a critic should be the desire to assume the author's point of view so as to take in at a glance the work as a whole. The same may also be said of the director. But as the naturalistic director deepens his analysis of the individual parts of the work, he fails to get a picture of the whole. Carried away with his filigree work—with the finishing touches of certain scenes which present favorable material for his creative imagination (a pearl of "characterization," for example)—he unwittingly destroys the balance and harmony of the whole.

Time is costly on the stage. If a certain scene, which the author intended to be unaccented, is protracted, it eats into the time of the following scene, which the author may have conceived as central. And the audience, whose prolonged attention is demanded by matters it must soon put aside, is wearied for the important scene. The director has thus given the scene too flashy a frame.

Such destruction of the harmony of the whole was evinced in the interpretation of Act III of *The Cherry Orchard* by the director of the Art Theater. The author conceives the act thus: the leitmotif of the act is Ranevskaya's presentiment of impending disaster (the sale of the cherry orchard). All around her, people somehow live vacantly. Here are the complacent people, moving to the monotonous rattle of a Jewish orchestra, and, in a nightmarish whirl, circling in some dull contemporary dance in which there is no enthusiasm, no excitement, no grace, not even lust. These smug individuals are unaware that the ground they dance on is slipping from under their feet. Only Ranevskaya foresees Misfortune, and waits for it restlessly, and for a moment stops the moving circle—this nightmarish dance of puppets in a farce. With an aching feeling she assigns faults to people; they only must not be "prigs," because through crime one may achieve sanctity, but mediocrity never leads anywhere. The harmony of the act is created from the plaints of Ranevskaya with her foreboding of imminent Misfortune (a fateful beginning in Chekhov's new mystical drama) on the one hand, and puppet buffoonery on the other. (Not for nothing did Chekhov have Charlotta dance among the "philistines" in the typical puppet theater costume— a black dress with checked trousers.) Translated into musical terms, the act would be part of a symphony. It contains a basic melancholy melody with changing *pianissimo* moods and *forte* outbursts (the experiences of Ranevskaya) and the background, a discordant accompaniment—the clanking monotone of a provincial orchestra and the dance of living corpses (the philistines). This, musically speaking, is the harmony of the act, and the scene with the tricks comprises only one of the discordant notes in the stupid dance whose dissonance breaks into the melody; thus, with the scenes of the dancing, it must break in only momentarily, then disappear and merge once more with the dances, which may, however, be heard as a background of continual, toneless accompaniment—but only as a background.[5]

The director of the Art Theater showed how the harmony of this act can be destroyed. Out of the [episode with the] tricks he made a whole scene with all kinds of bits and pieces. It is long-drawn-out and complicated. The audience is forced to concentrate on it and loses track of the leitmotif of the act. And when it is over, the background melody is remembered, but the leitmotif has been muffled and has disappeared.

In *The Cherry Orchard,* as in Maeterlinck's plays, there is a hero who is not seen on the stage, but who is sensed every time the curtain goes down. When the curtain descended on the Moscow Art Theater's performance of *The Cherry Orchard,* no such presence was felt. One could only remember "types." For Chekhov, the characters of *The Cherry Orchard* are a means, not the essence in themselves. In the Moscow Art Theater, however, the characters became the whole point, and the lyrical–mystical side of the play was left undisclosed. Apparently, Chekhov's impressionistically drawn images provide material which can readily be elaborated into figures (types).

* * *

This striving to exhibit everything whatever the cost, this fear of Mystery, of implication, turns theater into a mere illustrator of the words of an author.

"I hear a dog howling again," says one of the characters. And without fail, the howl of a dog is reproduced. The audience knows of a departure not only by the retreating sounds of bells, but also by the hoofbeats on a wooden bridge over a river. The patter of rain on an iron roof is heard. Birds. Frogs. Crickets.

In this connection, I would like to cite from my diary a conversation between Chekhov and a few actors. Chekhov had come for the second time to visit a rehearsal of *The Seagull* (September 11, 1898) in the Moscow Art Theater. One of the actors told him that during the play, frogs croaked backstage, dragonflies hummed, and dogs howled.

"What for?" asked Anton Pavlovich, sounding dissatisfied.

[5] These fleeting dissonances, which burst from the background into the leitmotif, can be found in the Station Master's reading of poetry, in the scene when Epikhodov breaks the billiard cue, and when Trofimov falls down the stairs. And see how closely Chekhov interweaves the two melodies: the leitmotif and the accompaniment.

Anya (Upset). There's some man in the kitchen now, who says that the cherry orchard has already been sold today.
Lyubov Andreevna. Sold—to whom?
Anya. He didn't say. He left. (She dances with Trofimov.)

"It's realistic," said the actor.

"Realistic," A. P. repeated with a laugh. And then after a brief pause, he remarked: "The stage is art. In one of [I. N.] Kramskoy's genre paintings he has some magnificently drawn faces. What if we cut the painted nose from one of these faces and substituted a live one? The new nose would be 'real,' but the painting would be ruined."

One actor proudly announced that, for the end of Act III of *The Seagull,* the director wanted to bring all the domestics out onto the stage, including some woman with a crying infant.

"Unnecessary," said Anton Pavlovich. "That would be tantamount to playing the piano *pianissimo,* and having the lid crash down at the same time."

One of the actors tried to object: "In real life, a totally unexpected *forte* will often burst into the *pianissimo.*"

"Yes, but the stage demands certain conventions," said A. P. "You have no fourth wall. Besides, the stage is art; theater expresses the quintessence of life. There is no need to introduce anything superfluous onto the stage."

Is it necessary to explain what kind of accusation was leveled at naturalistic theater by Chekhov in this dialogue? Naturalistic theater indefatigably sought the fourth wall, and this search led to a whole series of absurdities. Theater found itself at the mercy of the factory. It wanted everything on stage to be "like real life," and turned itself into some kind of antique shop.

Taking Stanislavsky's word that sometimes a theatrical sky can look real to an audience, theater directors agonized over ways to raise the roof over the stage as high as possible. And no one seemed to realize that instead of altering the stage (which is very costly) one ought to smash the basic principle of naturalistic theater; it was this principle alone which led the Art Theater into such absurdities.

Just because the actors' togas do not stir, one must never doubt that the garlands in the first scene of *Julius Caesar* are shaken by a breeze, and not by a stagehand.

In Act II of *The Cherry Orchard,* the actors walk through "real" ravines, across bridges, near a "genuine" country chapel. From the sky hang two large canvases, dyed blue and embellished with little tulle flounces, but in no way resembling either sky or clouds. Let the hills of the battlefield (in *Julius Caesar*) be designed to recede into the horizon, but why don't the actors diminish in height like the hills as they move upstage?

A conventional stage plan unfolds before the audience considerable depths of landscape perspective, but at the same time is not in a position to show human figures corresponding in size to the receding landscape. Yet this kind of staging pretends to be a true reproduction of nature! The actor, moving ten or twenty meters from stage front, looks just as big, is as distinctly visible as when he stood at the very footlights. And yet, according to the laws of design perspective, the actor should be moved as far upstage as possible. If he must be shown in proper relation to the trees, houses, and mountains surrounding him, then he must appear sharply diminished in height—by a silhouette perhaps, or just by a dot.[6]

A real tree will seem rough and unnatural next to a painted one, because its three dimensions do not harmonize with the two-dimensional reproduction. One might cite countless examples of absurdities that naturalistic theater has arrived at as a result of taking for its basic principle the exact reproduction of nature. The fundamental concern of naturalistic theater has been reduced to capturing the rationalistic element in an object, photographing, illustrating the text of a play by set design, copying historical style.

If naturalism has led Russian theater to the use of complicated technique, the theater of Chekhov, the other face of the Art Theater, witnessing to the power of mood on the stage, has created something without which the theater of Meininger would have perished long since. Yet naturalistic theater has been unable in the interests of its own further growth to take advantage of this new tone introduced into it by the Chekhovian music. The theater of mood was prompted by the creative work of Chekhov. When the Aleksandrinsky Theater performed *The Seagull,* they did not catch the mood he had suggested; but his secret does not at all lie in crickets, howling dogs, or real doors. When *The Seagull* was staged in the Hermitage quarters of the Art Theater, the machine had not yet been perfected and technics had not yet spread its tentacles into every corner of the theater.

The secret of Chekhovian mood is hidden in the rhythm of his language, and the actors of the Art Theater heard just this rhythm during the days when they rehearsed the first Chekhov production. They heard it through their affection for the author of *The Seagull.*

Had the Art Theater not caught the rhythm of Chekhov's works, had it been unable to re-create this rhythm on the stage, it never would have acquired this second face which created its reputation as the theater of mood. This was its real face and not a mask borrowed from the Meinin-

[6] Georg Fuchs, *Die Schaubühne der Zukunft* (Berlin, 1905), p. 28.

ger. I am profoundly certain that it was Chekhov himself who helped
the Art Theater successfully lodge the theater of mood under the same
roof which sheltered naturalistic theater. He helped by his presence at
the rehearsals of his plays, and by his personal charm. Through private
conversations with the actors, he influenced their taste and their approach to the problems of their art.

The theater's new personality was established by a certain group of
performers known in the theater as "Chekhovian actors." The key to
the acting of Chekhov's plays lay in the hands of this group which almost invariably made up the cast of a Chekhov performance. One
should consider these people to be the creators of Chekhovian rhythm on
the stage. Remembering the lively participation of the Art Theater's
actors in creating the images and moods of *The Seagull*, I begin to understand how I acquired such a firm belief in the actor as the principal
element of theater. *Mise-en-scène*, crickets, the tramp of hooves across
a little bridge—none of these created mood; it was born only of the
exceptional musicality of these performers. They grasped the rhythm of
Chekhov's poetry and were able to envelop their work in its moonlit
haze.

The harmony of Chekhov was not destroyed in the first two productions (*The Seagull, Uncle Vanya*). For the time being, the actors were
allowed complete freedom in their creative work. Later, the naturalistic
direction made the ensemble the essence, and thus lost the key to performing Chekhov's plays. Once the ensemble became the essence, each
actor became passive in terms of his artistry. The director, retaining his
role as conductor, had a pronounced influence on the fate of the new
tone, so recently acquired; but instead of deepening it, instead of pene-
trating its lyrical essence, the director of naturalistic theater created
mood by perfecting external devices such as darkness, noises, props,
character acting. Having once caught the rhythm of speech, the director
soon lost the key to directing (as exemplified by Act III of *The Cherry
Orchard*), because he did not notice how Chekhov had shifted from
subtle realism to a mystically intensified lyricism. . . .

The Art Theater had a chance to extricate itself from its blind alley,
to come to New Theater through the lyric talent of Chekhov. But in its
later work, this theater succeeded only in subordinating his music to
technical prowess and sundry tricks. Toward the end, the Art Theater
lost the ability to play its own author, just as the Germans lost the key
to performing Hauptmann when he began to write drama (*Schluck und
Jau, Und Pippa tanzt!*) unlike his realistic plays, and demanding a different approach.

Principles of Structure
in Chekhov's Plays

by A. Skaftymov

There is a rather large and in many respects substantial body of secondary literature on Chekhov's dramaturgy.

Contemporaries noted a peculiarity in Chekhov's plays at the time of the first productions. At first they interpreted this peculiarity as Chekhov's inability to manage the problems of continuous living dramatic movement. Reviewers spoke of "prolixity," of the lack of "stagecraft," of "insufficient action" and weakness of plot. In reproaching Chekhov, contemporaries wrote that "he himself does not know what he wants," that "he does not know the laws of drama," that he does not fulfill the "most elementary demands of the stage," that he writes some sort of "reports," that he gives little pictures with all the chance accidentality of photography, without any thought, and without expressing his own attitude.

K. S. Stanislavsky and V. I. Nemirovich-Danchenko noted the so-called "undercurrent," [1] the most essential principle in the dramatic movement of Chekhov's plays. They revealed the presence of a continuous, internal, intimate, lyric current behind the external, prosaic episodes and details; and in their endeavors at creative staging, they correctly directed all their efforts toward rendering this emotional current more perceptible to the spectator. The new, infectious force of Chekhov's plays became evident.

During this time critics ceased to speak of Chekhov's ineptitude in the field of drama. They reconciled themselves to the "absence of action" in his plays just as they did to the plays' evident strangeness; they defined Chekhov's plays as a special "drama of mood," and thereby seemed to answer all the questions for a time. Only a few critics continued to

"Principles of Structure in Chekhov's Plays" by A. Skaftymov. From *Stat'i o russkoj literature* (Saratov, 1958), pp. 313-338, in abridged form. Translated from the Russian by George McCracken Young. Skaftymov's essay was first published in 1948.

[1] V. I. Nemirovich-Danchenko, Predislovie "Ot redaktora" in N. Efros' *'Tri sestry' v postanovke Moskovskogo khudozhestvennogo teatra* (Petrograd, 1919), p. 10.

look back to traditional "dramatic laws," and as a mild reproof to Chekhov continued to speak of a "looseness" and of the "diffuseness of a Chekhovian scenario." [2] This reproof, however, no longer testified to dissatisfaction or ill will. They "forgave" Chekhov for his peculiarity. All the articles on Chekhov's plays now enumerated everything that contributed to the "mood": elements of lyric coloring in the characters' speeches, sound accompaniment, pauses, and so forth.

Later on these same devices and peculiarities were described in special studies (Yuriev, Grigoriev, and Balukhaty). S. D. Balukhaty's contributions to the study of Chekhov's dramaturgy were especially considerable. In two books and several separate studies, he traced the history of the writing and first productions of each play and gathered a great deal of material characterizing Chekhov's own attitude toward his activities as a dramatist and the attitude toward his plays on the part of the critics and public. He carefully described the structure of each play and thoroughly mapped out the process of gradual formation of those special features and devices which constitute the specific character of Chekhov's plays. All this aids considerably in the study of Chekhov's drama.

Regrettably, even Balukhaty presents all the peculiarities of dramatic structure merely in a descriptive manner. The question of the unity of form and content in Chekhov's plays remains altogether untouched.

Much remains unclear. Specifically, what was the nature of the new attitude toward reality which required new forms for its expression? What ideological kind of creative force drew Chekhov to put together this particular complex of dramatic peculiarities? What motivated Chekhov to devise new methods of dramatic movement? Why does everyday reality occupy such a large and free place in his plays? Why does he abolish tightness of plot and substitute for it episodic, disconnected scenes, and why does he change all forms of interaction of dialogue? And mainly: how is it that all these peculiarities harmonize with each other; what is the nature of their interdependence; what underlying defining principle do they have in common?

The statement that Chekhovian drama is not drama in the usual sense, that it is "lyric drama" or a "drama of moods," and more precisely of "melancholy moods," has only descriptive value. Furthermore, it has little concrete meaning. It is true that in such a description, functional explanations are found for such elements as sound accompaniment, pauses, etc. But why, for the purposes of lyricism, was it necessary to resort to indirect rather than direct expression of feeling, moods, and so forth? If it is a matter of "lyricism" or "moods" in general, with the

[2] Ju. Sobolev, *Chekhov* (Moscow, 1934), p. 241.

added note that this lyricism has a sad, melancholy character, then are the scattered quality of the everyday details, the absence of plot, and other purely Chekhovian features absolutely necessary for its expression?

Obviously, calling attention to the lyricism and melancholy mood of Chekhov's plays is inadequate as an answer to these questions. One must consider the qualitative substance of those "moods," that is, see what thoughts and ideas are connected with them. Only then will the essence of Chekhovian forms be revealed as the specific nature of content—a content which could only, and exclusively, be expressed through the given forms.

Balukhaty's suggestion that Chekhov, with his new type of drama, was seeking to supersede the old canon of the drama of everyday life explains little. It is true that Chekhov was dissatisfied with the "tried and true poetics" of the drama of everyday life, that he was "seeking to overcome the schematic character of the drama of everyday life" just by using new "elements and colors from everyday life," to "create in the theater the illusion of life," and "to construct new, fresh dramatic forms in place of the former, conventional typification of scenes and characters." [3] But one can hardly agree that Chekhov includes "facts, actions, intonations, and themes" in a drama merely because they were "new," "strikingly impressive," and because they had not yet been "utilized" on the stage; that merely for the sake of such "novelty," Chekhov "avoids vivid, dynamic elements," simplifies the plot fabric, and substitutes "an apparently unsystematic combination of facts and actions" for "the dramatically conceived, strictly motivated movement of themes one finds in the drama of everyday life." [4] Supposedly, Chekhov did all this in order to "tone down the customary 'theatricality' of plays and to revivify dramatic writing by *naturalistic* and *psychological devices* within the complex structure and relations of routine, ordinary life." [5]

The suggestion of a striving for novelty does not define the real nature of that novelty. If the term "naturalistic" is understood to mean Chekhov's striving not only toward novelty, but also toward the utmost truthfulness, that is, toward the closest approximation of the forms of life itself, then, of course, it would be generally correct to say that Chekhov discovered certain new aspects of reality, and in his creative work as an artist–realist sought to reproduce them. But a striving for truthfulness is insufficient as an explanation. . . . The crucial question is why Chekhov stubbornly and persistently sought to combine so many

---

[3] S. D. Balukhatyj, *Chekhov-dramaturg* (Leningrad, 1936), p. 113.
[4] *Ibid.*
[5] *Ibid.*, p. 18. [My italics—A. S.]

diverse elements of reality, the unity of which makes up the specific substance of his plays. He must obviously have perceived some sort of connection between all these elements of reflected life. . . . This article is
an attempt to reveal the structural peculiarities of Chekhov's plays as
an expression of a special dramatic quality of life discovered and interpreted by Chekhov as an attribute of his epoch.

As we know, theater critics reproved Chekhov most of all for introducing into his plays superfluous details from everyday life, and thus
violating the laws of stage action. The presence of such details was put
down to his ineptitude, to the habits of the writer of tales and short
stories, and to his inability or unwillingness to master the requirements
of the dramatic genre. These views were expressed not only by newspaper and theater reviewers who were distant from Chekhov and did
not know him, but even by those who clearly wished him well (for
example, A. Lensky and Nemirovich-Danchenko).

Chekhov himself, at the time he was writing the plays, apparently
experienced the greatest difficulty and confusion on this point. While
working on *The Wood Demon*, he saw that instead of a drama (in the
usual sense) he was arriving at something like a story. "*The Wood Demon*
is suitable for a novel," he wrote A. S. Suvorin October 24, 1888.

> I am perfectly well aware of this myself. But I haven't the strength for a
> novel. I might be able to write a short story. If I wrote a comedy, *The
> Wood Demon*, then not actors and a stage would be in the forefront, but
> literary quality. If the play had literary significance, it would be due to that.

After *The Wood Demon*, Chekhov turned away from the theater for
some time. Seven years passed. He was now at work on *The Seagull*.
His purpose was not to get rid of details from everyday life, but to overcome the seeming incompatibility between such details and the demands of dramatic genre and to effect a synthesis of these details. "Details" in the new play were, he knew, prevalent to a degree inadmissible
in the usual play, but obviously, he could not forsake them. While working on the play, he wrote: "I am afraid to make a mess of it and to
pile up details which will impair the clarity." And further: "I am
writing the play not without satisfaction, although I sin terribly against
the conventions of the stage. It is a comedy, three female parts, six male,
four acts, a landscape (view of a lake); much conversation about literature, little action, tons of love." And then again: "I began it *forte* and
finished *pianissimo*—despite all the rules of dramatic art. A story has
emerged. I am more dissatisfied than satisfied, and reading my new

play, I am again convinced that I am not at all a playwright." (Letters to Suvorin, October 21 and November 21, 1895.)

All of this indicates that for Chekhov in his excursions into drama, some sort of reproduction of the sphere of everyday life was an indispensable condition; he was unwilling to forsake it. . . . "They demand," he said,

> that the hero and heroine be ˄heatrically effective. But really, in life people are not every minute shooti˙ g each other, hanging themselves, and making declarations of love. And they are not saying clever things every minute. For the most part, they eat, drink, hang about, and talk nonsense; and this must be seen on the stage. A play must be written in which people can come, go, dine, talk about the weather, and play cards, not because that's the way the author wants it, but because that's the way it happens in real life.[6]
>
> Let everything on the stage be just as complex and at the same time just as simple as in life. People dine, merely dine, but at that moment their happiness is being made or their life is being smashed.[7]

At first glance, such statements seem incomprehensible. Was there not everyday life in the earlier drama of everyday life which had developed over the course of the entire nineteenth century? Take A. N. Ostrovsky (1823-1886)—whom, of course, Chekhov could not fail to know—don't people eat, drink, hang about, and talk nonsense in his plays? Can it be that his characters come, go, dine, talk, and so forth only because "that's the way it happens in real life"? Is not the entire structure of an Ostrovsky play directed toward the attainment of the greatest likeness in life? Are not all devices of plot, development, and denouement in Ostrovsky created in order to approximate the truth of everyday life? There were, of course, conscious deviations from this criterion. But these were unavoidable, an obligatory convention. And even in these instances the author's efforts were nevertheless directed toward achieving the closest resemblance to those situations which were regarded as possible in everyday life.

But let us not stop here. Are not the dramatic collisions which make up the heart and meaning of a play, drawn as belonging to everyday life? All images of people, types, and characters always have been represented as figures from everyday life, that is, as something established, of long standing, and characteristic of the general way of life in a given environment. At any rate, authors were always striving in this direction. . . .

---

[6] "Vospominanija D. Gorodetskogo," *Birzhevye vedomosti* (1904), No. 364.

[7] "Vospominanija Ars. G. (I. Ja. Gurljand)," *Teatr i iskusstvo* (1904), No. 28.

The principal justification for the nineteenth century play of everyday life was always one and the same: its closeness to reality and to the most universal and enduring qualities of life and people. Out of this demand arose the notion of "typicality," binding for all alike and accepted as the basis for all literary and dramatic judgments. It gave a common direction to everyone's efforts—one which met with varying success, to be sure, and brought about the creation of a peculiar but widely shared style of everyday life realism. In spite of all the variety of thematic and ideological problems, all the subtleties in ways of selecting and arranging material, everyone more or less had to present everyday life not only as a framework, but as a theme facilitating the most exact verisimilitude. One can scarcely point to any play of this kind where elements of the common flow of life are not represented, where, specifically, tea is not drunk, where there is no eating and drinking, and where quite "ordinary" conversations do not take place.

Chekhov, of course, knew this. It is clear that, when he spoke of the necessity for everyday ordinariness in a dramatic reproduction of life, he had in mind some other reality which he had observed, something unlike anything he had seen in his predecessors.

Wherein lay the difference?

One of the salient features of pre-Chekhovian drama is that everyday life is absorbed into, and overshadowed by, events. The humdrum—that which is most permanent, normal, customary, and habitual—is almost absent from these plays. Moments of the even flow of life appear at the beginning of the play, as an exposition and a starting point, but subsequently, the entire play, the entire fabric of dialogue is taken up with events; the daily flow of life recedes into the background and is merely mentioned and implied in places.

In plays of this type . . . where the stage situation serves merely as an occasion for the characteristic descriptive utterances of the *dramatis personae*, there are no entangling events. But these plays are not finished works of art; even for the authors they were no more than preliminary studies, episodic genre sketches. In most of the other plays . . . the elements of commonplace tranquility always, in essence, foreshadow an event and are directed toward it. They foretell an event, giving information about the conditions under which it will occur; or they comment on its meaning by revealing in dialogue certain traits in the characters without which the event would not occur. . . .

Furthermore, in the earlier drama, everyday life is nothing but the customary manners and morals of people. In each play the intent is to expose, display, and comment on some social vice or imperfection. Depending on the depth and breadth of the author's understanding and ability, the central event of the play absorbs into itself both the roots and manifestations of the evil at issue, as well as its consequences. Basically, the characters appear either as bearers of the vice depicted or as its victims. Some characters are introduced for subsidiary aims: to forward the intrigue, to reveal the qualities of the main characters, or to explain the author's point of view (the *raisonneur*). Within these limits there are countless variations. But despite all the variety of world views, talents, and objects depicted, and despite marked differences in the writers' mastery of drama, all the previous drama of everyday life is similar in its one objective: to mark and isolate some everyday traits in people, and for this purpose to show an event in which the characters act in accord with these selected traits.

The everyday elements of each play, then, are chosen only as they illustrate the social or ethical meaning of some feature of typical life like ignorance, despotism, acquisitiveness, flippancy, official swindling, social indifference, obscurantism, and so forth. . . . The result is a concentration of the ordinary dialogue on some morally significant trait or other which is embodied in the principal event. All other details of everyday life are merely extraneous, have no direct bearing on the problem, and could easily be omitted. The even humdrum of life is almost absent from these plays.

In Chekhov it is entirely different. Chekhov does not seek out events; on the contrary, he concentrates on reproducing the most ordinary features of day-to-day existence. Chekhov saw the drama of life being performed in that ordinary flow when things are left to themselves and nothing happens. The peaceful flow of life as it is lived was, to Chekhov, not simply a "setting" and not simply an exposition serving as a transition to the events, but the central area of life's dramas, that is, the direct and fundamental object of his creative act of representation. So, contrary to all traditions, Chekhov moves events to the periphery as if they were details; and all that is ordinary, constant, recurring, and habitual constitutes the main mass, the basic ground of the play. Events that do occur in Chekhov's plays do not fracture the general atmosphere of everyday conditions. Events spread themselves evenly throughout the interweaving of divergent interests, everyday habits and happenings; they are not knots where everything centers, but rather, they merge into the general multicolored fabric; each event serves as a thread, a detail in the pattern.

Chekhov's method of revealing everywhere—not only in the plot—
the substance of the play is not yet apparent in *Ivanov*. Ivanov's inner
drama, which organizes the play's principal movement, is brought out
in the event which integrates the plot—the story of Ivanov and Sasha
Lebedev. Much of the substance here, too, however, lies outside the
strict plot field: for example, scene v in Act I (Shabelsky and Anna
Petrovna), most of Act II (the guests at Sasha's estate), scenes i, ii, iii,
iv in Act III, with the conversations of Lebedev, Shabelsky, and Borkin
on political events in Germany and France, the conversations about
tasty foods and snacks, and the subsequent intrusion of Kosykh with his
passion for cards. None of this bears directly on the story of Ivanov and
Sasha. Everywhere in the play one is reminded of the permanent and
diverse aspects of life.

In *The Wood Demon*, this sense of an external, humdrum, protracted,
and ordinary atmosphere, conveyed through neutral, everyday, trivial
details, emerges quite distinctly. The play's event (the flight of Elena
Andreevna) has the status of a local episode. The most important and
larger part of the play's canvas is crowded with ordinary affairs, when
there is no special intention to attract interest to the central event.

In *The Seagull*, the most notable events are centered on Treplev.
But the play is not entirely concentrated around this most obvious pivot.
Its driving impulse is felt autonomously and independently in Nina
Zarechnaya, Trigorin's life, Arkadina's life, the lovesick Masha Shamraeva, the ill-starred life of Medvedenko, Dorn's weariness, and Sorin's
peculiar kind of suffering. Common life flows on and everywhere pre-
serves its common forms. Each of the participants has his own inner
world and sorrow, and each plays his own little part in the general
ensemble.

In *Uncle Vanya* and *The Three Sisters*, there are even fewer events.
In *Uncle Vanya*, the most prominently placed are Voynitsky's relations
to Elena Andreevna and Serebryakov; in *The Three Sisters*, the relations
of Masha and Vershinin and of Irina and Tusenbach. But these moments, so prominent, nevertheless do not provide a backbone of plot
for the play as a whole. In the general flow of the play these moments
remain episodes; they are seen as individual consequences of a way of
life that was formed long ago and is common to all, a way of life that is
sensed equally throughout the play and among all the characters in
situations that have long been chronic.

At the center of *The Cherry Orchard* stands the sale of the estate and
Ranevskaya's emotional upheavals and sufferings connected with it. But
throughout the play the drama of Ranevskaya is absorbed into the

flowing processes of common everyday life. From the first scenes, even Varya is shown to have her special anxieties and secret sorrows. Lopakhin is worried by the immediate business of the next day. Even Epikhodov, Firs, Simeonov-Pishchik, and Dunyasha have their minor, but still special inner worlds. And later, throughout the whole length of the play, everybody's common, everyday concerns continue to go on around Ranevskaya.[8]

In none of the plays do one or two persons bear the inner conflict all by themselves. Everyone suffers (except for a very few, cruel people).

* * *

. . . The bitter taste of life for these people consists not in a particular sad event, but precisely in the drawn-out, habitual, drab, monotonous dullness of every day. Workaday life with its outwardly tranquil forms is introduced into Chekhov's plays as the main sphere of the hidden—and most widespread—states of dramatic conflict.

What interests Chekhov in the humdrum of everyday existence is the general feeling of life, that state of pervasive inner tonicity in which man lives from day to day.

The dramatic characterization of everyday life, based on the depiction of customs, morals, and manners, proved unsuited to Chekhov's purposes. His choice of prosaic details was determined not by their ethical and thematic meaning, but by their significance in the general emotional content of life. But because this principle was not understood at first, it seemed that they had been deposited haphazardly, following no internal law.

* * *

At the end of Act I of Ostrovsky's *Let's Settle It Among Ourselves,* Bolshov, having a conversation with Rizhpolozhensky and Podkhalyuzin, picks up a newspaper, as if by accident, and reads there a declaration concerning "bankrupts." Now everyone can understand the reason for this episode because it is connected with the basic theme of the play. No one doubts the internal propriety of this seemingly "accidental" detail, because it so clearly corresponds to all that is happening and will happen to Bolshov.

---

[8] For further discussion on this point, see my essay "O edinstve formy i soderzhanija v 'Vishnevom sade' Chekhova" ["On the Unity of Form and Content in Chekhov's *The Cherry Orchard*"] in my collection of essays, *Stat'i o russkoj literature* (Saratov, 1958), pp. 356-390.

But consider: in Act II of *The Three Sisters,* Chebutykin reads from a newspaper: "Tsitsikar. Smallpox is raging here." Neither Tsitsikar nor smallpox bears any relation whatsoever to Chebutykin, or to any other person, or to anything that is happening or will happen on the stage. A newspaper report happens to catch his eye. He reads it through and it has no direct bearing on anything that is being said around him. Subsequently, it is left without any echo. Why is it there?

In Act I of *Uncle Vanya,* again without any connection to what is happening, Marina walks around the house and clucks: "Cheep, cheep, cheep." And again, one asks: what is its purpose?

In Act II of *The Seagull,* Masha stands up in the middle of a conversation, walks in a "lazy, limping gait," and announces: "My foot is asleep." Why is this necessary?

There are many such "accidental" remarks in Chekhov. The dialogue is continuously bursting, breaking, and becoming confused by some apparently unnecessary and altogether extraneous triviality. The result was bewilderment. People were astonished by the seeming incongruities, by the insignificance of the thematic content, and by the accidentality of much of the dialogue and many of the characters' individual remarks.

One can remain bewildered, however, only so long as one does not grasp the new dramatic principle whereby all these seemingly meaningless particularities are drawn in and unified. They take on life and meaning not by what they connote, but by the complex sense of life they convey.

When Chebutykin, immersed in his newspaper, reads: "Tsitsikar. Smallpox is raging here," this sentence is addressed to no one, and is not intended to provide information. It is simply one expression of boring tranquility, the idleness, sluggishness, and insubstantial character in the play's general atmosphere. Again, when Solyony and Chebutykin argue as to whether the word *chekhartma* or *cheremsha* means a meat or a plant of the onion family, this passing episode has meaning not for its thematic content, but simply because of the triviality and the stage of half-exasperation it expresses. . . .

The internal state of an individual is superimposed on the common variegated fabric and from it derives its particular meaning, background, and emphasis. Remarks are charged not only with particular meaning for the character who is speaking, but, when spoken neutrally, take on vast meaning that illumines the condition of the other characters present.

When Marina, during one pause, imitates a chicken's "cheep, cheep, cheep," it not only says something about Marina, but also gives expression to the tedium that weighs upon the other characters present: here the upset Voynitsky and the bored Elena Andreevna. When at the end of the play, Marina says: "I, sinner that I am, have not eaten noodle soup in a long time," her words are not especially meaningful and might even seem superfluous. But in the context of the play, they say less about Marina's homely desire for food than about the succession of pleasant and tranquil, but dull days which have now begun again for Uncle Vanya and Sonya.

Chekhov's methods of rendering the tedium of life were not created all at once, but rather they developed and grew complex according to the peculiar problems of each play.

In *Ivanov,* Chekhov points to the spiritual destitution and emptiness surrounding Ivanov and Sasha when he stuffs the dialogue with frankly boring conversations by Lebedev's guests (Act II), and Ivanov's guests (at the beginning of Act III). More of these conversations, their emptiness all the more obvious, filled the first versions of the play. Chekhov was thus faced with the danger that his depiction of tedium might itself become tedious to the audience. This danger compelled him to forgo some motifs and to shorten these episodes.[9]

Subsequently, Chekhov communicated the impression of emptiness and tedium in the everyday flow of life without emphasizing the tedious and uninteresting elements; he would merely touch on them, hinting at people's boredom through a gesture or intonation which revealed the direct, but also the hidden, emotional meaning of a seemingly insignificant sentence.

During a general conversation, Masha, in *The Seagull,* gets up and says: "It must be time for lunch. (Walks in a lazy, limping gait.) My foot is asleep. (Exits.)" The audience grasps not only Masha's boredom but the whole feeling of a scene on a typical endless day.

At the end of Act II of *Uncle Vanya,* when Elena Andreevna, upset by a conversation with Sonya about love, happiness, and her own fate, waits to hear whether or not she may play the piano, the watchman taps in the garden. Then he leaves, at Elena Andreevna's request, and his voice echoes in the silence: "Hey you! Zhuchka! Boy! Zhuchka!" This juxtaposition of a neutral, peaceful, ordinary detail with the pathos of a joy that is denied, opens a perspective on the calm, eternal indifference of the everyday flow of life: life—you have to recognize it—passes and goes its way.

By means of such juxtapositions as these, the homely detail in Chekhov acquires an enormous capacity for conveying emotion, and you feel

[9] See my essay "P'esa Chekhova *Ivanov* v rannikh redaktsijakh" ["The Early Versions of Chekhov's *Ivanov*"] in *Stat'i o russkoj literature,* pp. 339-355.

behind each detail the synthesizing force of a feeling for life as a whole.[10]

What is the source of the conflict? Who and what causes suffering? Until we arrive at the substance or the peculiar essence of Chekhovian conflict, we shall formulate it merely as the contradiction between what is given and what is desired, that is, the discrepancy between what a man has and what he strives for. Who or what brings about this breach between man's desired and real existence?

In other drama, the source of conflict, generally speaking, lies in the contradiction and conflict of human interests and passions. The conflict is based on a violation of moral norms, as when one will encroaches upon the resisting interests and wills of others. Therefore, the notion of some kind of guilt is always connected with the dramatic suffering. The source of the conflict, consequently, is the faulty, criminal, evil, or misdirected will of a person or persons; a battle of wills breaks out—the battle with obstacles, and all sorts of peripeteia.

Some defect in social relations always lies at the base of the dramatic conflict, and conflict consists of a collision between healthy and honorable human desires and a dark, evil force. Basically, one of two kinds of villains is involved: either the "domestic" oppressor, who, by his own despotic conduct, corrupts and disfigures life for those around him; or the newcomer, the bearer of evil. The latter is an adventurer or a swindler, and by deception he forces his own way into the confidence of his victims in order to achieve his mercenary and dishonest aims.

The poor who are dependent on the rich experience most of the dramatic suffering; or it falls on younger members of the oppressor's family, who are deprived of their rights: the daughter, the governess, or less often, the son or wife. The victims of the deception are honest, trusting people, primarily women, who for one reason or another attract the deceiver's interest, then, betrayed by blinded feelings, find themselves in his snare. . . . Social relations changed, customs changed, new vices arose, other problems were posed. . . . The drama of everyday life, however, remained the same, because it retained in every respect its

[10] In his representation of everyday life, Chekhov is sometimes thought to resemble Turgenev, especially as represented in *A Month in the Country*. It is true that one might see some analogy, notably in Act I in the insignificance of the conversation, in the remarks that cross and interrupt each other, in the general, peacefully bland mood as the characters play cards, wait for dinner, and so forth. But the substance of all these peculiar features in Turgenev bears no resemblance to Chekhov. In Turgenev the details are without relation to the essence of the characters' experience. The dramatic interest passes outside and around the details. Thus, the nature of the dramatic conflict in Turgenev is entirely different from that in Chekhov.

basic aims: to depict customs and morals, to edify, to expose and indict vice.

*   *   *

Chekhov is different and has an entirely different point of departure for his critique of reality. Chekhov's first mature play, *Ivanov*, does solve a problem having to do with social types, but at the same time it is polemically directed against preconceived and hasty judgment of people.

Ivanov perpetrates a number of acts which by their own outward appearance naturally arouse moral indignation. Everyone condemns him. Yet the play, by its dual illumination of Ivanov, outer and inner, cautions as it goes along against customary moral judgments and calls for a more complex understanding of those reasons, motives, and incentives which govern a man's behavior. . . . In *Ivanov*, instead of moralizing directly, Chekhov elucidates the emotional state of his hero and suggests the notion of involuntary guilt, as when one man causes another's misfortune without any desire whatsoever to do so. . . .[11]

In his second play, *The Wood Demon*, Chekhov was concerned with the same idea. The play again wars on the lack of attention people give to each other. It attacks preconceived labels and stereotypes which prompt one to judge people without any real basis for doing so. All the mutual suspicions and accusations which, ultimately, led to the misfortune turn out to be false. Everyone regrets his mistake (except Serebryakov, the most obtuse and self-satisfied of all the characters; and in the first draft of the play, even he is remorseful).

Dramatic conflicts in Chekhov consist not in the opposition of strong wills, but in contradictions inherent in the objective conditions of life, contradictions before which the individual will is powerless.

In *The Seagull*, in *Uncle Vanya*, in *The Three Sisters*, and in *The Cherry Orchard*, "no one is to blame," no one individually and consciously prevents another's happiness. Who is to blame that in *The Seagull*, Medvedenko loves Masha, and Masha loves Treplev, and Treplev loves Nina Zarechnaya, and Nina loves Trigorin, and so forth? Who is to blame that the professions of writing and acting do not in themselves bring happiness to Treplev and Zarechnaya? Who is to blame that Voynitsky regards Serebryakov as an idol worthy of the sacrifice of an entire life, and that when Serebryakov proves to be a hollow man

---

[11] We find this same thought in "Verochka" (1887), written at the time he was working on *Ivanov*: "For the first time in his life he [the hero] knew by experience how little man depends on his own free will, found himself in the position of a decent and sincere man who, against his own will, brings cruel and undeserved suffering to his fellow man."

Voynitsky's life goes by in vain? Who is to blame when Astrov cannot summon the feelings for Sonya that would make her happiness? Who is to blame for the lonely and inane life that tortures Astrov, disfigures him spiritually, and wears away his feelings to no purpose? Who is to blame in *The Three Sisters,* where, instead of leaving for Moscow, the Prozorov sisters begin to sink even further into the drabness and fog of provincial life? Who is to blame when their knowledge and sensibilities find no application and wither to no purpose? Who is to blame when Ranevskaya and Gaev, by virtue of their own moral and psychic condition, are unable to make use of Lopakhin's well-meaning advice? Who is to blame for the general state of life in *The Cherry Orchard,* where the characters wheel about in lonely suffering, where people do not and cannot understand each other. Who is to blame when people's sincere feelings and mutual good will do not give warming joy, but life remains drab, dirty, unhappy, and sad?

No one is to blame. Then, since no one is to blame, there are no real adversaries; and since there are no real adversaries, there are not and cannot be struggles. The fault lies with the complex of circumstances which seems to lie beyond the influence of the people in the play. The unfortunate situation is shaped without their willing it, and suffering arrives on its own.

It is not that Chekhov's people are not judged at all. It is not that there is no distinction between human virtues and defects, or that human conduct is not shown to be a source of evil. All that is there. But evil in Chekhov operates outside the sphere of direct, willful activity as if it were merely some involuntary fruit of life (though it is evil all the same). Even in the most negative of Chekhov's characters, it is not their wills that are presented first and foremost, but the quality of their feelings. Their wills do not create the action of the play. Wicked people in the plays only make worse a situation that is already bad in itself. The better people turn out to be powerless. A mass of petty, ordinary details entangles man; he flounders in them and is unable to extricate himself. Life passes irrevocably and in vain, continuously, inconspicuously giving out what people do not need. Who is to blame? This question resounds continuously throughout each play. And each play answers: individuals are not to blame, but the entire makeup of their lives. People are to blame only in that they are weak.

What is the substance of the conflict? It was defined generally above as the contradiction between what is given and what is desired. But such a definition still leaves out the specific Chekhovian quality. The contradiction between what is given and what is desired is to be found everywhere, and every play is structured on this conflict; but Chekhov established his own, specific sphere of the desired.

In the earlier, pre-Chekhovian drama of everyday life, the desired is projected as liberation from the vice that hinders life. In each of the given plays, the setting to rights of life is conceived to be limited to the areas encompassed by the evil operating in the play. The fate of people is considered with reference to that aspect immediately subject to the interference and influence of the given vice. The characters' individual desires, as a whole, are contained within these limits. Remove the action of the vice, and a state of happiness is obtained. The destructive influence may prove to be so profound, however, that the restoration of the "norm" proves impossible; then catastrophe results. But whichever way the characters' fate is structured, even in these cases, it remains within restricted thematic limits. That is what happens in all of Ostrovsky's plays. . . .

The particular conflict in which a Chekhovian character finds himself also proceeds from some perfectly concrete desire that has not been or cannot be fulfilled. In *The Seagull*, it is anguish over unrequited love or longing for the joy of a writer's or an artist's fame. In *Uncle Vanya*, suffering, caused by the consciousness of the irrevocable and joyless passing of life, moves into the main focus beside the motif of desired, but unattainable love (Voynitsky, Sonya, Astrov, and Elena Andreevna). In *The Three Sisters*, the concrete desire is a yearning to escape from the provinces to Moscow. In *The Cherry Orchard*, it is connected with the change awaited in the fate of the estate.

Yet it is not difficult to see that these concretely designated yearnings do not, in themselves, take in the entire scope of that longing for the better which is felt in the play. Each private desire is accompanied by expectation of a change in the entire substance of life. The dream of fulfillment of a given desire lives in the soul of each personage with a longing for the satisfaction of more poetic interests that embrace all of life. Each person's suffering consists in the fact that these higher spiritual elements do not find application and conceal themselves in intimate thoughts and daydreams. Thus the particular, private desires always have an extended meaning. They appear as vehicles for the inner longing for another, bright existence in which vague, lofty, poetically beautiful, secret dreams can be realized.

The melancholy of Masha Shamraeva and Sonya, the belated outbursts of Voynitsky and Astrov, the Prozorov sisters' continuously voiced yearning to move to Moscow, contain a suffering brought about by the general drabness and emptiness of the life they lead. They all want a complete transformation, they want to reject the present and set off for some new and bright horizon.

When Nina Zarechnaya aspires to be an actress she has a notion of some higher spiritual happiness which is not granted to mere mortals, about which one dreams only from a distance. For the Prozorovs, that many-featured daydream calling from afar is Moscow. What they will obtain in Moscow or what and how it will fill their lives—of this not a word. At the focal point of the play, one finds only a spiritual unrest, a feeling of life's incompleteness, a surging impulse, and an expectation of something better. The concrete forms in which this desire takes shape and becomes concentrated vary with each character. Each in his own way wants and expects something better. And in each case the inner unrest and dissatisfaction is expressed in a personal form: in Tusenbach it is different from what it is in Vershinin; in Solyony it is even more different; in Andrei Prozorov it is different again; and so forth. But in everyone, private desires are united with the common longing to begin some kind of different life. You feel an individual's distress only to feel the drabness and incoherence of life as a whole.

In *The Cherry Orchard,* personal and private outbursts are brought even more clearly into the realm of life's general disorder. The fate of the estate interests everyone in his own way, but behind each private interest, everyone thinks and feels desires of a more general character, as is obvious in the role of Petya Trofimov. Ranevskaya suffers not only because of the loss of the estate, but also because of the entire wasteland of her life. And even Lopakhin, in his dreams of summer cottages, in the end anticipates a general, fundamental change. "Oh, if it all would pass more quickly, if somehow our awkward, unhappy life would quickly change!" "Lord, thou gavest us immense forests, unbounded fields, and the widest horizons; and living here we should, by all that is true, be giants." This plea for eventual universal happiness finds passionate and overt expression in the lyric endings of the plays, in the words of Sonya, Olga, and Anya. . . .

The spectator is drawn into this lofty atmosphere of longing by various means, like things and sounds; and also by dialogue on subjects very different on the surface, but really in their emotional tone closely related and similar in meaning: love, happiness, nature, art, the past, and so forth. There are even theoretical discussions, usually inconclusive. They are cut short and abruptly left hanging in midair. Their significance lies not so much in their theoretical content as in the sense of helplessness and weariness which gives rise to them. They are symptoms of a dissatisfaction and inner upheaval which perhaps are not realized fully and equally by everyone all the time.

These lofty desires find strong resistance in the flow of life. . . .

The next question is that of the movement of the tragic element, of its development in the play. What are the progressive changes of situation that make up what we call "development of action"?

It is very characteristic of Chekhov that his selection of things to take place onstage and not offstage leans toward life's most constant and most time-consuming features. . . . The play opens with the characters already in a state of habitual, wearying discontent. The roots and causes of the present burdensome situation lie somewhere in the distant past. The chronic spiritual malaise is dragged out now day after day. This kind of suffering does not cease to be suffering, but has a peculiar character and its own discreet forms of expression. Hidden, it erupts and becomes noticeable only momentarily.

At the beginning of Act I of *The Seagull*, everyone but Nina Zarechnaya and, in part, Treplev (and Arkadina, who is always satisfied) has been only half-alive for a long time, can hardly endure life, and only frets and mourns after the happiness that has been denied to him. In *Uncle Vanya*, Voynitsky's situation was established long ago, and now, as his feeling for Elena Andreevna awakens again, it is only exacerbated. Astrov has long been sadly accustomed to the tedious, cold, and exhausting routine of his workaday existence and knows perfectly well that his situation is hopeless. Sonya, too, has languished for a long time. The Prozorov sisters have for years been yearning for Moscow. Life itself long ago conditioned the "unhappy" existence of the characters in *The Cherry Orchard*.

The development of the plays consists in the recurrence of hopes for happiness, followed by their being exposed as illusions and then shattered. Nascent hopes for happiness or at least for some improvement in the situation summon various persons to actions which have the character of events; but these events are never developed in the play. Chekhov quickly returns his hero to a new version of the everyday condition to be endured once again. The event provoked by the hero's enthusiasm for his new purpose occurs only behind the scenes. On the stage it makes itself felt only in the protracted and total tedium which has again set in.

In *The Seagull*, Nina Zarechnaya's fate changes. Illusions of happiness engulf her, an attempt to realize these hopes occurs (she draws nearer to Trigorin, she becomes an actress), and then the hopes are exposed as false. Happiness, she discovers, was not to be obtained even there. The moment of joy, however brief and illusory (her love affair with Trigorin), is not shown on the stage. Only the result is shown: the return to days of prosaic suffering. The false, happy excitement is already a thing of the past, life has become once more days to endure, and with this sad new humdrum state of things, Nina comes back on the stage. Masha Shamraeva, from act to act, hopes to overcome her melancholy by some new, decisive act (she gets married, again offstage). But there is no improvement. . . . *Uncle Vanya* contains almost no events. Voynitsky's feeling for Elena Andreevna is only an element in the final clarification and realization of his sealed fate. He struggles with no one and nothing. The shot at Serebryakov was only an indirect expression of his vexation at the mistake of his life which he had already realized. His joyless life is bound to remain the same as before. The play quickly restores him to his earlier, outwardly smooth, but bitter, humdrum existence. The same is true also of Sonya. Astrov, from the very beginning, knows that his situation is irremediable, and his drama is marked by bitter self-irony. "The entire meaning and drama of man are internal," Chekhov said apropos of *Uncle Vanya*. "Sonya's life had drama in it up to this moment; it will have drama in it after this moment, but the moment itself is simply an incident, a continuation of the shot. And the shot, after all, is not drama, but an incident." [12] . . .

[In *The Three Sisters*] Irina hopes for a renewal in life when she starts to work. She becomes a telegraph operator, then serves on the town council. The days are past when all this was new to her. . . . Chekhov takes up the situation when the new post has already become tedious, drab, and burdensome, when it is already clear that the changes which occurred have added no joy whatsoever. Andrei marries Natasha. But again, the event is not onstage when it is still something new; only its joyless result receives stage embodiment; we see the marriage only when illusions have already disappeared and the monotonous protraction of life's useless passing has already set in. . . . Chekhov presents the bitter thought, the bitter feeling, human suffering, not when they are fresh, but when they have passed within, have become part of an established state of mind, and are hidden from others by outwardly usual behavior. As a result, the movement of action acquires exceptional complexity. . . .

The resolution of the conflict corresponds to the specific nature of its content. The final chord has a double ring: it is both sad and bright.

If the dramatic tension has to do with the whole tenor of life, if no one individual is to blame, then one can expect that the way to some-

---

[12] L. Sulerzhitskij, "Iz vospominanij o Chekhove," *Shipovnik*, No. 23, p. 164.

thing better lies only in a radical unheaval of life in its entirety. The arrival of something better depends not on the removal of local obstacles, but on the transformation of all forms of existence. And until there is such a transformation, each person in the separateness of his being is powerless before the common fate. Therefore, in the end, Chekhov's heroes do not find their lot improved. Life remains dismal and drab. Nevertheless, all the plays end with an expression of a passionate dream and a belief in the future. Each play emphasizes the confidence that in time life will become different, clear, joyful, and rich with radiant feeling. Life, however, remains joyless—but only temporarily and only for those who are still weak. . . .

The double emotional chord at the end (sadness about the present, and the bright promises of the future) is the synthesis of that judgment on reality which is realized in the movement of the entire play: it is impossible to reconcile oneself to the view that people must live without joy, that everything vital and poetic in man must remain fallow, that it must die impotent inside; life must change, must become "beautiful"; one must build such a life, work. "Such a life is necessary to man, and if it does not exist at this time, then he must anticipate it, wait, dream, prepare for it."

*   *   *

Ivanov: An Analysis

by G. Berdnikov

The first of Chekhov's plays to be staged was written in 1887. It was finished very quickly. In the beginning of October, Chekhov told his brother that

> I wrote the play by chance, after a conversation with Korsh. I lay down to sleep, thought up the theme, and wrote. I spent two weeks on it, or, to be more honest, ten days—since there were days during those two weeks when I didn't work or was working on something else. (Letter to Al. P. Chekhov, October 10-12, 1887.)

The play was performed in the Korsh Theater in Moscow on November 19, 1887. It was the benefit performance for N. V. Svetlov, who played Borkin. The play was a reasonably solid success, although it evoked conflicting comment in the press.

How can we explain Chekhov's ability to write *Ivanov* so rapidly? By the fact that Chekhov was writing on a theme with which he had long been familiar, one which he had outlined roughly in his earlier play without a title. In the latter, he accurately caught the general contours of a gentry intellectual—a "superfluous man" of the 1880s—and the sketch was somewhat clumsy, but vivid after its own fashion.

Returning to an old theme with *Ivanov*, Chekhov stubbornly emphasized the originality of his conception. As he saw it, this originality lay in the fact that his main characters were "new in Russian literature," "not yet touched by anyone." (Letter to A. N. Pleshcheev, January 2, 1889.) What was Chekhov's basis for considering his theme, actually that of the "superfluous man," to be an untried novelty in Russian literature?

Categorically opposing his play to the contemporary "repertory piece," Chekhov insisted that his characters were "alive," represented "a slice of life," and were the result of the "observation and study of life." In this connection he persistently objected to attempts to interpret *Ivanov* in

"Ivanov: An Analysis" by G. Berdnikov. From *Chekhov-dramaturg* (Leningrad–Moscow, 1957), pp. 51-63, in abridged form. Translated from the Russian by Joyce C. Vining.

terms of the established conception of the "superfluous man." He always tried to make it clear that, in this play, he wanted to

> sum up everything that had been written so far about these whimpering melancholy people, and, with *Ivanov*, to put an end to this sort of writing. (Letter to A. S. Suvorin, January 7, 1889.)

Chekhov's attempt to differentiate between his nineteenth century intellectual hero and the traditional figure of the "superfluous man," as well as his intention to do away with the traditional theme, shows how profoundly conscious he was of history. Unquestionably, he had noted particular features of a hero of the new times, and tried to focus attention on them.

*   *   *

But what were these features?

> Ivanov is a gentleman, a university man, not unusual in any way; his is a nature easily stirred, ardent, strongly inclined toward enthusiasm, honest, straightforward—like most educated gentlemen. He has an excellent past, as is the case with most cultured Russians. There is scarcely a Russian gentleman or university graduate who could not boast of his past. The present is always worse than the past. (Letter to Suvorin, December 30, 1888.)

Ivanov's past is marked by attempts at a principled service of the people, fiery speeches, economic management of agriculture, creation of unusual schools, etc. His present shows a decline of his powers, apathy, laziness, utter indolence, and complete disillusionment. Chekhov considers all this typical of that class of people who barely see thirty or thirty-five and are already bored and tired. About such people, he writes,

> He hasn't even grown a decent moustache yet, but he already speaks with authority: "Don't get married, old man, trust my experience." Or, "What is liberalism anyway? Just between you and me, Katkov was often right." (Letter to Suvorin, December 30, 1888.)

Ivanov is one of these types; he appears to repudiate vehemently his past strivings and preaches a gray life in the spirit of the notorious liberal principle of "moderation and care." He lectures Lvov: "Pick yourself something ordinary, gray, with no bright colors or superfluous noises. In general, construct your whole life by a pattern—the grayer and more monotonous the background, the better." "My dear fellow," he exclaims,

> don't make war on thousands by yourself, don't fight windmills, don't beat your head against a wall. . . . God keep you from all kinds of economic management of agriculture, unusual schools, fiery speeches. . . . Retreat

into your shell and go about your own modest appointed way. . . . This is milder, healthier, more honest.

It is easy to see that this appeal of Ivanov's is completely in the spirit of Gaideburov's liberal publication, *Nedelya* (*The Week*), or "The Russian Consoler," as it was caustically and accurately nicknamed by Saltykov-Shchedrin.

In Ivanov, therefore, we find the traits of the newest hero in what might be called his purest form, when the evolution of the "Russian gentleman or university man" had run its course and really had come to its conclusion with a way of life which "bordered on villainy." Ivanov, too, would have been one of these gentlemen had Chekhov not set himself the task of making the character of his hero considerably more complex.

Life had shown Chekhov more than characters whose downfall was complete. Other variations on the ruin of this social type arose when the conscience of the "Russian intellectual" turned out not to be so compliant, when it did not and could not reconcile itself to the ignominious end to which the representatives of "cultural populism" had come. The first, classic case [of the gentleman whose downfall was complete] was perfect material for the merciless satire of a Saltykov-Shchedrin. But the other variation afforded excellent material for drama which mirrored the lives of many ordinary men of this kind, a drama of subjectively honest and respectable people who found themselves condemned—for reasons unknown to them—to an agonizing life "with nothing to do and with no rest."

Chekhov decided to make Ivanov precisely this subjectively honest person who tragically survives his downfall. The complexity of the task rested in the fact that this subjective honesty, while it remained unquestionably a real attribute of the hero, could not and did not change his highly unattractive life—one which signaled the ruin of the social tendency he represented. Chekhov concentrated all his efforts on the difficult problem of truthfully portraying this complex social phenomenon. But how did he cope with this problem?

When he had finished the play, Chekhov wrote to his brother:

My play has come out as light as a feather, with no tedious passages. The plot is unprecedented. (Letter to Al. P. Chekhov, October 10-12, 1887.)

In another letter, he stressed the essential distinction between his play and contemporary drama.

The playwrights of today begin their plays with angels, villains, and clowns, exclusively—go find these elements anywhere in the whole of Russia! Maybe

you'll find them, but not the extreme types that the playwrights need. . . .
I wanted to do something new: I didn't portray one villain or one angel
(although I wasn't able to refrain from clowns), didn't blame anybody,
and didn't exonerate anybody. (Letter to Al. P. Chekhov, October 24, 1887.)

And so Chekhov himself insisted on the unique, unstereotyped character
of his heroes, and on the originality of his plot: these features, and
especially the authenticity and lifelike character of the people in his
play, in Chekhov's view essentially distinguish his work from that of
other contemporary playwrights.

Actually, the originality of theme and idea made it necessary for him
to look for equally original artistic means of expression. He had to find
the structural and stylistic resolution which would make it possible to
avoid a one-sided portrayal of his characters (the "angel" or the "villain"),
so as neither to blame nor to exonerate. This concept did not mean,
however, that he avoided judging his characters. The contrary is true.
He tried to make the verdict pronounced on Ivanov final and uncondi-
tional. One might, Chekhov thought, in one way or another interpret
the subjective intent of the hero and the peculiarities of his nature, but
one could never ignore the fact of his undeniable bankruptcy in the
face of life, or the sentence which life had passed on him. Chekhov made
this idea the structural basis of his play.

However important the collateral lines of the play, the center of dramatic action is the fate of the hero, with his particular character traits.
Chekhov explains these traits as follows:

Ivanov is tired, doesn't understand himself, but life is unconcerned about
that. It makes its legitimate demands on him, and, whether he wants to or
not, he must decide the issues. The sick wife is an issue; the pile of debts is
an issue; Sasha drapes herself around his neck—an issue. How he resolves
all these questions must be evident in his monologue in Act III and in the
contents of the last two acts. People like Ivanov do not resolve problems,
but collapse under their weight. (Letter to Suvorin, December 30, 1888.)

Thus, the essence of the play's dramatic action turns out to be the ex-
posure of the decisive feature of the hero's character, one correctly noted
by Chekhov: his total inability to cope with life—the source of his ruin.
With this in mind, it would seem that there is no room in the play for
plot-complication, since the hero's relation to life is passive.

The originality of composition of *Ivanov* lies nevertheless in the
existence of a plot, one indeed which is clearly pronounced. Its foundation is Ivanov's relationship with his wife, and the later relationship
with Sasha in which the others see an attempt on Ivanov's part to
straighten out his shaken financial affairs through an advantageous

marriage. They think he has miscalculated, since his wife's parents gave not one kopeck with her, and that he is trying to arrange a new marriage to a wealthy heiress.

It must be said that the plot of the play develops most consistently. At first, it emerges in provincial gossip, to which no one attributes real importance. An example would be the conversation, in Act II, between Zinaida Savishna, Babakina, Avdotya Nazarovna, and the other guests about the adroit adventurer Ivanov who worries his dowerless wife to death, and who is able to extricate himself from a difficult financial situation only through the crooked operations of the manager Borkin. In Act III, Ivanov's friend Lebedev still keeps aloof from this gossip and is merely perplexed. "Really, now, where does this gossip come from!" he says to Ivanov. "So much of it is going around the district about you that you'd better watch out that the district attorney doesn't come for you. It seems you're a murderer, and a blood-sucker, and a thief." But the gossip increases. With the help of Lvov, who for his part stubbornly insists that Ivanov is a scoundrel, the gossip reaches Ivanov's wife Anna Petrovna. Deeply wounded by Sasha's unceremonious visit to their home, Anna Petrovna accuses Ivanov of behaving dishonorably and of chasing after money. This is the background for the final, highly dramatic scene of Act III—Ivanov's explanation with his wife.

In the first version of the play, the gossip theme reappears again at the beginning of Act IV in the conversation of Kosykh and Dudkin. They still regard Ivanov as an adventurer but express sympathy for him since they think that Zyuzyushka will betray Ivanov and give no dowry with her daughter. The gossip theme arises again in Lebedev's conversation with the daughter, when Lebedev, though in an evasive sort of way, lends credence to the unfavorable gossip about the wedding. "Shurochka, forgive me," he says, "but something's not aboveboard here. A lot of people are talking already. Somehow or other this Sarah of his died, then somehow and for some reason he suddenly wants to marry you." Shura does not listen to him, and the gossip does not crop up again until the end of the act. Lvov's insulting outburst, when he pronounces Ivanov a villain, deals the hero his final blow. He dies of a broken heart.

After his play was produced at the Korsh Theater, Chekhov came to the conclusion that although it had seemed so successfully written, his play was not understood, and that he had not managed to embody his idea in clear artistic forms. Mikhail Pavlovich Chekhov, recalling the first performances of *Ivanov*, writes,

The play had a mixed reception: some hissed, others—the majority—applauded loudly and called for the author. But in general, they did not understand *Ivanov* and for a long time the papers were explaining the personality and character of the hero.[1]

Thus, disappointment followed Chekhov's initial satisfaction with his work, and he found essential revisions necessary. These revisions were difficult, and the work dragged on for a long time. Chekhov produced the third and final version only in 1889, and even this verion later underwent further, though not basic, emendations, which were not completed until 1901.

Chekhov began revising the play in October of 1888 when it was to be produced at the Aleksandrinsky Theater as a benefit performance for the theater's director, F. A. Fedorov-Yurkovsky. On December 19, 1888, enclosing the new edition of *Ivanov*, Chekhov writes to Suvorin:

> Now my Mr. Ivanov is much more intelligible. I am not completely satisfied with the finale (except for the shot, everything is sluggish), but I take comfort in the thought that this is not yet its final form.

However, Chekhov was to suffer a serious disappointment this time, too. As reviews of the new version indicated, the main characters were again misinterpreted. Once more, Chekhov had to introduce substantial changes.

The chief purpose of the revisions was to clarify Ivanov's character. Professor A. P. Skaftymov writes that "while reworking the play, Chekhov was mostly concerned with making Ivanov's character clear. Chekhov felt it was important not to allow sympathy for Ivanov's pessimism, and, at the same time, not to make Ivanov morally at fault." [2]

In making a series of changes for the second and third versions, Chekhov concentrated on Act IV, which twice underwent radical revision. The plot became even better defined as a result of these rewritings. In the very beginning of Act IV, two plot lines hostile to Ivanov merge. Lvov, who condemns Ivanov from what he thinks is a position of high principle, joins forces with Kosykh at this point. The latter, although critical of Ivanov, is really far from condemning him, because the sins attributed to Ivanov strike him as the perfectly natural acts of a man who is no fool and is looking out for himself. Now, after a talk with Kosykh, who confirms his belief that Ivanov is a "schemer," Lvov decides

[1] M. P. Chekhov, *Anton Chekhov i ego sjuzhety* (Moscow, 1923), p. 40.
[2] A. P. Skaftymov, "P'esa Chekhova *Ivanov* v rannikh redaktsijakh," in his collection of essays, *Stat'i o russkoj literature* (Saratov, 1958), pp. 344-345.

to "unmask" him once and for all; the "unmasking" occurs at the finale, when Lvov publicly insults Ivanov.

In the second version, this plot line was further strengthened. Sasha, till now Ivanov's only steady supporter, at this point all but joins his maligners. She wavers after the above-mentioned conversation with her father, and when Ivanov appears and suggests that she give up the idea of getting married, she quickly consents.

Even without this intensification of the plot, which Chekhov discarded in the final version, the complication is clear enough. Moreover, both the development and denouement could create the impression that Ivanov was the victim of intrigue, and the play was even interpreted this way by some of the critics. For example, in the *Novoe Vremya* review of the Korsh Theater production it was said of Ivanov that

> he is an ordinary man, honest, but weak in character. . . . He has many good inclinations, but they are only seen and understood by those who are close to him and who love him. . . . Gossip takes advantage of this and works on it, making a scandal out of it.[3]

Of course, nothing could please Chekhov less than this kind of approach, which reduced his play to a flat, mediocre theatrical trifle. Yet, when he revised the play, he did not reject the plot-complication, but strengthened it. What role, then, did the author give it in the play?

It has been noted above that a fundamental trait of Ivanov is his passivity, an inability to make decisions. But he does not live in a vacuum. As Chekhov puts it, life cares nothing about Ivanov's weakness; it keeps on putting its questions to him. Under these conditions, Ivanov's passivity, his total inability to cope with the problems of life, leads him to do things which, as he himself realizes, no decent person would do. At this point those nuances appear which Chekhov strove to bring home to his audience. Of course, the conviction of Lvov and the others that Ivanov is trying to do away with his wife because she brought him no fortune is ridiculous and absurd. Chekhov succeeds in convincing us that this is nonsense. Nevertheless, Ivanov really does destroy his wife by his inattentiveness, his crudeness, and his romance with Sasha; he drives her to consumption. Is Ivanov guilty on this account? Subjectively, Chekhov says, he is blameless, since he assuredly did not desire the death of his wife. But objectively, he is certainly guilty, because his wife died and her death was the result of a series of unlovely deeds on Ivanov's part.

The same may be said of his romance with Sasha. Aware, deep in his

[3] *Novoe vremja*, No. 4215, November 20, 1887.

heart, of his own real worth, Ivanov knows that this marriage will bring Sasha only unhappiness. He even tries to dissuade her from it at the last moment. Nevertheless, he agrees to the wedding in the end. Even here the motive is not mercenary calculation or pursuit of Zyuzyukina's money; it is simply again a matter of Ivanov's passivity and inability to stand his ground before the trials of life. Again, he acts as no decent man could or should.

In other words, Ivanov reacts to all these situations without feeling guilty and without active evil intent. But he lacks the will to oppose wrong actions, and so they are carried out. The gossip which haunts him throughout the play may be explained as merely a philistine version of his undeniable guilt. It is the guilt of a man who, thanks to his inertia, his lack of will and moral fibre, wallows in deeds which lower him to the level of the philistines around him. Ivanov fully understands this only at the end. Hence his line, "For a long time you careened down an incline; now stand still! It's time you learned honor!" Hence too the suicide, which, under the circumstances, was the only thing that could save him from complete submersion in the world of the Borkins, Lebedevs, Babakinas, Zyuzyukinas, and the other provincial philistines. And that is why Ivanov's declaration before his suicide conveys precisely his spiritual state at the end: "The youth in me has awakened, the old Ivanov has begun to speak."

In this way, the role of the plot-complication within the play proves to be more profound than it might seem at first glance. The plot is not at all the buildup of provincial gossip which conquers an innocent man, but a kind of exaggerated expression of a real slide down an incline which ends in a complex moral collapse. Ivanov, it is true, recollects himself, but only momentarily, and because he discerns in this gossip, to his own horror, his true image—if not today's, then tomorrow's.

Thus Chekhov resolved the main problem in his new play—the creation of a complex and contradictory character for the hero. After long, unrelenting work, he managed to portray a typical character. Both spectator and reader recognized in Ivanov a representative of the liberal intelligentsia, who, in the conditions of the 1880s, soon degenerated into pitiful parasites and philistines. The critics had to recognize this directly or indirectly, as we can see from letters that Chekhov received: "I get anonymous and signed letters," he wrote in this regard to Suvorin, February 8, 1889. "Some socialist (obviously) is full of ire in his anonymous letter, reproaches me bitterly; he writes that some young person perished after my play, that the play is harmful and so on. They obviously understood that I am very glad." Of course, he was referring to those socialists who, as he put it, "got married and criticized the district council." It was just this sort of "socialist" that he had in mind when he wrote *Ivanov*.

The structure of *Ivanov* is centripetal in character, as is plainly evident from the plot outline. The same centripetal pull may be observed in the portrayals of the characters, most of whom in one way or another gravitate toward Ivanov.

Lvov reveals this peculiarity clearly, even though at first glance he seems to be not only Ivanov's antagonist, but his opposite as well. Chekhov describes his most important traits in a letter to Suvorin, December 30, 1888.

> Doctor Lvov is one of those honest, straightforward, frank, but narrow rectilinear people. . . . Anything like breadth of view or spontaneity of emotion is foreign to him. He is pattern personified, a walking trend. . . . He was raised on Mikhailov's novels, saw "new people" on the stage, that is, the kulaks and sons of the century who are portrayed by the new playwrights, the "men of profit.". . . He was impressed by all this, so profoundly that he could not read [Turgenev's] *Rudin* without asking himself, "Is Rudin a villain or not?" Literature and the stage has trained him so well that he approaches everyone with this question. . . .
>
> When he came into the district, he was already biased. He immediately saw a kulak in every prosperous muzhik, and a villain in the Ivanov whom he could not comprehend. A man has a sick wife, and he rides over to a rich young neighbor—well now, isn't he a villain? Obviously, he kills the wife so he can marry the rich one. . . .
>
> Lvov is honest and frank; he spares nothing and nobody. If necessary, he will throw bombs under carriages, punch inspectors in the nose, and call a person a scoundrel. He will stop at nothing.

While he was working on this character, Chekhov also ran into serious difficulties. In the same letter to Suvorin, Chekhov responded to comments on his play:

> If I make Ivanov appear a villain or a superfluous man, and the doctor a great man . . . then my play evidently didn't come off.

Chekhov wanted least of all to make Lvov "a great man"—a fearless and irreproachable knight. But he did not want to caricature him, since he saw Lvov as the representative of a democratic tendency, despite all his narrowness and personal limitations. Had Chekhov chosen to mock Lvov, it would have marked him as belonging to the tribe who played into the hands of the reactionaries by their "antinihilistic" writings. Chekhov could never have made such a choice, and he spoke frankly about it to Suvorin, who seems to have suggested that he resort to caricature:

> These people are necessary, and quite nice for the most part. It is dishonest to caricature them, even for a stage effect, and there's no good reason for it anyway. True, caricature is more biting, and therefore gets across better, but a vague sketch is preferable to a smear.

Chekhov chose another way; he tried to introduce scenes that would explain the peculiarities of Lvov's character as he, the author, understood them. Thus, the third version of the play saw a new episode in scene iv of Act II, which, after a minor correction in 1897, became part of the definitive text. This scene contains the conversation between Shabelsky, Ivanov, and Lebedev in which Lvov is broadly characterized along lines similar to Chekhov's description in his letter. Not content with this scene, Chekhov greatly enlarged the dialogue in Act II when Lvov and Anna Petrovna are at Lebedev's house. In this new episode Anna Petrovna further elaborates on Lvov's character. Her evaluation is extremely important because it is based on a contrast of Lvov and Ivanov, which makes it possible to understand better Lvov himself, as well as his place in the scheme of the play's imagery.

Like the others, Anna Petrovna mentions Lvov's tendency to be dry and doctrinaire, which makes even his honesty unsympathetic. "Listen, Mr. Honest Man!" she addresses him.

> It's not polite to escort a lady somewhere and talk to her about nothing but your honesty the whole way! Maybe it's true, but it's boring, to say the least. Never talk about your virtues to women; let them find out for themselves. My Nikolai, when he was like you, only sang songs and told stories in feminine company, and yet every one of us knew what kind of man he was.

Anna Petrovna's remark brings out not only the contrast between Lvov and Ivanov, but also establishes the community between them. Is Anna Petrovna's statement that Ivanov was once like Lvov really accidental? That it is not accidental comes out in Ivanov's way of warning Lvov exactly as though he were speaking to a man just setting out on the road he—Ivanov—has already traveled. . . .

What is the origin of Lvov's narrow views, which Chekhov persistently stresses and which certainly lower Lvov's stature? His tendency to be narrow and doctrinaire is less a question of character than of background. The explanation for it, Chekhov insisted, is that "he was raised on Mikhailov's novels"—that is, in the spirit of populist fiction, and moreover, of populist ideology in general. That is why faint notes of disillusionment appear in Lvov which further point to his resemblance to Ivanov. These notes of disillusionment do not stem from any weakness in Lvov's character, but from the instability and poverty of the doctrine on which he had been brought up. Their community in ideological areas, therefore, does not lessen the sharp distinction between them as "psychological types." No doubt, Chekhov was trying to depict in Lvov a psychological type from that part of the nonaristocratic intelligentsia which not only had preached about "the people" a short while before, but even threw real bombs under real carriages. Considering Lvov in the light of conditions left by the collapse of the populist movement, Chekhov still tries to isolate those psychological traits which distinguish him from representatives of another wing of the liberal, populist intelligentsia. Chekhov ranks Lvov's consistency in his convictions and his impulsiveness among those traits. When he says that Lvov will stop at nothing, Chekhov underlines the fact that Lvov is a man of deeds as well as words. These traits engendered populist heroes in the not too distant past, but in the populists of the 1880s—those who survived the collapse of the movement—these traits acquired a new character. They bore the marks of donquixotism. . . .

Chekhov's *Seagull*:
The Empty Well, the Dry Lake, and the Cold Cave

by Robert Louis Jackson

Art is at the center of *The Seagull*. Four characters in the play are actresses or writers. Everybody talks about art. Everybody embodies or lives out a concept of art. The problem of talent—what it takes and means to become an artist—is a fundamental theme of the play.[1] Illusion and reality, dream and fulfillment in art and life constitute the inner-most concern of the author. Finally, art in its most basic form as myth gives expression to the underlying dramatic conflicts and realities in the play: the myth of creation, the Oedipal syndrome and the metaphor of the journey.

In his myth-play in Act I of Chekhov's *The Seagull* the young writer Konstantin Gavrilovich Treplev pictures a bleak future for the world: thousands of centuries have passed and all life has vanished. The bodies of living beings have long ago crumbled into dust, and eternal matter has turned them into stone, water, and clouds; their souls have merged into one. A doleful moon vainly sheds light on this desolation. And desolation it is: "Cold, cold, cold. Empty, empty, empty. Terrible, terrible, terrible."

Konstantin's play itself, as commentators on *The Seagull* have observed, is also terrible. It is a concoction of melodramatic posturing and mannered symbolism. Yet—though bad art—it is, paradoxically, full of Chekhov's art. The action, the character-symbols and portents—all the devices which fail so miserably in Konstantin's play taken by itself and which seem merely a Chekhovian parody of a "decadent" theatrical

[1] For a wide-ranging analysis of *The Seagull*—one which posits the central importance of the problems of art and talent in the play—see V. Yermilov's discussion in his *Dramaturgija Chekhova* (Moscow, 1948), pp. 3-54.

style—have a distinctly allegorical character in the context of the larger play, *The Seagull.* Just as in Shakespeare's *Hamlet,* so in *The Seagull,* the play within the play reaches out into the psychological drama.[2] But while the import of Hamlet's theatrical is immediately evident, both before and after the performance, the significance of Konstantin's play is only fully apparent by the end of *The Seagull.* Chekhov's use of Konstantin's play is crucial to his whole development of the character of Konstantin and to the expression of some of the central ideas of *The Seagull.* A discussion of Chekhov's play, then, may properly begin with an analysis of the play within the play.

"Cold, cold, cold. Empty, empty, empty. Terrible, terrible, terrible."

The state of Konstantin's world of tomorrow, unpromising as it appears at first glance, is not entirely without hope. On closer investigation it becomes apparent that Konstantin is dramatizing in mythopoetic language a physical world that is delicately poised between death and life, between sterility and creation, between the negative force of the "father of eternal matter, the devil," and the beneficent, life-stimulating power of "spirit." We have here, essentially, a dramatization of un-liberated life and creation; and, it is further apparent, this is also a crucial self-dramatization. The author Konstantin not only projects a vision of a universe in biological limbo; he, or his alter ego, also inhabits it. But what is not quite clear or established is the poet–narrator's exact status in this created legend.

At the end of the first half of his soliloquy—after referring to the merging of the souls into one—the poet identifies himself directly with the force of spirit and creation which continues to inhabit the universe.

> The universal world soul—that's me, me. In me there is the soul of Alex-
> ander the Great, and of Caesar, and of Shakespeare, and of Napoleon, and
> of the last worm. In me the consciousness of people is united with the in-
> stincts of animals, and I remember everything, everything, everything, and
> I experience anew every life in myself.

This is the high point of the soliloquy. His self-centered exaltation is not without a sort of naïve charm. The poet completely identifies himself with his muse. And this muse is ascendant.

But at this point—and we are now halfway through Konstantin's play—the "marsh fires" (will-o'-the-wisp) appear. (The reader will recall that Konstantin's mother, the actress Irina Nikolaevna Arkadina, ex-

---

[2] For an interesting discussion of allusions to *Hamlet* in *The Seagull,* see Thomas G. Winner's "Chekhov's *Seagull* and Shakespeare's *Hamlet*: A Study of a Dramatic Device," in *The American Slavic and East European Review,* XV (February, 1956), 103-111.

claims at this juncture: "This is something decadent"—to which Konstantin replies with a pleading "Mama!") The marsh fires, it is evident, take on the character of some kind of robot creature-symbols which have depressing import to the poet. Indeed, their appearance signals the collapse of his poetic ego: the "universal soul" metamorphoses into a petty anthropomorphic soul. "I am alone. Once in a hundred years I open my lips to speak and my voice echoes gloomily in this emptiness, and nobody hears me." The pale fires, born from the rotten bog, wander mindlessly and without will or beat of life, toward the dawn. Fearing that life will awaken in them, the poet tells us, the "father of eternal matter, the devil" keeps the atoms in these fires in constant flux. "Only spirit remains constant and unchangeable in the universe." But now spirit seems to be keeping very much to itself. The poet, plainly, is abandoned by his muse.

> Like a prisoner thrown into an empty, deep well, I do not know where I am or what awaits me. One thing, however, is not concealed from me: in stubborn, savage struggle with the devil, with the element of material forces, I am destined to conquer, and then matter and spirit will unite in a beautiful harmony and the kingdom of the world will is to arrive.

Konstantin's play gives expression to the *pro* and *contra* in his nature. It dramatizes his creative yearnings, the flight of his poetic muse, but in the final analysis it is paradigmatic of the downward spiral of a hopelessly crippled creative spirit. "There's something in it," Dr. Dorn observes after seeing Konstantin's play, something "fresh, naïve." The play, indeed, partakes of poetry, as the audience realizes in Act IV when the young actress Nina Mikhailovna Zarechnaya recites again the opening lines from Konstantin's youthful work. But apart from revealing a propensity for abstractions and symbols ("not a single character that's alive," Trigorin later observes of Konstantin's writings in general), the play discloses Konstantin's tendency toward grandiose dreams and impetuous challenges, on the one hand, and passive retreats and sterile reconciliations on the other. The movement of the play—all appearances to the contrary—is precipitous from self-exaltation to a depressed posture of defeat. Here in his well the poet prophesies "stubborn, savage struggle with the devil" and eventual victory. But this is empty prophecy: the well is dry. The poet himself is inwardly aware of the emptiness of his prophecy, of the utopian character of his mythic dream of "beautiful harmony" and of a "kingdom of world will." He resolves the contradiction between the reality of his nature (his weakness of will, his impotence) and his fantastic dream in the manner of a familiar Chekhovian type.

But all this will only take place when, little by little, through long, long
series of millennia, both the moon, and the bright Sirius, and the earth will
turn into dust. And until then, horror, horror.

The "horror" here is, in a sense, an intuition: the self's forereading of
its own tragic emptiness.

It may be argued that our analysis of the inner direction of Konstantin's
play—the view that it moves toward compromise and defeat—must be
permanently flawed by the fact that we are analyzing an incomplete
drama: the play within the play, as we know, is cut short by a flurry of
argument between mother and son. There is no question that the outcome of the poet–narrator's struggle with the "devil" cannot be deduced
with complete certainty from Konstantin's text alone, just as it is impossible at the outset of *The Seagull* clearly to anticipate the denouement
of Konstantin's struggle to become a mature artist. Both destinies are
to a large extent "open." But in the action that brings Konstantin's play
to an end Chekhov subtly prefigures the sad fate of Konstantin and, at
the same time, indicates the inner direction of Konstantin's play, that is,
discloses that *conclusion* which is embryonic in the play's development.
This action is so ordinary and so distracting as to conceal its profound
meaning. We have in mind Konstantin's altercation with his mother.

This altercation is the momentary point of intersection of two lines:
the line of the poet–narrator's struggle with the "devil" in the play within
the play, and the line of Konstantin's permanent psychological duel with
his mother. The duel—one marked throughout *The Seagull* by alternat-
ing acts of hostility, magnanimity, and submission—forms a real-life prologue to Konstantin's play; it bisects the play at its halfway point (the
appearance of the bog fires and the deflation of poetic ego—the painful
exchange between mother and son); finally, it is the immediate cause of
the play's ending. "My mighty opponent, the devil, is now approaching,"
the poet declares. "I see his fearful, crimson eyes. . . ." At this point
Konstantin's own mighty antagonist, his mother, once and for all shatters
his magic lantern with some disruptive, sarcastic comments on the play.
Put out by this cruel teasing, Konstantin declares: "The play is finished!
Enough! Curtain!" And in a childish fit he retires from the scene. His
retreat, of course, constitutes an ironic commentary upon the bold resolve
of his fictional alter ego. In the context of Chekhov's subtle juxtaposition
and interplay of real and fictional lines in the episode of the play within
the play, we recognize that Konstantin's announcement, "the play is
finished," anticipates the abortive ending of his life drama; it constitutes
a dramatic rehearsal for the ending of *The Seagull.*

The negative attitude of Madame Arkadina toward her son—unfavorable circumstances, indeed, for the artistic as well as psychological development of Konstantin's personality—cannot be underestimated in any evaluation of his personal tragedy. But in the final analysis it is Konstantin himself who chooses to ring down the curtain on his own life, as he does on his own play. We may note in passing, here, that Konstantin's impulsive retreat before his mother's jibes contrast pointedly with Nina's efforts, in the midst of the quarrel, to continue the play. Konstantin's behavior in this episode, then, reveals fundamental character weaknesses which will manifest themselves in his life at large. Konstantin's confrontation with his mother is of a very petty nature. Yet as Chekhov once observed: "Let everything on the stage be just as complex and at the same time just as simple as in life. People dine, merely dine, but at that moment their happiness is being made or their life is being smashed." So, also, here—in an ordinary quarrel, in a single moment, Chekhov discloses the compound character and fate of his hero.

Konstantin created for himself in his play a legend not too different in character from the typical fairy tale, with its demons, its embattled and enchanted knights, and its golden kingdoms at the end of the trail. As in a fairy tale, so in Konstantin's legend we are in a world of magic, of the supernatural. The hero in this legend, plainly, finds himself imprisoned by some evil force (the devil). But how will he get out? In stubborn, savage struggle, he declares, "I am destined to conquer" (*mne suzhdeno pobedit'*). The passive structuring of this thought is revealing. Who has destined this victory? What fairy of fate, what magic is going to liberate the hero from his dry prison-well? The appeal here on the part of the poet to a force, fate (*sud'ba*), outside of self points to the tragic flaw in Konstantin, this modern pseudo-tragic hero of *The Seagull*: his refusal to recognize his essential freedom and to accept the responsibility that it implies.

Chekhov alludes to this refusal at the very outset of the play when Konstantin casually tries his fortune by an age-old means: "(Picking petals from a flower) She loves me, loves me not, loves me, loves me not, loves me, loves me not. (Laughs.) You see, my mother doesn't love me. You can say that again!" A search for authority, for a decision-maker outside of oneself, of course, is characteristic of all immaturity. The young actress Nina also reveals a penchant for fortune-telling: "Even or odd," she asks Trigorin at the beginning of Act III. "No," Nina sighs, "I have only one pea in my hand. I was trying my fortune: should I become an actress or not? I wish somebody would advise me." Trigorin's

reply—and we have no difficulty recognizing Chekhov in these words—
is that "in this sort of thing nobody can give advice." We are free. Nina
must accept her freedom: the choice must be one's own. "No general
ethics can show you what is to be done," Sartre wrote in *L'existentialisme
est un humanisme* in connection with another case of decision-making.
"There are no omens in the world." This is a painful lesson that many
of Chekhov's heroes experience. It is of the essence of Chekhov's conception of Nina that she ultimately accepts a world without omens, that,
in a very real sense, she takes her fate into her own hands. "Boris
Alekseevich," she exclaims to Trigorin at the end of Act III, "I have
made an irrevocable decision; the die is cast; I am going on the stage.
Tomorrow I will not be here any longer; I am leaving my father,
abandoning everything; I am beginning a new life." Nothing is fated,
nothing postponed here; a choice is arrived at lucidly. If anything, Nina's
decision constitutes a challenge to fate, to the force of circumstances (her
family life) which is so hostile to her choice of an artistic career. "The
main thing is to give a new turn to life," Sasha tells Nadya in Chekhov's
last story, "The Betrothed" (1903). And Nadya leaves her provincial
town, breaks out of the rut. The tragic consequences of this kind of
challenge to fate are part of the story of Nina in *The Seagull*. But it is
tragedy in which the consequences are surmounted and a new vision
attained.

Chekhov sees in the individual's attitude toward "fate"—whether expressed in discussion or in casual or unconscious acts—a measure of the
individual's own capacity to respond to the sum total of forces acting
upon him, to necessity, to the *given* in life. Chekhov's focus in his brilliant story, "A Woman's Kingdom" (1894) is upon the interrelation of
this factor of the given (background and environment) and individual
will, character, and fate, in the life of the heroine. She was not to blame
for the fact that she never married, the young factory owner Anna
Akimovna muses one Christmas morning. Chekhov takes us into her
inner consciousness. "Fate itself had flung her from a simple worker's
setting where, if one can believe memories, she had felt so comfortable
and at home, into these huge rooms where she was completely unable to
imagine what to do with herself, and could not understand why so many
people were darting in front of her." But it is her passive character, her
lack of courage that seals Anna's destiny. Her daydream that, if her
father had lived longer, he would "surely have married her to a simple
man, for example, to Pimenov"—would have "ordered her to marry him
—and that would be that"; her general belief that "love will define my
obligations, my work, illuminate my world view"; her conviction that

"nobody will take me"; the symbolic scene at the card table when she asks to be "matched" with Pimenov, and then jumbles the cards—all this is symptomatic of Anna Akimovna's deep malaise, her inner impotence. "A man's character is his fate." "A Woman's Kingdom" embodies the insight of this maxim of the ancient Heraclitus.[8]

Those characters in Chekhov who accept the notion of fate, of a force acting independently and capriciously outside of human will, seem to bear within themselves the element of defeat. The fatalistic philosophy of Tusenbach, so poignantly expressed in Act II of *The Three Sisters,* is an ingredient of his tragic fate. "The die is cast," he exclaims in connection with his decision to retire from the army. But his decision to take charge of his life comes too late. This amiable but weak man is the victim, quite ironically, of the meaningless universe that he posits as a philosopher. His would-be partner in life, Irina, also relates passively to life; like Konstantin Treplev in *The Seagull,* she reveals the character of her world view in her casual play with cards: "It's coming out right, the patience, I see. We shall be in Moscow." Fate, chance, luck, of course, is not going to bring the sisters to Moscow, any more than Charlotta Ivanovna's tricks (in *The Cherry Orchard*) will save the orchard. Chance is never productive, creative in the world of Chekhov. On the contrary. When the owners of the cherry orchard renounce their option to decide upon the fate of the estate, when they renounce their freedom actively to participate in their own fate, the estate and their lives are ceded both literally and symbolically to the caprice of chance— the auction block. We discern in the magician Charlotta Ivanovna a symbol of that haphazard universe for which Lyubov Andreevna Ranevskaya and her brother opt (the scattering of money, the game of billiards are symbolic). It is the merchant Lopakhin—no relier on chance or the help of others, but a man who lifts himself by his own bootstraps— who takes fate into his own hands and who triumphs.[4]

[8] The theme of chance or accident—with its correlative idea of a meaningless or perverse universe—saturates the content of "A Woman's Kingdom." It is only when this theme is perceived that the real inner structure and meaning of this story— philosophical, social, and psychological—emerges. Strictly speaking, nothing "happens" in this story; yet in the course of twenty-four hours, held as within the classical unities, the fate of the heroine is determined; put in other words, she (and the reader) discover that fate which is already embodied in her character but which has not yet crystalized in consciousness. The story—and it is largely a psychological one—is the account of the feeble inner struggle (turning centrally on a chance encounter, but involving the heroine's Christmas charity activities) which results in the defeat for self-determination.

[4] It is perfectly true, of course, that the freedom of the estate owners is, *historically,* severely limited. Chekhov plainly depicts the estate owners—in the context of their suffering humanity, to be sure—as representatives of a moribund class which is im-

The objective passiveness of the three sisters in fact leaves everything open to counter-productive chance: their weak brother *gambles* away their money; his wife, Natasha, and her lover Protopopov, untroubled by any fate or a sense of the meaninglessness of life, reap the benefits of this play with the wheel of fortune. "It's all the same," mutters the defunct doctor Chebutykin throughout the tragic Act IV of *The Three Sisters*. But whatever meaninglessness, chaos, or nonsense exists in the world outside of Chebutykin's will, he generously contributes to it through his own action or inaction. He himself, in his renunciation of knowledge, his philosophy of nonexistence, his bankruptcy as a doctor, and his indifference to the fate of Tusenbach (and therefore, for all practical purposes, to the fate of Irina), is the agent of blind, accidental fate. The life of Tusenbach and the half-happiness of Irina are sacrificed to Solyony's bullet of chance. "He was sentimental," Dostoevsky observed of Fyodor Karamazov, "he was evil and sentimental." These words might have been applied by a sterner Chekhov to Chebutykin.

Chebutykin's refrain, "it's all the same," is juxtaposed at the end of the play with the theme of knowledge, of knowing. "If we only knew, if we only knew!" Olga exclaims. "A man must be a believer or must seek some belief," Masha says in the same play, "otherwise life is empty, empty. . . . Either he knows what he's living for, or it's all nonsense." Whether or not Chekhov believed that absolute insight into the meaning and purpose of life was attainable, he did believe that a creative life had to be based upon a striving for that knowledge. Happiness or despair, truth or void, lie not outside man, not in Moscow or in the falling snow,

---

potently being overcome by the movement of time and history; on the other hand, the ability to "decide" and to act is given to a representative of a historically new class—Lopakhin. But Anya and Trofimov also take advantage of the option to shape their own lives. Are we pawns of history and circumstance? It is doubtless Chekhov in "An Anonymous Story" who suggests that "in nature, in man's environment nothing happens indifferently. Everything has reason and is necessary." But we are not thereby relieved of responsibility for, or participation in, our fate. For all Chekhov's undoubted pessimism over the human condition he is not an adherent of a theory of implacable determinism. Lopakhin's constant reiterations to "decide," "think seriously about it," "definitely decide," "decide once and for all," "think about it" point to the constant potential for freedom in man's life. The sense of doom and of guilt that weighs upon Lyubov Ranevskaya and Gaev is not alone in the force of circumstances, in ineluctable "history"; it is *in* them, in their passive nature, in their philosophy. They have become their own history and, no less than Oedipus, are the source of their own undoing. "I am continually waiting for something, as though our own house must collapse over us." Chekhov significantly juxtaposes this observation of Ranevskaya with her brother's random (in form and content) billiard talk. "Today my fate is being decided, fate. . . ." she remarks in Act III. Her fate is indeed out of her hands at this moment, but it is she who has cast it to the winds, as surely as she has scattered her wealth.

but in man, in his choices, and in his attitude toward the world about him. "I am destined to conquer," Konstantin's protagonist declares. We are not *a priori* destined for anything—is Chekhov's reply in *The Seagull*. Nor is the universe *a priori* a meaningful one. Man creates meaning, he gives embodiment to his "history," his destiny. His first step, everywhere, must be to recognize his fate in himself, his past in his present, and so come to grips with the only real *given* in history: man. This step Konstantin Gavrilovich Treplev is incapable of making.

"I love you just as tenderly and devotedly as in childhood," Konstantin tells his mother. "Except for you there's nobody left me now." The neurotic deadlock that constitutes his relation with his mother remains unbroken from the beginning to the end of *The Seagull*. "Can you imagine anything more hopeless than my position in her house?" he asks his uncle Sorin, in Act I. But, unlike Nina, who wrenches herself free from the stifling confines of her family, Konstantin chooses to remain with his dilemma. His last words, in Act IV, after Nina runs out of the house and out of his world once and for all, point to his peculiar oedipal paralysis. "It would be too bad if anybody met her in the garden and then told Mama. That might upset Mama."

Konstantin cannot leave the illusory "magic lake"; he cannot step out of the magic circle of his love–hate relationship with his mother; he cannot cease being a child. He finds himself surrounded by successful people whom he despises and who, so he believes, despise him as the son of a "burgher of Kiev." Certainly imagination, as much as reality, feeds his hypersensitivity. "*It seemed to me* that with their glances they measured my insignificance, *I guessed* their thoughts and suffered from humiliation" (italics mine—R. L. J.). He has contempt for the stale, though glamorous theatrical world of his mother. He is convinced that "new forms are necessary"; yet it is characteristic of his frayed and offended ego that he is equally convinced that "if we don't get them then nothing is necessary." Maupassant, he observes, "ran away from the Eiffel Tower which oppressed him with its vulgarity." But Konstantin himself does not run away from the vulgarity of his world: he stays with it, sinks ever more deeply into it, with his rankling ambition and sniveling self-depreciation, his wounded pride and peevish vanity.

He clearly seeks a kind of surrogate-mother in Nina. Yet the tragedy of his emotional quest is not that he seeks warmth and affection, love, but that this love becomes a kind of *sine qua non* for any sustained interest and progress in art. As he broods over the "failure" of his play (significantly this is his own judgment), he complains to Nina about her coldness. "Your coldness is terrible, unbelievable, it's as though I woke up and looked out and saw this lake suddenly dried up or sunk into the earth." And later, embracing his mother after his quarrel with her, he exclaims: "If you only knew! I have lost everything. She does not love me, I can no longer write, all my hopes have been smashed."

"Love," Chekhov jotted down in his notebook, "is either the remnant of something long past which is dying out but was once tremendous, or it is a part of something which in the future will develop into something tremendous; at the present time, however, it doesn't satisfy, offers far less than one expects." "If you fear loneliness, then don't marry," reads another note. In his well-known letter to his brother Nikolai in March 1886, in which he defines a cultured person, Chekhov remarks that if the cultured person possesses talent he respects it, he sacrifices "peace, women, wine, vanity to it." The creative personality does not passively subject itself to the love relationship. Love alone, Chekhov suggests in *The Seagull*, does not provide a firm foundation for a creative life. The tragedy of Masha in *The Seagull* is that, unlike Nina, she desires nothing but love.

Chekhov, however, does not adopt a monastic attitude toward the love relationship. Nina, in her final talk with Konstantin (Act IV), indicates her readiness to plunge back again into the maelstrom of life. She says of Trigorin at this point: "I love him. I love him even more than before. 'An idea for a short story.' I love, I love passionately, I love to desperation." This is active love: love that is combined with a readiness to face life; it may not carry Nina to Arcadia, but it is love without illusions, love which seeks to envelop and not to be enveloped in warm self-oblivion.

Konstantin, on the other hand, seeks to be enveloped in love. He is "cold" and desires warmth; he yearns for the waters of the womb. Psychologically, he finds himself trapped in the "oedipal situation." But if he is trapped, he has nonetheless, like Oedipus or Hamlet, the option of self-discovery in art or action. This option he rejects, for he lacks the courage to face himself, his talent. The self-knowledge that he attains in the end is too incomplete and too incidental to his real condition to grant him any tragic stature. Like so many Chekhovian heroes, his tragedy consists in his inability to rise to the level of tragedy. He is far from being a Hamlet. And for all the noise of his departure from this world, the real truth is that he leaves this life—to borrow the words from T. S. Eliot—"not with a bang but a whimper."

The real knowledge of self, the blinding vision, the tragic perception, on the other hand, is granted to Nina. Her drama in its painful dialectic is symbolized in the complex image of the seagull; in its living and dead incarnations this image enters her being as a *pro* and *contra*. "I'm a seagull. No, that's not it. I'm an actress." In her anguished outpouring to Konstantin in Act IV she speaks of her growing spiritual strength. "Now I know, I understand, Kostya, that in our work—it makes no difference whether we are on the stage or writing—the main thing is not fame, not glory, not what I dreamed of, but the ability to endure. Be able to bear your cross and have faith. I have faith and it doesn't hurt me so much, and when I think about my calling, I do not fear life."

Just before the performance of Konstantin's play, Medvedenko matter-of-factly observes that Nina "will do the acting, while the play is written by Konstantin Gavrilovich." It is, indeed, Nina who *acts* in Konstantin's play and in the broader drama of life, who summons the will to confront the devil in "stubborn, savage struggle," who emerges in *The Seagull* as the embodiment of Konstantin's "world soul."

The myth of Plato's "cave" and its inhabitants may or may not have been a conscious allegorical point of reference for Chekhov when he wrote *The Seagull*, especially its last act. But the fundamental elements of this myth nonetheless inform Chekhov's play (as they do Gorky's later play, *The Lower Depths*) on its deepest level of meaning—that level in art where character and idea merge with archetypal pattern and source. The central problem here is unquestionably that of illusion and reality and man's necessary movement from the former to the latter; the relevant metaphor, appearing in art and epic, is the *journey*. It is Nina, like Plato's wanderer, who leaves the magic world of illusions to make the difficult journey—the Platonic "steep and rugged ascent" [5]—to reality, to knowledge, to quintessential meaning; while it is Konstantin who chooses to remain forever secure in his world of shadows, illusions, and disembodied forms. "You have found your road," he declares to Nina in Act IV, "you know where you are going, but I am still moving in a chaos of dreams and images, not knowing for what or for whom this is necessary. I do not have faith and do not know where my calling lies."

Two worlds are juxtaposed in the last act of *The Seagull* (as they are in the first scenes of *Hamlet*): the inner, comfortable world of warmth and the outer world of dark, threatening reality. "Evening. A single lamp with a shade is lighted. Semidarkness. The sound from the outside of trees and rustling and the wind howling in the chimney. The night watchman is knocking." Outside, behind the glass door to the terrace

[5] Citations are from the Benjamin Jowett translation of *The Works of Plato*.

which faces the audience, the garden is dark. Nina, like the wanderer in Plato's myth who revisits his den of old, returns to her native nest. She observes: "It's warm, nice here," and again: "It's nice here, warm, comfortable. Do you hear—the wind outside? Turgenev says somewhere: 'Happy is he who in such a night sits under the roof of a house, who has a warm spot.' I'm a seagull. No, that's not it. Where was I? Yes, Turgenev. 'And God help all homeless wanderers.'" And Nina, in her tears of pain and anguish, tears evoked by the contrast of past and present, recalls her "clear, warm, joyful, pure life," her naïve dreams of fame, and her dreamlike love. But Konstantin misunderstands Nina's feelings. He begins to speak—trying to pick up the threads of the past, to reweave the old pattern; he reaffirms his love for her. Nina is brought up with a start. "Why does he talk that way, why does he talk that way?" The question is a pertinent one. Konstantin answers the question. "I am alone, not warmed by anybody's affection, I am cold, as in a cave, and no matter what I write it's dry, harsh, and gloomy. Stay here, Nina, I beg of you, or let me go away with you. (Nina quickly puts on her hat and cape.)"

Why is Nina in such haste to leave? Socrates, discussing the return of the wanderer to the cave, observes that the wanderer would find it easier "to endure anything, rather than think as they do [in the cave] and live after their manner." Men in the cave would say of the wanderer, according to Socrates, that "up he went and down he came without his eyes; and that it was better not even to think of ascending." But for the wanderer—"he would rather suffer anything than entertain these false notions and live in this miserable manner." It is in these terms that we can understand Konstantin's view of Nina as a failure (his story of Nina's two years away from home) and Nina's attitude toward his appeal to remain with him. There can be no return to the innocence and illusions of the past. Nina's reply to Konstantin's plea is replete with real and symbolic meaning. "My horses are standing at the gate. Don't see me off. I'll make it by myself. (Through her tears) Give me some water." Nina dashes into the play on a horse—"A red sky, the moon is already rising, and I raced the horse, I raced it." Nina's horse —Pegasus, winged horse of inspiration—stands ready to carry her away. Brutal reality ("we have both been drawn into the maelstrom") is preferable to Konstantin's sterile cave. "Give me some water." Nina's request for water—over and above its perfectly ordinary meaning—takes on special poetic significance in the context of the rich water imagery in *The Seagull* (Nina's name, Zarechnaya—"beyond or across the river," the "magic lake"). Water is creation, life. Konstantin offers Nina some water to drink. Yet in the arid world that he still inhabits there is none of the water for which Nina craves and upon which art and life flourish. The "magic lake" toward which Nina once had been drawn "like a seagull" has vanished. All that is left is a cold cave, a dry lake, an empty well.

The personal tragedy of Konstantin is that he chose not to make the journey of his life; overwhelmed by his character, he remained forever in the shadow of his fear of life. The triumph of Nina is her free choice of the journey, her willingness, finally, to *endure*. One may say, of course, that this is a very narrow, precarious triumph. And so it is. But Chekhov, like Dostoevsky, was a realist where man is concerned. He knew that the only triumph that counts is the precarious one, the one, in short, that is organically fused with tragic knowledge and experience.

The painful relinquishment of golden childhood and the dream of innocence before the bitter necessity of knowing reality—this is the poignant and tragic side of Nina Zarechnaya's journey into life. Art, or, at least, "pure art" with its efflorescence of beauty, is somehow permanently linked with that dream of innocence. In this sense Nina's awakening in real life reenacts the tragedy of the fall. Yet it is clear that Chekhov does not envisage the renunciation of art or illusion (in the deepest creative sense) in the journey to reality. In the lucid confrontation with reality—the "paradox of the fortunate fall"—lies all realistic hope, the hope once again of reappropriating the dream.

Uncle Vanya:
The Play's Movement

by V. Yermilov

The main theme of the play—the theme of beauty and its destruction—is struck immediately, almost with the first words in Act I. It echoes right away in the dialogue between Astrov and Marina, when the nurse answers Astrov's question about whether he has changed a great deal in eleven years. "A great deal," Marina answers. "Then you were young, handsome, but now you've aged. And your good looks now are not what they were. One might also say you've taken up drinking."

These words contain what we will find later as the play develops: both Astrov's fear of becoming a "vulgarian" and Sonya's begging him not to destroy himself. She asks Astrov to stop drinking.

> It doesn't suit you! You are refined; you have such a gentle voice. Besides, you are different from all the people I know; you are beautiful. Then why do you want to be like ordinary people who drink and play cards? Oh, don't do that, I beg of you! You always say that people don't create but only destroy what is given them from above. Then why, why are you destroying yourself? Don't, don't, I implore you, I entreat you!

Sorrow for beauty that has been destroyed is another theme that is set with Astrov's very first appearance on stage.

Act I provides the main theme and motifs of each of the characters and indicates all the play's conflicts leading to the culmination in Act III. We meet the play's heroes on a day that is overcast and stifling before a storm. Clouds are gathering over them. Misfortune threatens both Sonya and Uncle Vanya, with the beginning of the relationship between Astrov and Elena which will shock them so. Only blissful Waffle does not feel the storm in the air or notice the clouds, and for some unknown

"Uncle Vanya: The Play's Movement" by V. Yermilov. From a chapter on *Uncle Vanya* in *Dramaturgija Chekhova* (Moscow, 1948), pp. 105-116, in abridged form. Translated from the Russian by Elizabeth Henderson.

reason he rejoices: "The weather is charming, the little birds sing, we all live in peace and harmony—what more do we need?" . . .

Even conversations about the weather have a hidden meaning in Chekhov's writing. [It was shown earlier that] Waffle and Elena Andreevna echo one another like sentinels in their desire for general reconciliation—though Waffle's desire to reconcile is both active and comically absurd, while Elena Andreevna's is indolent. They echo one another, too, in Act I when they talk about the weather. "But the weather's fine today, not hot," says Elena Andreevna, trying to smooth over the awkward pause which ensues after Uncle Vanya's sharp words about Serebryakov. But Uncle Vanya erases all these conciliatory efforts with a short, morose rejoinder: "It's fine weather to hang yourself."

Act II unfolds against the background of the storm. The storm colors all the words and all the heroes' experiences in this densely emotional act so full of dramatic exchanges.

The heaviness before the storm permeates the entire opening of Act II. Thus, Serebryakov's "legs throb," as Marina says, and he torments Elena Andreevna as though every word, moan, gesture intensifies the unbearable closeness of the air. Now Marina leads him away—and how many events unfold before us! We hear Uncle Vanya's declaration of love to Elena Andreevna heightened by the background of the storm; in his tragic words about his life in ruins we can already sense a smoldering rebellion. We hear Uncle Vanya's speech about how life has deceived him. We hear Astrov, rebellious, too, in his own way, ordering Telegin to play the guitar and singing with a drunken flourish. "Go away hut, go away stove!" Astrov finds escape only in drink, yet he talks in a fascinating way about "benefits to humanity" and "the broad plans of the future." This act contains Sonya's reproach to Uncle Vanya for "getting drunk with the doctor," and Uncle Vanya's weeping at the memory of his dead sister whose image Sonya's words recall like the memory of lost purity, of hope. . . . We hear Sonya's declaration of love to Astrov, his confession, Sonya's false premonition of happiness, and how in a lyric mood she is reconciled with Elena Andreevna and ventures on a conversation about Astrov: she cannot help talking about him; his dream, his call to beauty fill her soul with music. But Elena Andreevna also finds Astrov attractive. She is overcome by nostalgia for the useless passing of her life, for her wasted youth, for love. She feels a sort of vague jealousy of Sonya. . . . She is sorry for herself; she is resentful that she never in her life felt that free, full happiness of love which carries Sonya away. "There's no happiness for me in this world. No!" she grieves, "why are you laughing." Sonya (Laughing, covering her face): "I am so happy, so happy!" Both dream of one man. The one who pleases him says she is unhappy. And the one who is fated to learn so soon that he does not love her, is happy. . . .

"I am tedious," Elena says of herself. We may speak of a certain inner resemblance between Elena Andreevna and Serebryakov: both are tedious people who kill any light, joy, or gaiety around themselves. All the same, Elena is a young, beautiful woman, a musician, a pianist whose soul inclines toward poetry and beauty. And all of her yearning, her dissatisfaction with life, her pity for herself, all, all must pour forth in music. . . . "It is a long time since I've played. I shall play and cry, cry, like a fool."

Elena Andreevna's music, which should ring out joyfully, is instead a lament for an absurd life with an old, capricious egotist; it is anguish over lost happiness. Sonya's music, which sounds within her and should fill the entire world around her, is a music of hope, youth, exultation. And both of them hear the music of the voice of a wonderful man. "I cannot sleep. Do play something!" says Sonya, embracing Elena Andreevna. Longing for music might be the title for the finale of Act II. Everything is caught up in the expectation of music, as during a drought everything waits for rain. Music is necessary as a sum, as a conclusion, a solution of all that has accumulated here in this story atmosphere where people grieve over wasted lives awaiting fulfillment of their desire for happiness. A theatrical production might stress this musical theme, single out in the darkness the piano and the beautiful hands of Elena Andreevna from which we in the audience expect a miracle: the birth of music. "Your father isn't sleeping," she says to Sonya, "when he is ill music irritates him. Go ask. If he is all right then I'll play. Go on." Sonya goes out and the tension of the pause is filled with the expectation of an answer, filled with the growing desire for music. Then—a quick blow:\ one phrase which Sonya brings from Serebryakov: "It is forbidden!"

This brief sentence signifies many things. The ban on music is a ban on happiness, on youth, on life. The Serebryakovs are those who say: it is forbidden. Everyone is forbidden to strive for joy. The Serebryakovs smother the music of life. "It is forbidden!" is a central phrase: it refers to Sonya's dream of happiness, and to Elena Andreevna's anguish, and to Astrov's strivings, and to Uncle Vanya's rebellion. Everything is forbidden so long as the Serebryakovs, "men in a shell" ["The Man in the Shell," 1898] hold sway over people.

How different the deep, internal, natural musicality of this brilliant finale of Act II is from the external, superficial, meretricious "musicality" of those plays in which music serves as a supplement to the text. . . . In Chekhov's plays music is born in the depths of the text itself and the heroes' experiences; it is an accompaniment to those experiences, an organic part of the text. Music in Chekhov's plays expresses the experiences of the characters which are not expressed in words. Music is a subtext, and expresses the hidden essence of the action, the inner meanings of the words, thoughts, and feelings of the characters. Even unsounded music is part of the development and movement of the play, an active part of the action, and never merely ornamentation. . . .

Yet there is a profound artistic reason that the music does not sound on stage. It would have been a discharge, a resolution, a sum. But nothing has been decided for the play's heroes. . . . The storm outside the windows has passed, been resolved in a refreshing downpour, but within, the storm still broods over the play's action and the souls of the heroes.

"The rain will be over right away," Uncle Vanya says to Elena Andreevna, "and everything in nature will be refreshed and breathe easily. Only I will not be refreshed by the storm. Day and night, I am suffocated, as if by a tormenter, with the thought that my life is hopelessly lost." The heaviness of a storm continues to oppress him.

Then Act III unties all the knots, though without easing or brightening the heroes' fates; instead, it heaps upon them a new, even heavier burden which they will bear to the end of their lives, without any hope of relief.

The composition of Act III is admirable for its complexity. Everything in it is drawn toward the central moment of this central act, and, consequently, to the central moment of the entire play: the "conference" organized by Serebryakov. . . . The scene opens with Uncle Vanya's words: "Herr Professor deigned to express a wish that we all gather today in this living room by one o'clock. (Looks at the clock) Quarter to one. He wishes to announce something to the world."

In the quarter of an hour remaining before the conference, so many dramatic events take place that by the time of the conference people are already different from what they were a quarter of an hour before it. The "fifteen minutes" prove to be extraordinarily paced with action and everything that happens in this brief interval prepares and strengthens the explosion which takes place at the conference.

What then takes place in the course of these "fifteen minutes"? With particular insistence and passion Uncle Vanya impresses on Elena Andreevna that she should, at last, "let yourself go for once in your life," "plunge headfirst into a whirlpool." And it is obvious from the anger with which she greets these hypnotic suggestions of the tempter, and especially from her reply: "How cruel that is!" that Uncle Vanya's words fall this time on thoroughly prepared soil, strike home. After all, she already has reached the point of carrying out Uncle Vanya's advice, but still hesitates, afraid—and now Uncle Vanya lacerates what is most painful and troubling in her soul. We know that Uncle Vanya's words make a profound impression on Elena Andreevna from the reflections she makes while she is alone waiting for Astrov, and we see her terribly agitated over the forthcoming "interrogation": "To give in to the charm of such a man, to forget yourself. . . . Uncle Vanya suggests that a water nymph's blood flows in my veins. 'Let yourself go for once in your life.' Well then? Perhaps it must be so. But I am cowardly, shy. My conscience will torment me."

Thus, Uncle Vanya adds fuel to the fire in which he himself will be consumed. An exchange takes place between Elena Andreevna and Sonya; Sonya agrees to the interrogation of Astrov. We hear Elena Andreevna's explanation with Astrov; then Uncle Vanya is witness to their embraces. He had left to fetch a bouquet of roses for Elena Andreevna, and now these roses, alone and absurdly abandoned, lie on a chair, useless, like Uncle Vanya's love. Meanwhile, behind the scene, Sonya is waiting for the decision on her fate, Astrov's answer.

The participants in the conference, then, come to it shaken by what has taken place already in this fateful quarter of an hour. Uncle Vanya is stunned by the embraces he has seen. Sonya is crushed by the answer brought to her by Elena Andreevna that Astrov will not come around to the house any longer. Everything is prepared for an explosion of extraordinary force, and the "conference" itself appears before us in a completely different light and with a completely different meaning from the way it appeared at the beginning of the act. If the conference had begun immediately after the curtain opened, if there had been no intervening fifteen minutes, everything would have gone on much more quietly, without sharp dramatic effect. Jealousy, anger, hatred, consciousness of a wasted life—all of Uncle Vanya's feelings have reached the boiling point as a result of the scene, terrible for him, in which Elena Andreevna and Astrov declared their love. Elena Andreevna would not have insisted so vigorously on a speedy departure from the estate if Uncle Vanya had not caught her with Astrov at an awkward moment. A curious detail: Elena Andreevna orders Uncle Vanya "to use all his influence, so that my husband and I can leave here today." And Uncle Vanya really does "use all his influence" to fulfill her command: he fires at Serebryakov and so makes it impossible for the Serebryakovs to stay. Ironically, things turn out as though Uncle Vanya had done everything he could to accomplish the will of the woman he loved.

Thus, the "conference" becomes the focus, the center where all the play's lines, all fates cross. Against this background, the conceited Serebryakov's total insensitivity to all that surrounds him appears particularly striking. He delivers his speech like a deaf-blind man, like a strange apparition from some other world that hears and sees nothing that is happening around him.

The storm has broken and has proved not purifying, but consuming and devastating to everything and everyone. In Act IV we see Chekhov as the great master of transitions. The entire act gives us a picture of all the turning points, all the transitions the characters have made from one mode of life to another, from one psychological state to another, all those which have already taken place or are completed before our eyes. The characters begin to live out the life that remains to them. The last hopes that they could expect something from life died out in Act III: the events of this act already seem far away, as though they were not hours, but years distant. This sense of remoteness, of the removal into the distant past of everything that just now was seething, stirring, and burning, constitutes the inner content of the last act. It is the result of many details given to us stark, deep, and strong in the Chekhovian manner.

"And I feel sad that they are gone," Sonya observes. The remark is striking in its unexpectedness but at the same time full of profound truth. Sonya is already so far from the dramas, agitations, hopes, and losses which have just stormed by, that she remembers everything that has happened as if it were in the distant past. Sonya's statement is her formula for transition into another mode of life.

Each character has his own "formula for transition." With Uncle Vanya it is "to work, to work!"—getting down to the everyday, habitual things which he forgot while the professor and his wife were there: "The bill . . . to Mr. ———," "February 2nd, vegetable oil. . . ."

About Astrov's formula for transition, Gorky wrote to Chekhov:

> In the last act of *Vanya*, when after a long pause, the doctor speaks of the heat in Africa, I trembled with admiration of your talent and with fear for people for our colorless, wretched life. How magnificently you struck at the heart of things here and how very much to the point! [1]

[1] M. Gor'kij i A. Chekhov, *Perepiska, stat'i i vyskazyvanija* (Moscow-Leningrad, 1937), p. 11.

A map of Africa that no one here needs, hangs for some reason in the room which serves both as office and domicile for Uncle Vanya. Perhaps Sonya studied it as a child. Astrov walks up to the map, examines it, and declares: "And it must be fearfully hot now in this very Africa—really something awful!". . .

Astrov had just argued bitterly with Uncle Vanya. He demanded that Vanya return the little jar of morphine which he had taken from Astrov's traveling medicine bag. Uncle Vanya was still thinking of suicide. But then even this last echo from the past died. Ordinary days, only ordinary days remained ahead—"buckwheat, vegetable oil." Astrov is ready to leave; his carriage is waiting for him at the door. And this remark about Africa conclusively transports everything that has happened here a moment before far, far away: it is as though Africa symbolized the immeasurable distance separating the heroes of the play from the dramas in which they so recently participated. . . . After the remark about Africa, everything that has taken place on the estate becomes conclusively just as distant as Africa. The fact alone that Astrov is capable of speaking about the heat in Africa, and Uncle Vanya of answering him, makes it particularly evident how far everything has receded into the remote past.

Among the formulas for transition is the glass of vodka which the nurse offers Astrov. He replies to this offer indecisively: "Well, maybe." Just recently he promised Sonya that he would never drink. He has not forgotten this promise yet, and for that reason he answers Marina indecisively. She leaves to get the vodka, and the pause that follows is, like all Chekhov's pauses, saturated with content. Sonya is silent. She, of course, could not have forgotten her conversation with Astrov and his promise not to drink. In this pause they both say goodbye to the past and to one another forever. And, as always, when parting demands decisiveness, courage, Astrov interrupts the farewell pause: "My side horse is lame for some reason." After the exchange of everyday remarks with Uncle Vanya about how he will "have to stop at the blacksmith's," Astrov goes up to the map of Africa. In this way Africa wipes out, erases once and for all, the pause whose content was the farewell between Sonya and Astrov; so when Marina returns with the glass of vodka, it is no longer the same glass of vodka as before the pause, before the farewell, before "Africa." Then it signified the parting with Sonya; in Astrov's indecisiveness there remained some trace of a link with the past, with Sonya. But while Marina is bringing it here, the glass of vodka acquires a new significance: it points, alas, to Astrov's future. What can restrain him now from "destroying himself"? He drinks the vodka; he is already completely free of any thoughts of the past or of Sonya. He takes a swallow from that bitter cup of life which remains to him to drain, or rather, to bring to an end. In his rejection of Marina's proposal that he "take a piece of bread"—"No, just the vodka"—we sense that he no longer has any sort of concern for himself or for his life. *"Finita la commedia!"* He had reason for saying this when he parted with Elena Andreevna.

These are some of the features of Chekhov's dramaturgy: the amazing capaciousness of scenic time, when fundamental psychological processes, transitions from one qualitative state to another, take place in very short intervals; an unprecedented richness of pauses; the pithiness of all the details, all the objects, and their meanings; the miraculous transformations of objects (as in the case of the glass of vodka which is transformed from a token of parting with the past into a token of complete estrangement from the past); the flexibility and at the same time the precision of the transitions.

It is interesting to note the correlation of the final act with that *earlier life* on the estate, which existed here "beyond the limits of the play," even before Act I and the Serebryakovs' "intrusion." As always in Chekhov's plays, we see this "prehistorical" life as clearly as though it had been shown to us onstage; and what takes place in Act IV is an apparently complete return to the way of life on the estate before the Serebryakovs' arrival. The circle has been closed.

"We'll live again the way it used to be in the old days," says Marina. Voynitsky, parting with the Serebryakovs, announces: "You will receive punctually what you used to receive. Everything will be as before." Sonya says to Uncle Vanya: "It's a long, long time now since we have sat together at this table"; and Astrov, looking at Uncle Vanya and Sonya, who, as in the old times, are working together at the table, observes what seems to him an old, familiar picture: "It's quiet now. Pens are scratching, crickets are chirping. It's warm and cozy. I don't feel like going away from here." Even the parting between Sonya and Astrov is, on the surface, like the usual parting for the winter: formerly they also separated for the winter, because of "difficult distances." So everything is as it was "in the old days," and once again, Uncle Vanya and Sonya remain alone together with their old friends, Marina and Telegin.

This external sameness accentuates with particular force the changes that actually have occurred as a result of the Serebryakovs' "intrusion" into the life of the estate. Everything has returned to the old course, and yet things are completely different. Everyone is different; even the cricket, it seems, chirps in a new way.

This is Chekhovian action: on the one hand, the absence of change, even the apparent negation of change, an emphatic impression of the unchanging character of life; on the other hand, the reality of internal, qualitative changes, altering the entire structure of life as it was. The most important thing has passed from life: hope. And it seems that Uncle Vanya and Sonya have been buried alive on this estate, where snowstorms will soon whirl and snow will blot out everything.

The Three Sisters
in the Production
of the Moscow Art Theater

by M. N. Stroeva

"Following the success of *The Seagull* and *Uncle Vanya*, the Moscow Art Theater could no longer get along without a new Chekhov play," wrote K. S. Stanislavsky. "Thus, our fate from that time on was in the hands of Anton Pavlovich: if a play arrived, there would be a season; if not, the theater would lose its flavor." [1]

The Three Sisters was the first play written by Chekhov specifically for the Moscow Art Theater, "commissioned" by it, as it were.

Work on the production began under the direction of Stanislavsky. After a preliminary talk, Nemirovich-Danchenko went abroad and Stanislavsky himself now carried on the rehearsals. . . . The first striking thing in Stanislavsky's new direction is his view of the play as an integral whole, as a symphonic work unfolding harmoniously. In *The Seagull* there were still individual bits which functioned only as external "transitions" for the actors, while in *Uncle Vanya* certain characteristics of the *dramatis personae* did not always tie in with the general mood of the play. This time all these elements were drawn systematically into the general fabric of the production and given logical coherence through the integral thinking of the director which disclosed the idea of the whole performance.

One might define this idea as representation of the inner struggle of man with the "power of banality." Stanislavsky had dealt before this with man's confrontation of his environment but neither in *The Seagull* nor in *Uncle Vanya* did it come so plainly into the foreground. The

"*The Three Sisters* in the Production of the Moscow Art Theater" by M. N. Stroeva. From *K. S. Stanislavskij: materialy, pis'ma, issledovanija, Teatral'noe nasledstvo*, I (Moscow, 1955), pp. 653-670, in abridged form. Translated from the Russian by Robert Louis Jackson.

[1] K. S. Stanislavskij, *Moja zhizn' v iskusstve* (Moscow, 1954), p. 234.

main thing, though, is that this confrontation now acquired an entirely new character.

Formerly, in *Uncle Vanya* and especially in *The Seagull,* the prosaic background tended to have a passive, descriptive function; it only explained the reasons for one kind of mood or behavior in people as opposed to another kind. In *The Three Sisters,* however, in full accordance with the author's thought, banal everyday life becomes an active, aggressive, far more dangerous force. It almost eats into people's lives, gradually enveloping everything, even the most intimate aspects of their lives, dogs all their actions, at every step smothers their dreams, with indifferent mockery reduces to nought their bursts of energy, their strivings. But no richly gifted Chekhovian man of sensibility can remain static. His inner life has the same dramatic intensity as the inner life of the heroes of *Uncle Vanya*; but now this inner activity all the more demands resolution in the external world, is imbued with an even greater sense of purpose. The purpose or goal here is to find the true path to happiness, to a free and bright life of labor.

The clash of two hostile forces constitutes the dramatic pivot in the director's prompt book. This clash begins in the second act. The first act, as is always the case with Chekhov, makes up a bright, joyous prelude —the "nameday, spring, high spirits; the birds are singing; the sun is shining brightly." [2] "Branches with buds barely turned green" peer into the windows "which have just been opened after winter." Irina is preparing feed for the birds; one can hear their "chirping outside beyond the bay window." "Andrei, full of spring feeling, is playing some melodious sonata off in the wings." [3] . . . There are lots of flowers on the stage and from time to time one hears music, loud laughter, joyous exclamations. The mood of contemplation is quickly broken off; tears are erased by a smile. Stanislavsky even introduces entire scenes of laughter, of good-natured quarreling and unexpected bursts of gaiety, in his effort to heighten the mood of buoyancy and good cheer. Dreams about Moscow easily muffle the sadness arising from recollections of the past. The struggle between these two motifs and the quick triumph of vernal hopes for the future lies at the basis of the director's development of the beginning of the performance.

This resolution of the first act shows how correctly the director understands the unique way in which a Chekhov play is put together. In

[2] V. I. Nemirovich-Danchenko, *Iz proshlogo* (Moscow, 1938), p. 168.

[3] K. S. Stanislavskij, *Prompt Book of Act I of* The Three Sisters. Photocopy. Obtained from the *Prague Drama Theater.* Museum of the Moscow Art Theater, No. 5646, pp. 4, 12.

The Three Sisters (just as in *The Seagull* and in *Uncle Vanya*), the first act, full of hopes and confidence, is followed by a second in which reality—the banal everyday life enveloping the heroes—replaces the dream. Later on, in the third act, there is a clash between these two planes of the play and an explosion which leads to the complete defeat of all the hopes of the heroes to realize their dreams in actuality; only the self-sacrificing faith in a better future for mankind remains intact.

In full accord with this development, the second act—in contrast to Stanislavsky's first act (in the director's prompt book)—begins almost somberly; at the very outset the director, in the handling of lights and sound alone, conveys the feeling of anxiety that has crept into the house which till now had been warmed by joyous hopes.

> The beginning: It is dark in the living room; the fire in the stove is going out, only a streak of light falls from the open door leading to Andrei's room. From time to time Andrei's shadow flickers in this streak of light; he is walking up and down in his room, recalling his lectures. One can hear Andrei's footsteps as well as the sound of conversation, the monotonous undertone, occasional coughing, sighs, blowing of the nose, the shifting of a chair. Everything falls silent; he stops at his table and leafs through a notebook (the rustle of pages). Perhaps a sound hinting at tears, and once again a blowing of the nose, steps, a lower murmuring, and his shadow on the stage. The lamp is about to go out in the dining room; it flares up, then again begins to die out. The windows are frozen over. Snow on the roof. Outside it is snowing. A storm. The piano has been moved and it obstructs the bay window.[4]

And, as if to explain the reason for the changes that have taken place in the house, the director points out: "The appointment of the room is in Natasha's taste." It immediately becomes clear that she has filled the place with herself; her Bobik is everywhere: "A child's blanket, baby sheets, cushions, swaddling bands, and the like are strewn over the sofa. On the table next to the sofa are toys: a little barrel-organ (with a squeaky sound), a harlequin clapping cymbals together. On the floor next to the piano—a large rug; on it are pillows from the sofa, toys—a child's harmonica, a top, a little wagon. On the piano are pieces of material, scissors, a towel." One gets the impression that not a single space is left in the room which has not been taken over by Natasha's philistine existence. Light and air have been banished. The only sounds in the darkness are the "monotonous strokes of the pendulums of two

---

[4] K. S. Stanislavskij. *Prompt Book of* The Three Sisters. Museum of the M. A. T., No. 22, p. 3. Hereafter page references to the director's prompt book will appear in parentheses in the text after citations.

clocks"; "the wind howls in the chimney of the stove," while the snow-storm "beats at the windowpanes." And as though to make this atmos-phere of hopeless anguish heavier still, the "sound of a harmonica drifts in now and then"; "a troika rushes down the street to the sound of drunken shouts" and you hear "far off the drunken singing of a stray reveler" (p. 3).

It becomes clear now why Andrei's shadow shifts about the room so restlessly, why Anfisa, "her slippers scraping," drags herself along so despondently "as she carries a pitcher with kvass into Andrei's room." "Anfisa has changed," the director emphasizes. She has become shrunken, pale; she gathers up the toys, gets down on her knees, expresses exhaus-tion, weariness." When Natasha appears, Anfisa in a state of fright sets about putting away the toys, while "a fat custodian zealously gives her a dressing down" (pp. 4 and 5). Natasha, according to the notation of Stanislavsky, only enters in order to extinguish all the lamps. It gets quite dark. Andrei is obliged to light a candle and by its uncertain flickering light he carries on a conversation with Ferapont, or more correctly, a conversation with himself: "How terribly life changes, de-ceives one!" . . .

One should note that in Stanislavsky's direction of *The Three Sisters,* he adheres rigorously and consistently to the principle of introducing only ideologically important, necessary details from everyday life. The sounds of the harmonica and the drunken voices which invade the room are justified not only on the plane of everyday life (it is Shrovetide), but also on the ideological plane (they emphasize, in the director's think-ing, the hopeless banality and crudity of the surroundings).

The scene of Masha and Vershinin, for example, is constructed as follows. On their appearance in the room "it grows lighter." But the elated, dreamy conversation–confession of the two lovers has at the basis of its construction the fact that the conversation is interrupted; during the pauses, for instance, "the scraping of a mouse" is occasionally heard, and they chase it away, knocking on the sofa, while from Andrei's room there is heard at first "a frightfully plaintive melody on the violin," then the "sound of a saw. . . ." "Overcome by depression in his room, he is obviously casting about now this way, now that, but nothing holds him," explains the director (p. 7). In this context Vershinin's bitter and unanswerable question inevitably comes to mind and becomes relevant: "A lofty way of thought is characteristic of the Russian man in the high-est degree, but tell me why it is that in life he strikes so low? Why?"

The idea of the disjunction between dream and reality seems to be graphically confirmed at every step. Thus Irina declares despairingly:

"Work without poetry, without ideas—" And in the pause—the dreary "scratching of the mouse." Irina once again begins to dream of Moscow, but at this moment Vershinin "picks up a toy lying on the table—Petrushka with the cymbals—and makes a noise with it—then he holds this toy in his hands and every now and then makes a noise with it," thus producing as it were an ironic accompaniment to his words. Irina doggedly continues. "We are moving there [to Moscow] in June"—once again one hears the mocking "noise of Petrushka" (p. 8). Here Stanislavsky employs quite the same device as Chekhov does in Act I of the play when Olga's words, "One longs so passionately to go home," are accompanied—seemingly accidentally, but actually with clear mocking intent—by a rejoinder of Chebutykin: "The devil take it!"

The same device of contrasting details is introduced even more clearly by the director in the "philosophizing" scene which follows: "Let's at least philosophize a bit," suggests Vershinin. Tusenbach has found a little music box, plays it. "About what?" "Let's dream—for example, about what life will be like when we are gone, in two or three hundred years." Pause. Tusenbach turns the music box two or three times, it emits some vague sounds. "And in a thousand years man will be sighing the same: 'Ah, how hard it is to live!'" Tusenbach holds the music box in his hands and now and again gives it a turn; it emits plaintive sounds (p. 9). But Vershinin energetically retorts: "In two or three hundred years, or even in a thousand years—it's not a matter of a particular time —a new, happy life will come into being. We will not participate in this life, of course, but we live for it now, we are working, well, suffering, we are creating it—and in this alone is the purpose of our being and, if you will, our happiness." And Stanislavsky notes: *"It is very important to stir up the audience, [speak with] spirit, raise the voice."* But just here, opposite those same words of Vershinin, he writes: *"In the distance the harmonica and the drunken voices seem deliberately to bring to mind the thought that everything about which Vershinin speaks is a long way off"* (p. 10—italics are Stanislavsky's).

It is striking to see how profoundly Stanislavsky penetrates into the author's conception, into the intense drama of the scene. Chekhov convinced people that "a new, happy life will come into being" not at all in order to calm and lull in them the feeling of protest against the system of life of those times; on the contrary, he aroused it. And it is remarkable that Stanislavsky, who considered it "very important" to convey to the spectator an inspiriting faith in the future, simultaneously instills in him a sense of distress by creating the oppressive atmosphere of the everyday world surrounding Chekhov's heroes.

Obviously in such conditions joy cannot be complete. It would seem that Masha is happy in this scene; she is cheerful, laughing. But the director notes: "Masha's laughter is nervous, she could as well burst into tears; therefore she quickly puts out both candles." The scene that follows is without light: "Darkness. Snow. The moon. Only the glow of the cigarettes is visible." And how expressive it is: the lonely glow of cigarettes in the gloom as people dispute "passionately" about happiness, work, the future. But the dispute gradually dies down and ends with the "quiet singing—some song about wasted youth." Then even the "singing somehow gets out of tune and stops. All fall silent" (p. 10). And when Masha does not want to give up and tries again to talk with Vershinin about happiness, about Moscow, she is interrupted by an "ominous ring from the anteroom" (p. 12). The letter to Vershinin ("the wife has taken poison again") tears him from Masha.

The whole second act is worked out in this way by the director. There is constant emphasis upon the contrast between the people's inner state, their strivings, impulses, and that life which in every detail seems to say to them: "No." But for Stanislavsky it was important to show that people do not give up, that their thirst for life does not die out, but, on the contrary, revives, as appears in the structure of the encounter between Natasha and the guests who have gathered at the house of the Prozorovs. The director introduces a whole "laughing scene" after Natasha's French phrases: "Some hiss; others rock with laughter" (p. 15). After she goes, Tusenbach feels somehow liberated and starts to sing, dances a little waltz on the proscenium, . . . laughs, leaps about gaily, and goes to the piano: 'I'm sitting down to play!' Masha hears the waltz, jumps up, and begins to dance—singing to herself, she dances alone and in despair. Roday takes hold of her and they go on dancing together." Then when Natasha unceremoniously sends the guests packing, the director stresses that this is a "comic, cheerful departure" (p. 17).

The "appearance of the maskers" was transformed by Stanislavsky into a whole scene; in just the same way, he meant it to introduce a fresh breath of life into the desolate semidark atmosphere of the house. "You see them; you hear gay voices—the sound of bells." But (on Natasha's orders) the maskers are not allowed in: "Silence. All the gaiety is shattered; somebody whistles. A pall descends upon the gay spirits of the crowd. They are even sort of embarrassed" (p. 17).

The entire finale of the act is dominated now by Natasha and Protopopov. The bells of Protopopov's troika ring out and stifle the sound of voices: "In the course of the Kulygin–Irina–Olga–Vershinin scene one can hear the troika standing at the front gate; the horses are shaking their manes; their bells are jingling" (p. 19). Thus the anguished despair of Irina in the finale is prepared and justified: "Irina stands motionless —sadly she makes her way to the piano. Natasha walks past. The departure of the troika. Pause. The lamp in the dining room starts to go out, flickers; a mouse scratches. Irina groans as though in pain: 'To Moscow, to Moscow.' She leans against the piano. The pendulum" (p. 20).

The clash of hostile forces increases in the third act. The whole atmosphere of the action becomes extraordinarily tense. Stanislavsky makes a special point about it: "Wherever possible one must accent the sense of nervousness and the tempo. Do not abuse the pauses. Everybody's transitions and movements are nervous and rapid" (p. 30). Gone now are the scraping mouse, the squeaking sounds, the music box and revelers' singing—these do not create the "mood." The "ever intensifying heavy-sounding bell of the fire alarm" (p. 30) clangs through the entire act, "the firemen thunder past the house, across the yard" (p. 46), "a red light falls in patches on the floor" (p. 30).

Taking advantage of everybody's anxiety and distraught condition, banality takes the offensive. Natasha takes over as sovereign mistress of the house. In the second act she could still deal with Andrei or Irina "very tenderly" (p. 5), "almost caressingly" (p. 17). But now, in the scene with Anfisa, she "speaks without shouting, but very commandingly and boldly drives her out with a gesture" (p. 30). And later with Olga she begins to speak "without shouting, but firmly; at Olga's slightest movement she gets more and more irritated. She ends up with a squealing hysterical scream. She squeals with tears in her voice" (p. 34). And, after establishing herself in this manner as mistress of the house, Natasha walks by from time to time without looking at anybody, crosses the room, candle in hand, angrily slamming doors (pp. 43-46). It should be noted that the last *mise-en-scène* was close to what the author wanted when he wrote Stanislavsky: "Better if she [Natasha] crosses the stage, in a straight line, without looking at anybody or anything, *à la* Lady Macbeth, with a candle—this would be simpler and more terrible." [5] Originally it was proposed—as Stanislavsky wrote Chekhov—that "Natasha, while making the rounds of the house, at night, should extinguish all the lights and look for burglars under the furniture."

In these circumstances the dissatisfaction with life that Chekhov's heroines feel reaches a point of unbearable suffering. Irina "groans with misery, clutches her head, agonizes—throws herself on the bed, sobs behind the screen" (p. 41). "I can't, I can't bear any more! I can't, I can't!"

[5] A. P. Chekhov, *Polnoe sobranie sochinenij i pisem*, XIX (Moscow, 1944-1951), p. 8.

She hasn't the strength to tear herself away and, pleading with the others to help her, "with a groan she almost shouts: 'Throw me out, throw me out, I can't stand it any longer!'" After this, "veritable hysteria breaks out behind the screen, growing more and more intense (only, for God's sake, not in real!!!!!!!!!!)" writes Stanislavsky (p. 41).

Act III for the sisters is marked by a search for a way out, a search for action. Masha, stronger and bolder, seems to have found this way out; she has decided to break with the cheerless, tedious banality of her life. Here is how the director set up her confession to her sisters: "Masha quickly gets up, agitated, in a state of decision; she is nervously excited, nervously stretches out her arms, gets on her knees, just as does Olga, at the head of Irina's bed, embraces Irina with one arm and Olga with the other. She speaks quietly ("I love that man, in a word, I love Vershinin"), drawing the heads of Olga and Irina closer to her own. The three heads of the sisters are close to one another. Masha looks upwards with an ecstatic look, recalls her whole romance" (p. 44). After the words of Olga: "Please stop this. I'm just not going to listen," Masha, "with vexation brushing off her dress, gets up, briskly goes up to Olga; the tone is desperate; she's turning her back on everything; she's come to a decision" (p. 44).

Stanislavsky stresses that Olga, in essence, understands Masha, sympathizes with her (something which Chekhov does not reveal in this scene). "Olga tenderly caresses her, the sinner, as she does the innocent Irina. Olga tenderly kisses Masha, strokes her." The director felt it was important to show that common strivings unite the sisters; it is interesting in this respect to note his instruction: "Masha is solicitous over Irina, although this is not in her character" (p. 44). Again the sisters' community of strivings in their struggle to find a way out is revealed with special clarity in the scene of Masha's departure: "The departure of Masha—hurriedly, impetuously, very nervous and upset, she embraces Olga firmly and talks as she moves toward the door. At the door Olga kisses Masha tenderly, in a motherly way. In reality she understands her; in the depths of her heart she acknowledges that she would act the same way. Now she does not censure her, but pities her. Therefore she kisses her tenderly, as a mother would" (p. 46). And as though to emphasize the importance of this moment, so crucial to Masha's fate, the sounds of the conflagration are carried in again from the street: "The firemen thunder past the house and across the yard: the clatter of hooves, bells, empty barrels, the shouts of two voices; against the background of this tumult—the kiss of Olga and Masha" (p. 46).

Act IV brings a shattering of all hopes; the dream about a possible happiness must be relinquished. "There is no happiness; there should not be and will not be for us. We should only work and work, and as for happiness—that is the lot of our distant descendants"—this is the leitmotif of the last act. In contrast to the first act with its springlike atmosphere, Stanislavsky notes here: "The mood. Autumn. It is cool, everyone is wearing coats (the light summer kind). Here and there yellow leaves are falling from trees during the whole act" (p. 54).

The curtain rises at a moment when one hears a treble peal of bells (after Mass—prayers on the occasion of the departure of the troops)" (p. 54). The director creates the troubled and confused atmosphere surrounding departure by introducing the activity of many people: porter, orderly, cook, maid, all seeing the officers off. They are hauling all sorts of things. The garden gate is being slammed all the time (p. 59).

Each of the heroes bears his suffering, the sorrow of departure. Tusenbach continually has a troubled look; he looks at his watch frequently and coughs nervously. Irina is aware of his state and looks at him anxiously (p. 59). He knows that the duel is inevitable and senses its tragic end; but when he says goodbye to Irina, he tries to stifle his sorrow and vainly strives to appear gay. This is the way the director structured the farewell scene:

> The music comes closer. Violin and harp. Tusenbach caresses Irina, smooths her hair, wraps her more warmly in her shawl, kisses all the fingers of her hand. Irina is tense, does not take her eyes off Tusenbach. He pats her on the head. She presses more closely to him. Tusenbach: "I'm happy"—he becomes much more cheerful, inspirited, livelier. "It's time for me to go now"—quickly kisses her hand, leaves, takes hold of the gate handle, opens the gate. Irina runs after him with an anxious glance, grabs him by the hand and holds him back. Tusenbach makes an effort to smile. Irina embraces him and nestles close to him. Tusenbach pensively looks off toward the garden (p. 64).

We find Masha also in the same state of waiting for unhappiness. "The cranes fly by; Masha gets up with a start. She is distraught; tears well up. Harp and violin in the distance. Masha rubs her forehead, sighs deeply, shakes her head. She looks at her watch, is very nervous, pensive" (pp. 61-62).

While the troubled, unhappy atmosphere of departure gradually deepens outside in the garden, the house lives its own, special life, quite alien to these suffering people. Natasha and Protopopov now reign undisputed there. From time to time, echoes of this life carry their loud, indifferent dissonance into the garden. In order to shut herself off more completely from what is now taking place out there, Natasha "draws a curtain over

the balcony" and from time to time one hears loud laughter; moreover,
"a deep bass, obviously that of Protopopov, can be distinguished amidst
the laughter" (p. 67).

On the stage—the delicate, restrained lyricism of sorrow; but it is
lacerated by indifferent, happy "voices, the sound of a top, the sound of
a large ball bouncing on the floor, the noise of a wooden sphere rolling
on the floor. Frequent laughter—a bass may be distinguished" (p. 68).
Stanislavsky considers it necessary to show how this balcony world penetrates into the garden: "At one point a ball bounces from the balcony;
the nurse picks it up in the garden and returns to the balcony." The
director even went so far as to consider bringing Protopopov himself
out onto the stage. "Make a try at having Protopopov himself pick it
[the ball] up; in this way he would appear before the public for a moment. It might turn out magnificently or dreadfully. It should be tried
at one of the dress rehearsals," writes Stanislavsky, sketching the image
of Protopopov in several strokes. "This would be a marvelous role. Just
imagine: suddenly a fat man with a cigar between his teeth would unexpectedly leap from the balcony; he would run after the ball, bending
over several times since he could not catch it at once. Then he disappears
forever with the ball" (p. 68).

But when the most trying period of the departure arrives and human
sorrow fills the scene, the director banishes banality from the stage. "Up
to this moment [i.e., the moment when Masha bids farewell to Vershinin
—M.S.] one can still hear conversation and the noise of the ball and
games on the terrace, though it does not interfere with the action; after
this moment, a calm sets in, things gradually come to a halt, and the
balcony empties" (p. 72).

"Masha, all distraught, comes rapidly along the garden path. Vershinin: 'I came to bid farewell.' Masha: 'Farewell'—sobs in Vershinin's
arms; he himself barely restrains his tears; he is deeply moved. Olga
wants to comfort Masha. Irina advises her not to interfere and to let her
weep" (p. 74).

The surmounting of suffering is, for the director, the most important
thing in the finale. He sees "an inspiriting thought of the author" in the
fact that Chekhovian heroes even in a moment of profound sorrow find
the strength to raise themselves to dreaming of people's future happiness.
The director accompanies the concluding monologue of Olga with an
emphatic note: *"As much as possible, speak more spiritedly"* (p. 72).

In the first version of Chekhov's play, which Stanislavsky worked with,
Olga's words, "If we only knew" are followed by this stage direction of
the author: "The music gradually dies down; in the background of the

stage there is a bustle; one can see a crowd watching the baron, killed at the duel, as he is being carried away; Kulygin happy, smiling, carries a hat and cape; Andrei is pushing another pram in which Bobik is sitting."

Stanislavsky, as he finished his work on the director's plan, came to the conclusion that the body of Tusenbach must not be carried across the stage. The director gave detailed reasons why it seemed important to him to change the author's stage direction:

Call Anton Pavlovich's attention to the fact that in his version it would be necessary to insert a scene involving the populace, the chatter of the crowd which is accompanying Tusenbach; otherwise we would have a ballet. During the procession across the narrow stage all the scenery would rock. The crowd would make a racket with their feet, bump into things—all this would produce an anticlimactic pause. And as for the sisters—is it possible to leave them indifferent to seeing Tusenbach carried away? One would have to think up something for them. I am afraid that, after chasing so many hares, we shall lose what is most important: the final inspiriting thought of the author which atones for many of the somber parts of the play. The removal of the body will either turn out to be boring, anticlimactic, unnatural, or (if we succeed in overcoming all these obstacles) terribly oppressive, and would only reinforce a feeling of oppression" (p. 78).

The reason for Stanislavsky's reluctance to intensify the "feeling of oppression" of the play was, first of all, that he wanted to emphasize its affirmative aspect. This fully accorded with the desires of the author himself who, as we know, even at the first reading of the play in the theater objected to the view of *The Three Sisters* as "an oppressive drama of Russian life," and affirmed that he had written a "comedy." [6] For this reason Chekhov gladly agreed to strike out the episode with the carrying of Tusenbach's body;[7] he had had doubts about it even earlier but had left it in on the insistence of Stanislavsky ("Even at that time," he wrote Olga Knipper, "I had said that it would be inconvenient to bear away the corpse of Tusenbach across your stage, but Alekseev [Stanislavsky] insisted that there was no getting along without the corpse.").[8]. . .

Stanislavsky understood the idea of Chekhov's play as being the clash between two hostile forces in the milieu of the Russian intelligentsia of that period. The social significance of this clash consisted in the fact that, in spite of the external triumph of "banality," that is, the philis-

[6] Cf. K. S. Stanislavskij "A. P. Chekhov v Moskovskom khudozhestvennom teatre," *Ezhegodnik MKhAT* (1943), p. 130; K. S. Stanislavskij, *Moja zhizn' v iskusstve*, p. 235; and V. I. Nemirovich-Danchenko, *Iz proshlogo*, p. 169.

[7] A. P. Chekhov, *Polnoe sobranie sochinenij i pisem*, XIX, 20.

[8] *Ibid.*, p. 24.

tine, bourgeois element, moral victory rested on the side of the anti-
philistine, antibourgeois elements, that is, on the side of the three sisters
who had inwardly liberated themselves from the "power of everyday
environment." Thus, the performance was supposed to be a rebellion
against the "external slavery" of the Chekhovian heroes, and was intended to arouse a feeling of social protest. At the same time the
affirmative aspect of the play is clearly emphasized in Stanislavsky's
prompt book—the dream of Chekhov's heroes which is opposed to the
horror of reality. . . .

In a way, as he worked on the director's plan for *The Three Sisters*,
Stanislavsky in a practical sense came close to realizing his concept of
"a through-line of action." This made it possible for him to show in a
Chekhovian manner the natural "current of life," not simply as a chain
of accidental episodes, details from everyday life strung together, but
in movement, when each seemingly accidental word that is dropped,
everything that strikes the eye, emphasizes and brings out the author's
thought.

*   *   *

Stanislavsky sought to concentrate heavily around Chekhov's heroes
such a crushing and stifling atmosphere—expressing itself everywhere,
even in the tiniest details—that the thought would of itself arise: how
unbearable this existence is—and a conflict with reality would inevitably
take shape. But this conflict could only really become the *active* pivot
of the performance if the people drawn into it stepped forward as an
active force of opposition. And herein lay the chief difficulty of rehearsal
with the actors. Because really: how is one to disclose this active element
in people who do not come out in open struggle with the banality surrounding them, who, so it seems, only suffer and yearn, and in this way
are doomed to inaction?

Stanislavsky found the correct answer—as he writes—"unexpectedly"
at one of the rehearsals, and only then did "Chekhovian people come
to life." "It turned out that they are by no means moping about in
anguish but, on the contrary, are seeking gaiety, laughter, animation;
they want to live and not just vegetate. I sensed that this was the true
approach to Chekhov's heroes, it inspired me, and I intuitively understood what had to be done." [9] It should be emphasized that all of Stanislavsky's preparatory work on the director's prompt book led him to this
resolution of the question.

It might appear that this assertion contradicts Stanislavsky's statement

[9] K. S. Stanislavskij, *Moja zhizn' v iskusstve*, p. 236.

cited above, that it was only at rehearsals that the main idea was found. But, first of all, the path from conception to realization is always complex and contradictory. Now, for example, if Stanislavsky immediately, at the first rehearsal, had set before the actors the task of "seeking gaiety, laughter, animation," then one can say for certain that Chekhov's idea would not have been disclosed. Through such an approach it would have been impossible to perceive and transmit the genuinely Chekhovian inner action, the activity of the heroes. It was first necessary for the actors at rehearsals to live deeply into this unbearable state of a life without exit, in order then to feel a hatred for it, to feel the necessity for inner liberation. . . .

It is characteristic that the performance began to live a full life when its "supertask" was defined—Stanislavsky's formulation that "Chekhovian people . . . are seeking gaiety, laughter, animation; they want to live and not just vegetate." Only such an active, operative "supertask" could help the actors to "live" on the stage, and not to "act," because truth of life in the theater is born through correctly discovered stage action. One of the important achievements in the rehearsal work on *The Three Sisters* lay in the fact that—basing themselves on the work on *Uncle Vanya*—the actors and directors of the Moscow Art Theater now came close to mastering on a practical plane the central principle of the "art of experience"—not to act, but to live, i.e., to feel and live.

In his book *From the Past*, Nemirovich-Danchenko writes that in its work on Chekhovian performances the Moscow Art Theater came close to the goal advanced by Chekhov himself when he said at a rehearsal for *The Seagull* in St. Petersburg: "There is too much acting, everything must be as it is in real life." "Nothing must be acted"—this is how Nemirovich-Danchenko defined that basic demand which he and Stanislavsky made to the actors at that time. "Absolutely nothing. Neither feelings, nor moods, nor situations, nor words, nor style, nor images." [10]

This is a decisive refutation of the false notion that a certain "mood" was a goal in itself for the directors of Chekhov performances in the Moscow Art Theater. In fact, what Stanislavsky and Nemirovich-Danchenko understood by the notion "mood" was the realistic atmosphere of the performance; it served only as a means for re-creating on the stage the truth of life as refracted through the prism of Chekhov's world view.

"The difference between the stage and life is only in the world view of the author," wrote Nemirovich-Danchenko in reporting to Chekhov on the progress of rehearsals of *The Three Sisters*. "All *this* life, the life

[10] V. I. Nemirovich-Danchenko, *Iz proshlogo*, p. 131.

shown in this performance, has passed through the world view, sensibility, temperament of the author. It received a special coloration which is called poetry." [11]

Nemirovich-Danchenko began to take part in rehearsals only in the middle of January 1901 (the first performance was given January 31), i.e., at a time when Stanislavsky had carried the work on the performance to the point of rough dress rehearsals.

* * *

[In a letter to Chekhov of January 22, 1901] Nemirovich-Danchenko disclosed his understanding of the essence of the future performance. . . . "The fable: the house of the Prozorovs. The life of the three sisters after the death of the father, the appearance of Natasha, her gradual taking possession of the whole house, and, finally, her complete triumph and the isolation of the sisters. The fate of each of them—take the fate of Irina—runs like a red thread: 1) I want to work, [she is] happy, gay, healthy; 2) a headache from work, it doesn't satisfy; 3) life is smashed, youth passes, she agrees to marry a man who doesn't appeal to her; 4) fate trips things up, and the bridegroom is killed." [12]

This interpretation of the play differs considerably from the one which is revealed to us on the pages of Stanislavsky's prompt book. Of course, the basic design is the same. But what is obviously missing in Nemirovich-Danchenko's interpretation is the element of struggle, an emphasis upon the active side of Chekhov's heroes who try to resist the onslaught of banality. Quite the contrary, he emphasizes their passive submission to their fate: "These people are like chessmen in the hands of unseen players." [13] (It should be noted that in his production of *The Three Sisters* in 1940, Nemirovich-Danchenko reexamines the old traditions precisely in this manner.)

Thus, Nemirovich-Danchenko comprehends the Chekhovian "current of life" more in the way of epic narration which broadly and fully embraces all life, not merely its "heaving heights and falling depths." "The events in the play seem to creep along, like life itself in that epoch —sluggishly, without any apparent logical connection. People act more under the influence of chance happenings, they are not themselves the builders of their life," [14] wrote Nemirovich-Danchenko later on; he was setting forth his view of the unique character of the play, a uniqueness

---

[11] Nemirovich-Danchenko. Letter to A. P. Chekhov of January 22, 1901. *Ezhegodnik MKhAT* (1944), I, 134.

[12] *Ibid.*, p. 133.

[13] Nemirovich-Danchenko, *Iz proshlogo*, p. 168.

[14] *Ibid.*

—so it seemed to him—created by the peculiar features of the epoch. While rehearsing the play, he stressed the following in a letter to Chekhov: "The fable develops, as in an *epic* work—without those stimuli which were supposed to be used by the old-style dramatists—in the midst of a simple, faithfully perceived current of life. The nameday, Shrovetide, the fire, the departure, the stove, the lamp, the pianoforte, pies, drunkenness, twilight, night, the living room, the dining room, the girls' bedroom, winter, autumn, spring, etc., etc., etc." [15]

But if we recall that the performance occurred on the boundary-line of the new century (December 1900–January 1901), on the threshold of the first Russian revolution, then it becomes clear that the characterization of the epoch given by Nemirovich-Danchenko, far from being accurate, is one-sided. We must acknowledge that Stanislavsky's position in this case was more progressive, since the intense dramatic character of the clash of two hostile forces in modern society better reflected the progressive moods of the epoch than the passive-epic narrative about how "some splendid people could fall into the clutches of a most common vulgar woman." [16]

As a whole, Stanislavsky's direction of the performance strove to represent through *The Three Sisters* the tragedy of the Russian intelligentsia of that day, to awaken in the audience a protest against unbearable conditions of life and at the same time to see to it that faith in man himself did not perish—in that man who was straining toward a renewal of life, who was expending himself in dreams of the bright future of his country.

*   *   *

[15] *Ezhegodnik MKhAT* (1944), I, 133.
[16] *Ibid.*, p. 134.

The Cherry Orchard:
A Formalist Approach

by S. D. Balukhaty

What prompted Chekhov to undertake in *The Cherry Orchard* a dramatic work with new thematic dimensions, one strikingly different in key from his preceding dramas? The answer must be sought in the attitude of the critics toward the thematic content—not the style—of *The Three Sisters,* as well as in Chekhov's own responsiveness to the social and aesthetic demands of the time.

Even when working on the new play, Chekhov was critical of his manner of writing. "I have the feeling that my style has grown old." Or, "I feel that as a writer I have already outlived my time; every sentence I write strikes me as completely worthless and unnecessary." Chekhov sought "renewal" of his dramatic technique in devices of the *comic genre.*

Let us consider Chekhov's observations on vaudeville at the time when he was writing *The Cherry Orchard,* his penchant for a comic tone: these reveal to us the sources of the unique compositional features of *The Cherry Orchard,* especially as they relate to tone.

Directly following the staging of *The Three Sisters* early in 1901, Chekhov notes: "The next play that I write will be, without fail, funny, very funny, at least in its conception." Or: "At times I am overcome by a strong desire to write a four-act vaudeville or comedy for the Moscow Art Theater." And again: "I still dream of writing a funny play, where the devil is running loose." "I'd like to write a vaudeville, but I just can't get organized." "I really want to write a vaudeville, but there is just no time; I can't pull myself together. I have some kind of presentiment that vaudeville will soon come back into fashion." At this very time Chekhov was revising his old vaudeville, *On the Harmful*

"*The Cherry Orchard:* A Formalist Approach" (original title: "*The Cherry Orchard*") by S. D. Balukhaty. From *Problemy dramaturgicheskogo analiza. Chekhov* (Leningrad, 1927), chap. VII, pp. 148-161 in abridged form. Translated from the Russian by James Karambelas.

Effects of Tobacco. . . . While shaping the new play and developing the characters, Chekhov wrote to O. L. Knipper "If my play doesn't come out as I have conceived it, then clout me on the head. There's a comic part for Stanislavsky, for you too." "The last act will be gay, light-hearted." Apropos the comic role of Charlotta Ivanovna, Chekhov wrote: "Ah, if only you were to play the governess in my play. It's the best role; the other ones don't appeal to me." In characterizing the play as a whole, Chekhov wrote again: "I have a feeling that there is something new in my play, however boring it may be. Incidentally, there's not one shot in the entire play." "I'm calling the play a comedy." "It turned out to be not a drama, but a comedy, in places even a farce." . . .

Let us turn to a concise dramatic analysis of the play. . . .

Characterization. In the *dramatis personae,* there is a tendency to indicate by the first and last names of the characters whether they belong to the "intelligentsia" or not. The characters in the play are delineated through 1) recurrent themes in their dialogue and 2) peculiarities of individual speech and gesture. We may single out by way of example Lyubov Andreevna Ranevskaya. She is characterized by Lopakhin (p. 59),[1] Gaev (p. 73), Anya (p. 63), her own words (pp. 80-81, 93-94, 102); by an incident from everyday life (she drops her purse, the money scatters); by her relations with Varya, Trofimov, Gaev, and with "him" [her lover] living in Paris who sends her telegrams (pp. 68, 94, and others). Open, "joyous" emotions, excitability, rapid transitions from tears to laughter—all this is typical of Ranevskaya. Her movements, intonation, patterns of behavior are set forth in Chekhov's stage directions. . . .

Composition. The movement of themes. There is no division of the act into scenes. We may single out as follows, in the order of their appearance within the act, the basic themes that recur in the dialogue.

Act I. The initial and characterizing themes arise in the context of Ranevskaya's arrival at the estate. Thus: the theme of Lopakhin with a flashback and a view of Ranevskaya, as well as a partial development of the theme of Dunyasha. Transition: the arrival of Epikhodov. The theme of Epikhodov and, partially, that of Dunyasha. Transition: the scene of the arrival of Ranevskaya, speeches and special characterizations of Ranevskaya and Varya. The theme of Anya and, partially, that of Dunyasha. The theme of Anya, characterization of Ranevskaya by Anya, with a general flashback, and with the introduction of the everyday plot element [the bankruptcy and impend-

[1] Page citations are from Chekhov, *Uncle Vanya. The Cherry Orchard.* Translated and edited by Ronald Hingley. Oxford Paperbacks, No. 89 (London, 1965)—ED.

ing sale of the estate]. The theme of Varya. The dialogue between Varya
and Anya is interrupted by a brief exchange between Yasha and Dunyasha.
The dialogue concludes with a flashback by Anya. The theme of Firs. The
theme of Gaev. As we progress—with all the characters introduced—the
characterizing themes recur and interchange, though there is no full development of these themes. Thus: the themes of Ranevskaya and Lopakhin,
with the exposition of the plot, with the settlement on a general theme,
and with a preliminary clash of the characters (Lopakhin, Ranevskaya, and
Gaev on the sale of the cherry orchard); the themes of Gaev, Pishchik,
Charlotta, Pishchik, Firs, Ranevskaya. The arrival of Trofimov. The theme
of Trofimov and the termination of the theme of Pishchik. A new grouping
of characters. The theme of Yasha, the characterization of Ranevskaya as
seen by Gaev. The theme of Anya and Gaev with a general exposition. The
theme of Varya. In the finale we have a genre scene lyrically presented.

We shall designate the main themes in Act I with capital letters: A—
Lopakhin; B—Ranevskaya; C—the sale of the estate. We shall use small
letters to indicate the other themes. We get a picture of an unsystematic
movement of themes in a pattern where the repetition of letters indicates
recurrent themes: a A B b c b B d e C b e B f g h B A c h i j k g B C l m
B C e h C f.

Act II. The characterizing themes are these groupings: Charlotta and
Epikhodov, Dunyasha and Yasha. Transition: the arrival of new characters.
Episodic scenes. Themes and speeches of Gaev, Ranevskaya, Lopakhin; the
theme of the sale of the estate serves as a stimulus for the characterizing
theme of Gaev and Ranevskaya. The theme of Ranevskaya, with self-exposi-
tion. The theme of Lopakhin. Episode with the theme of Firs. Arrival of
new characters. Characterization of Lopakhin by Trofimov. Trofimov's
theme of the proud man, of the intelligentsia, of life, all of which is picked
up by Lopakhin. Later, successive interchange of episodes with internal
themes: Gaev's declamation, the falling bucket, characteristic replies of
Firs, of the Passer-by, and the characterizing theme of Ranevskaya. Termination of the themes and the exits of characters. In the finale—the theme of
Anya and Trofimov, with disclosure of the general synthetic theme of the
play, lyrically interpreted.

The themes move in the pattern: a b c d C e B A f A g A h i f k B l m.

Act III. The background is the ball, with music (prepared for in Act II).
The theme of Pishchik, which is broken off by the start of the episode of
Trofimov and Varya. Start of the movement of the basic theme in the act—
the sale of the estate, which is broken off by the start of the episode "Charlotta and her tricks," and later by the end of the episode of "Trofimov and
Varya," which is interpreted as the theme of the relationship of Lopakhin
and Varya. The recurring, basic theme of the act is again replaced by the

theme of Trofimov and Ranevskaya, settling on the overall, "synthetic" theme, which is interrupted by the themes of Ranevskaya and Trofimov, and which is concluded by a vivid, [lyrically] expressive scene. Conclusion of the scene. Start of the theme of Firs and Yasha. Recurrence of the basic, "synthetic" theme. Interchange of episodic themes: Pishchik, Charlotta Ivanovna (silent scene), Dunyasha, Epikhodov and Dunyasha, Epikhodov and Varya, Varya and Lopakhin. Recurrence of the basic theme, with pointing up of the theme of Gaev. The theme of Lopakhin, which terminates the basic theme of the act, settling on the overall, "synthetic" theme. In the finale—the theme of Ranevskaya as seen by Anya, with a lyrical treatment of the overall theme.

The themes move in the pattern: a b a C c b C B d e f C e f g h i j k C l A B m.

Act IV. The movement of the themes occurs in the context of the dialogue of departure and farewell. . . . The introductory dialogue between Lopakhin and Yasha, the theme of Lopakhin. The theme of Trofimov and Lopakhin with a partial movement toward the overall, "synthetic" theme. Start of the movement of the episodic theme of Firs, which moves through the entire act. The theme of Dunyasha and Yasha, which concludes their relationship. The theme of Gaev, Ranevskaya, and Anya, with quasi-final exposition. Final theme of Charlotta and Pishchik. Recurrence of the theme of Firs. The theme of Lopakhin and Varya. Start of the departure scene, with the themes of Gaev, Ranevskaya, Epikhodov, Yasha, Anya, and Trofimov standing out. Termination of the plot line and of the distinctive themes-in-pairs: Gaev–Ranevskaya and Anya–Trofimov. The finale presents the termination of the theme of Firs.

In the following pattern, D is the new theme of Firs which moves through the act and partly organizes its composition: a A D b c B d e f g D h i k . . . B D.

Thus, the movement of themes through the acts is accomplished according to the principle of unorganized articulation, of a kind of *disintegration* of composition in which the devices of interruption, severance, and recurrence of themes clearly stand out. Each act, however, acquires its compositional unity through the primary movement of one basic theme in the act. Thus, Act I gives, in abundance, the themes characteristic of Ranevskaya and only partially introduces the sale of the estate. Act II distinguishes the theme of Lopakhin. Act III is organized on the principle of an uninterrupted and intensifying movement of the theme of the sale of the estate. Act IV is constructed by distinguishing the episodic theme of Firs.

The functions of the acts in the general structure of the play are not unusual: Act I discloses the background in everyday life, gives the disposition of characters and their basic characterizations, and partially points up the plot line of the play (in the encounter of Lopakhin and Ranevskaya). Act II brings out the themes of the preceding act but complicates the thematic sequence with the new general themes of Trofimov [the need for work, censure of the intelligentsia, dream of happiness, etc.]. Act III dramatizes, partially along personal lines, the basic theme of the play (Trofimov–Ranevskaya, p. 93), reveals fully the synthesizing role of Lopakhin (p. 100), and terminates the plot line. Act IV rounds out the fates of the characters: Lopakhin, Trofimov (p. 103), Ranevskaya, Anya (pp. 106-107), Varya (p. 109), Firs (p. 112), and partially hints at a continuation of the action beyond the play (pp. 106, 109).

Plot. The principle of dramatic effectiveness and the dramatic function of the characters. The play has no dramatic plot, that is, the play has no such correlation of "events" as would make it possible to develop or bring out the characters, or disclose the phases of their "movement." Therefore, there are no dramatic moments in the play. The fate of characters, their actions and behavior, are motivated entirely by common everyday situations and "events." The basic everyday "event"—the sale of the estate—is predetermined from the start of the play (p. 63) and . . . is the motive force which organizes the characters and the plot structure of the play, that is, the background against which the characters unfold. There are no love themes and relationships in the play: the relationship of Trofimov to Anya is qualified as one which is not a love relationship (pp. 87, 93); the relations of Lopakhin and Varya are not revealed; the love theme of Ranevskaya—of which there are clear hints—also is not spelled out in the play; the love themes of Dunyasha and Epikhodov or of Dunyasha and Yasha come across as plain comedy, almost on the plane of parody.

The plot line is developed through the contrasting movement of the characters; these are arranged in two opposing groups: Ranevskaya and Gaev, on the one hand, and Lopakhin, Trofimov, and Anya on the other. There is a common ground: the sale of the estate. Both groups are disclosed in their thematic and tonal relationships: that is, the sale of the estate serves to bring out the individuality of the characters; in time these characters become polarized in patterns representing a thematic (ideological) contrast (Ranevskaya–Lopakhin), and they are presented in contrasting, lyrically expressive tones (the speeches and conduct of Ranevskaya and Gaev introduce a minor tonality; those of Lopakhin, Trofimov, and Anya, a major tonality). Each group of characters is differentiated within itself according to the principle of antithesis. Ranevskaya is more vigorous in self-expression and address than Gaev. Expressive emotional speech in Lopakhin is distinctively local and individual, whereas the expressive emotional element in Anya and Trofimov partakes of their general grasp of the "questions of life."

The play has a "synthetic" theme: a psychological pattern and then a social one are superimposed on a pattern of everyday life. The "synthetic" theme is established through the relationships of the characters to a single, everyday matter; the exact motivation of these relationships, of course, is different with each character and has a different tone color. The author develops the basic theme of the play dialectically; at the same time he suggests its markedly synthetic character in his mastery not so much of individual scenes and speeches, as of the harmonious thematic composition of the whole play. The synthetic catalyst is indicated on the comic—not the dramatic—plane of the play, in the predominantly major key of the speeches of Anya and Trofimov. Lopakhin (pp. 68, 100) and Trofimov (pp. 83-84, 87, 88, 93, 103-104) carry the central speeches which reveal the general theme. But though their speeches coincide in theme, their point of departure is different. . . . (Cf. Lopakhin, p. 68, and Trofimov, p. 87.)

The function of other characters is to create a background of everyday life. The relationships among the characters in the play are notably unresolved Lopakhin–Varya; Yasha, Epikhodov–Dunyasha).

The absence of a dramatic plot and of dramatic treatment of the majority of characters (Ranevskaya and Gaev are the exceptions), together with the abundance of comic scenes and situations, allows the acts to unfold without pressure from plot or dramatic requirements. The single crisis in the play—in Act III when the sale of the estate might have been a moment of dramatic disclosure of Ranevskaya and Gaev— is presented in a dramatically weakened, lyrically expressive form; on the other hand, the highly dramatic action preceding this moment, with its heightening emotional tension, is veiled by an element of everyday comedy. In short, the action is developed in the unique style of the grotesque.

The same technique for lessening dramatic intensity may be observed in the design—generally lyrical—of the ends of the acts.

Composition of the dialogue. As a rule themes are not extensively developed, but only hinted at in speeches of various characters, and then broken off. The intervening theme or episode can lead to a return to one which was dropped or not fully developed. The alternation of themes is generally without motivation, except of the most common kind.

Observations grow out of ordinary situations. Rejoinders often are laconic in style and unrelated to any particular theme in the dialogue. The dialogue is rich in incidents and situations drawn from everyday life.

There is a conscious and extensive disposition of expressive forms of dialogue. We may distinguish some typical examples: 1) The direct, vivid lyrical utterance which signifies an open but tense emotional state; thus, Ranevskaya [looks at the orchard through the window]: "Oh, my childhood, my innocent childhood!" and so on (p. 71). See also pp. 61, 62-63, 74, 75, 87, 106-107. 2) The lyrical, passive utterance (Gaev, p. 85). Large, overarching themes are conveyed lyrically. Thus, Trofimov: "Yes, the moon is rising (Pause). Here it is! Happiness is here. Here it comes, nearer, ever nearer. Already I hear its footsteps. And if we never see it, if we never know it, what does that matter? Others will see it!" (p. 88). 3) The short, expressive comment which reveals basic themes; for example, Anya: "Goodbye, house! Goodbye, old life." Trofimov: "And welcome, new life!" (p. 111). 4) The expressive monologue: Lopakhin's (p. 100) and Anya's (p. 101). 5) The expressive, charged dialogue: the episode of Trofimov and Ranevskaya (pp. 94-95). 6) Play with contrasting overtones: Gaev and Ranevskaya as opposed to Anya and Trofimov in the finale. 7) The buildup of emotions which is lyrically, though not dramatically, resolved (Act III—Ranevskaya). 8) The lyrical endings of the acts. 9) The expressive parody forms: Gaev's speech to the bookcase (p. 69); Gaev declaiming (p. 85); Gaev (p. 110).

The extensive use of pauses conditions the lyrical character of the dialogue. Pauses are introduced as a sign of "reflection"—usually with Lopakhin—(pp. 59, 73, 77, 81, 82, 87, 102); as a sign of a change of theme (pp. 59, 73, 78, 82, 85, 102, 109); as an indication of troubled speech (pp. 108, 109); as an indication of an emotion that is being revealed (pp. 80, 87, 109).

There is an abundance of pauses containing sounds—sounds that have nothing to do with the dialogue (pp. 75, 82, 85, 88, 90—she "hums" [Ranevskaya], 107—she "sings" [Charlotta]), or which form a kind of lyrical accompaniment to words (pp. 76, 82, 99); music, waltzing in Act III. The general pause with some sound which is related to the plot is of special significance. This kind of pause emphasizes the symbolic level of meaning in the strong sound effect; e.g., the sound of the "breaking string" (pp. 85, 112), the sound of the "axe striking a tree" (pp. 104, 112). The general pause which is taken up by the ordinary business of life has a plot function; for example, the moment following Lopakhin's brief remarks about the purchase of the estate. Other pauses with everyday life content bear functions having to do with staging.

The pauses are distributed through the acts as follows: 10, 17, 1, and 15. The almost complete absence of pauses in Act III is explained by the compositional requirements of the act. The dialogue proceeds against the background of the ball, in the intervals between dances and amidst comedy scenes. The general decrease in pauses as compared with the peak in pauses in the preceding play [*The Three Sisters*] can be explained, over and above the realization of the theme of the play on a different (comedy) level, by the small scope of the entire play, but especially of the final act.

The lyrical conception of the acts extends even to the formulation of stage directions; the latter not only are designed for the stage, but have a *literary,* narrative function. Here are some examples from Act I and Act II:

(Act I) Dawn is breaking and the sun will soon be up. It is May. The cherry trees are in bloom, *but it is cold and frosty in the orchard.*

(Act II) In the open country. A small, tumble-down old chapel long ago abandoned. Near it a well, some large stones *which look like old* tombstones, and an old bench. A road can be seen leading to Gaev's estate. Dark poplar trees loom on one side and beyond them the cherry orchard begins. There is a row of telegraph poles in the distance and *far, far away* on the horizon are the dim outlines of a big town, *visible only in very fine, clear weather.* It will soon be sunset.

Everyone sits deep in thought. It is very quiet. All that can be heards is Firs's low muttering. Suddenly a distant sound is heard. It seems to come from the sky and is the sound of a breaking string. It dies away sadly.

One might also note the stage directions in the other acts, and also directions of the following type: Anya "has reverted to a calmer mood and is happy" (p. 74). . . .

Stage composition. We find wide use of everyday *mise-en-scène,* of common entrances and exits of characters, the double playing areas (Act III—the arch which divides the reception room from the ballroom), and the introduction of silent scenes saturated with the mood of everyday surroundings (pp. 61, 101). The lyrical background of the action is created through lyrical pauses and sound effects, and also by silent lyrical scenes (pp. 75, 88) and through the alternation of "natural" background (in Act I it is May; in Act IV, October).

What is original in the composition and style of *The Cherry Orchard* as a whole—in comparison with the preceding plays—is the under-structure of comedy: comic situations and episodes in the play's ensemble, a large number of comic characters, the introduction of a general major tonality. This style of comedy did not exclude a dramatic treatment of the emotions of the separate characters, but it forms a leitmotif to this dramatic treatment throughout the course of the play.

We may speak of another new feature of the play: through the technique of dialogue and the disposition of characters . . . Chekhov wrought an organic, frankly *social theme*—but one which is nevertheless structured within a psychological framework of everyday life. . . .

The devices for character drawing and of successive, unmotivated interchange of dialogue themes, the everyday motivations of dialogue and plot, devices for treating the dialogue lyrically—all hark back in nuance and detail to the stylistic practices, chiefly, of *The Three Sisters,* which was closest in time to *The Cherry Orchard.*

However, other facets of the new play give evidence that Chekhov set new dramatic tasks in his last dramatic experiment. The play's "plotless" quality, together with the absence of love entanglements (which usually organize, dramatically, the overall actions of the characters in a psychological drama of everyday life), and the absence of "events" (which usually dramatize the sequence of happenings in daily life); the absence of any visible organization of the episodes and speeches in an act (composition without the usual dramatic principle of composition); the use of expressive lyrical transitions . . . these all solved particular tasks in the spirit of a compositional–stylistic system to which the author was already accustomed. The new general and particular tasks of the play did not destroy the principle which Chekhov had mastered in his other plays, but the combination of them in one scheme gave rise to "mixed," distinctively grotesque forms.

The features of *The Cherry Orchard* which we have noted are reflected in the evolution of the text of the play and in Chekhov's reactions to various correspondents. An examination of the evolution of the text brings into relief the author's extremely careful reworking of the dialogue and those elements of the new composition which, as Chekhov repeatedly acknowledges, were "difficult." The letters disclose those aspects and areas of *The Cherry Orchard* which draw Chekhov's attention. Chekhov observes: "The play . . . is making slow progress, which I explain . . . by the difficulty of the plot." Or: " . . . how hard it was for me to write the play!" Defining the scope of the play, Chekhov writes: "My *Cherry Orchard* will be in three acts. That's how it looks to me, but I have not made the final decision yet." Or: "I wanted to make *The Cherry Orchard* into three long acts, but I can do it in four. It's all the same to me, whether there are three or four acts—the play will be the same anyway." And later: "The fourth act in my play, in comparison with the other acts, will be meager in its content, but effective." And again: "The fourth act is coming easily, almost smoothly." In these remarks Chekhov in a way was underscoring the following compositional feature of his play (which we find also in the preceding plays): the plot of the play is brought to a close in Act III; the final act in its combination of common everyday affairs and lyric mood has the character of a finale: it emphasizes the fact that the problems and relationships of the characters are not resolved and it projects the action beyond the limits of the play into a realm of everyday life.

As he worked over the play, the author was troubled principally by the second act with its exclusively lyrical design. "It was hard, very hard, to write the second act. . . ." He writes again: "The third act itself is not boring, but the second is boring and monotonous, like a spiderweb." Then again: "I was mainly frightened by the lack of movement in the second act." At the same time Chekhov was worried by the weakening of those devices for obtaining lyrical effects which he had used in preceding plays: "It will be necessary . . . very likely, to change two or three words at the end of Act III, otherwise it will probably be like the end of *Uncle Vanya.*"

We have already seen that Chekhov, in his letters, defined the formal problem of the play as an attempt at providing an understructure of comedy, with corresponding comic characters. He paid a great deal of attention in his letters to explaining the comic and dramatic functions of the characters. When comparing, apparently, the number of people in the new play to the larger group of people in *The Three Sisters,* Chekhov wrote: "I am making an effort to limit the number of characters as much as possible; it will be more intimate this way." And later, in various letters, we find characterizations of people that Chekhov defined as being, in a stage sense, "live characters"; comic characters are affirmed and comic traits singled out (Gaev, Lopakhin, Charlotta, Varya, and others). Chekhov stresses the importance of maintaining a gay and lively tone in the play and gives an exact interpretation of the roles of the different characters, especially Lopakhin—in Chekhov's view the "central role in the play." Chekhov gives special attention to the stage interpretation of gesture and external appearance of characters, to expression in the roles of the characteristic themes, as well as to the environment surrounding the performance and to sound effects. Chekhov was himself present at the rehearsals of the play and frequently corrected parts of it in the interests of clarity and expressiveness.

The Cherry Orchard was performed at the Moscow Art Theater while Chekhov was still living. The thematic conception of the play had demanded a new structural framework; it had been realized on a new plane of comedy; it had been implemented by well-tried methods of Chekhov's dramatic style. The directors of the Moscow Art Theater interpreted the thematic conception of the play according to the principle which they had used in earlier Chekhov plays. But in acting by analogy and in transferring to Chekhov's last play the directing practices used in earlier plays . . . the Moscow Art Theater somehow ignored the original conceptions and new dramatic perspectives of *The Cherry Orchard*. And Chekhov sharply censured the staging of the play in this theater: "How terrible this is! Act IV, which should last twelve minutes maximum, runs forty minutes with you. I can only say that Stanislavsky ruined the play for me." Or again: "Why is my play so insistently called a drama in the playbills and the newspaper announcements? Nemirovich and Alekseev [Stanislavsky] simply don't see what I have written in my play, and I am ready to bet that not once has either of them read my play attentively."

The Cherry Orchard:
A Theater-Poem of the
Suffering of Change

by Francis Fergusson

The Plot of The Cherry Orchard

The Cherry Orchard is often accused of having no plot whatever, and it is true that the story gives little indication of the play's content or meaning; nothing happens, as the Broadway reviewers so often point out. Nor does it have a thesis, though many attempts have been made to attribute a thesis to it, to make it into a Marxian tract, or into a nostalgic defense of the old regime. The play does not have much of a plot in either of these accepted meanings of the word, for it is not addressed to the rationalizing mind but to the poetic and histrionic sensibility. It is an imitation of an action in the strictest sense, and it is plotted according to the first meaning of this word which I have distinguished in other contexts: the incidents are selected and arranged to define an action in a certain mode; a complete action, with a beginning, middle, and end in time. Its freedom from the mechanical order of the thesis or the intrigue is the sign of the perfection of Chekhov's realistic art. And its apparently casual incidents are actually composed with most elaborate and conscious skill to reveal the underlying life, and the natural, objective form of the play as a whole.

In Ghosts, . . . the action is distorted by the stereotyped requirements of the thesis and the intrigue. That is partly a matter of the mode of action which Ibsen was trying to show; a quest "of ethical motivation" which requires some sort of intellectual framework, and yet can have no final meaning-in the purely literal terms of Ibsen's theater. The Cherry

"The Cherry Orchard: A Theater-Poem of the Suffering of Change" (originally untitled) by Francis Fergusson. From The Idea of a Theater (Princeton, N. J., 1949), pp. 161-177. Copyright © 1949 by Princeton University Press. Reprinted by permission of Princeton University Press.

Orchard, on the other hand, is a drama "of pathetic motivation," a theater-poem of the suffering of change; and this mode of action and awareness is much closer to the skeptical basis of modern realism, and to the histrionic basis of all realism. Direct perception before predication is always true, says Aristotle; and the extraordinary feat of Chekhov is to predicate nothing. This he achieves by means of his plot: he selects only those incidents, those moments in his characters' lives, between their rationalized efforts, when they sense their situation and destiny most directly. So he contrives to show the action of the play as a whole—the unsuccessful attempt to cling to the cherry orchard—in many diverse reflectors and without propounding any thesis about it.

The slight narrative thread which ties these incidents and characters together for the inquiring mind, is quickly recounted. The family that owns the old estate named after its famous orchard—Lyubov, her brother Gaev, and her daughters Varya and Anya—is all but bankrupt, and the question is how to prevent the bailiffs from selling the estate to pay their debts. Lopakhin, whose family were formerly serfs on the estate, is now rapidly growing rich as a businessman, and he offers a very sensible plan: chop down the orchard, divide the property into small lots, and sell them off to make a residential suburb for the growing industrial town nearby. Thus the cash value of the estate could be not only preserved, but increased. But this would not save what Lyubov and her brother finds valuable in the old estate; they cannot consent to the destruction of the orchard. But they cannot find, or earn, or borrow the money to pay their debts either; and in due course the estate is sold at auction to Lopakhin himself, who will make a very good thing of it. His workmen are hacking at the old trees before the family is out of the house.

The play may be briefly described as a realistic ensemble pathos: the characters all suffer the passing of the estate in different ways, thus adumbrating this change at a deeper and more generally significant level than that of any individual's experience. The action which they all share by analogy, and which informs the suffering of the destined change of the cherry orchard, is "to save the cherry orchard": that is, each character sees some value in it—economic, sentimental, social, cultural—which he wishes to keep. By means of his plot, Chekhov always focuses attention on the general action: his crowded stage, full of the characters I have mentioned as well as half a dozen hangers-on, is like an implicit discussion of the fatality which concerns them all; but Chekhov does not believe in their ideas, and the interplay he shows among his *dramatis personae* is not so much the play of thought as the alternation of his characters' perceptions of their situation, as the moods shift and the time for decision comes and goes.

Though the action which Chekhov chooses to show onstage is "pathetic," i.e., suffering and perception, it is complete: the cherry orchard is constituted before our eyes, and then dissolved. The first act is a prologue: it is the occasion of Lyubov's return from Paris to try to resume her old life. Through her eyes and those of her daughter Anya, as well as from the complementary perspectives of Lopakhin and Trofimov, we see the estate as it were in the round, in its many possible meanings. The second act corresponds to the agon; it is in this act that we become aware of the conflicting values of all the characters, and of the efforts they make (offstage) to save each one *his* orchard. The third act corresponds to the pathos and peripety of the traditional tragic form. The occasion is a rather hysterical party which Lyubov gives while her estate is being sold at auction in the nearby town; it ends with Lopakhin's announcement, in pride and the bitterness of guilt, that he was the purchaser. The last act is the epiphany: we see the action, now completed, in a new and ironic light. The occasion is the departure of the family: the windows are boarded up, the furniture piled in the corners, and the bags packed. All the characters feel, and the audience sees in a thousand ways, that the wish to save the orchard has amounted in fact to destroying it; the gathering of its denizens to separation; the homecoming to departure. What this "means" we are not told. But the action is completed, and the poem of the suffering of change concludes in a new and final perception, and a rich chord of feeling.

The structure of each act is based upon a more or less ceremonious social occasion. In his use of the social ceremony—arrivals, departures, anniversaries, parties—Chekhov is akin to James. His purpose is the same: to focus attention on an action which all share by analogy, instead of upon the reasoned purpose of any individual, as Ibsen does in his drama of ethical motivation. Chekhov uses the social occasion also to reveal the individual at moments when he is least enclosed in his private rationalization and most open to disinterested insights. The Chekhovian ensembles may appear superficially to be mere pointless stalemates—too like family gatherings and arbitrary meetings which we know offstage. So they are. But in his miraculous arrangement the very discomfort of many presences is made to reveal fundamental aspects of the human situation.

That Chekhov's art of plotting is extremely conscious and deliberate is clear the moment one considers the distinction between the stories of his characters as we learn about them, and the moments of their lives which he chose to show directly onstage. Lopakhin, for example, is a man of action like one of the new capitalists in Gorky's plays. Chekhov knew all about him, and could have shown us an exciting episode from his career if he had not chosen to see him only when he was forced to pause and pathetically sense his own motives in a wider context which qualifies their importance. Lyubov has been dragged about Europe for years by her ne'er-do-well lover, and her life might have yielded several sure-fire erotic intrigues like those of the commercial theater. But Chekhov, like all the great artists of modern times, rejected these standard motivations as both stale and false. The actress Arkadina, in *The Seagull,* remarks, as she closes a novel of Maupassant's, "Well, among the French that may be, but here with us there's nothing of the kind, we've no set program." In the context the irony of her remark is deep: she is herself a purest product of the commercial theater, and at that very time she is engaged in a love affair of the kind she objects to in Maupassant. But Chekhov, with his subtle art of plotting, has caught her in a situation, and at a brief moment of clarity and pause, when the falsity of her career is clear to all, even herself.

Thus Chekhov, by his art of plot-making, defines an action in the opposite mode to that of *Ghosts.* Ibsen defines a desperate quest for reasons and for ultimate, intelligible moral values. This action falls naturally into the form of the agon, and at the end of the play Ibsen is at a loss to develop the final pathos, or bring it to an end with an accepted perception. But the pathetic is the very mode of action and awareness which seems to Chekhov closest to the reality of the human situation, and by means of his plot he shows, even in characters who are not in themselves unusually passive, the suffering and the perception of change. The "moment" of human experience which *The Cherry Orchard* presents thus corresponds to that of the Sophoclean chorus, and of the evenings in the *Purgatorio. Ghosts* is a fighting play, armed for its sharp encounter with the rationalizing mind, its poetry concealed by its reasons. Chekhov's poetry, like Ibsen's, is behind the naturalistic surfaces; but the form of the play as a whole is "nothing but" poetry in the widest sense: the coherence of the concrete elements of the composition. Hence the curious vulnerability of Chekhov on the contemporary stage: he does not argue, he merely presents; and though his audiences even on Broadway are touched by the time they reach the last act, they are at a loss to say what it is all about.

It is this reticent objectivity of Chekhov also which makes him so difficult to analyze in words: he appeals exclusively to the histrionic sensibility where the little poetry of modern realism is to be found. Nevertheless, the effort of analysis must be made if one is to understand this art at all; and if the reader will bear with me, he is asked to consider one element, that of the scene, in the composition of the second act.

Act II: The Scene as a Basic Element in the Composition

Jean Cocteau writes, in his preface to *Les Mariés de la Tour Eiffel*: "The action of my play is in images (*imagée*) while the text is not: I attempt to substitute a 'poetry of the theater' for 'poetry in the theater.' Poetry in the theater is a piece of lace which it is impossible to see at a distance. Poetry of the theater would be coarse lace; a lace of ropes, a ship at sea. *Les Mariés* should have the frightening look of a drop of poetry under the microscope. The *scenes* are integrated like the *words* of a poem."

This description applies very exactly to *The Cherry Orchard*: the larger elements of the composition—the scenes or episodes, the setting, and the developing story—are composed in such a way as to make a poetry of the theater; but the "text" as we read it literally, is not. Chekhov's method, as Stark Young puts it in the preface to his translation of *The Seagull*, "is to take actual material such as we find in life and manage it in such a way that the inner meanings are made to appear. On the surface the life in his plays is natural, possible, and at times in effect even casual."

Young's translations of Chekhov's plays, together with his beautifully accurate notes, explanations, and interpretations, have made the text of Chekhov at last available for the English-speaking stage, and for any reader who will bring to his reading a little patience and imagination.[1] Young shows us what Chekhov means in detail: by the particular words his characters use; by their rhythms of speech; by their gestures, pauses, and bits of stage business. In short, he makes the text transparent, enabling us to see through it to the music of action, the underlying poetry of the composition as a whole—and this is as much as to say that any study of Chekhov (lacking as we do adequate and available productions) must be based upon Young's work. At this point I propose to take this work for granted; to assume the translucent text; and to consider the role of the setting in the poetic or musical order of Act II.

The second act, as I have said, corresponds to the agon of the tradi-

---

[1] The quotations from *The Cherry Orchard* are taken from the translation by Stark Young (New York: Samuel French). Copyright © 1947 by Stark Young. All rights reserved. Reprinted by permission of the author and Samuel French.

tional plot scheme: it is here that we see most clearly the divisive purposes of the characters, the contrasts between their views of the cherry orchard itself. But the center of interest is not in these individual conflicts, nor in the contrasting versions for their own sake, but in the common fatality which they reveal: the passing of the old estate. The setting, as we come to know it behind the casual surfaces of the text, is one of the chief elements in this poem of change: if Act II were a lyric, instead of an act of a play, the setting would be a crucial word appearing in a succession of rich contexts which endow it with a developing meaning.

Chekhov describes the setting in the following realistic terms. "A field. An old chapel, long abandoned, with crooked walls, near it a well, big stones that apparently were once tombstones, and an old bench. A road to the estate of Gaev can be seen. On one side poplars rise, casting their shadows, the cherry orchard begins there. In the distance a row of telegraph poles; and far, far away, faintly traced on the horizon, is a large town, visible only in the clearest weather. The sun will soon be down."

To make this set out of a cyclorama, flats, cut-out silhouettes, and lighting effects would be difficult, without producing that unbelievable but literally intended—and in any case indigestible—scene which modern realism demands; and here Chekhov is uncomfortably bound by the convention of his time. The best strategy in production is that adopted by Robert Edmond Jones in his setting for *The Seagull*: to pay lip service only to the convention of photographic realism, and make the trees, the chapel, and all the other elements as simple as possible. The less closely the setting is defined by the carpenter, the freer it is to play the role Chekhov wrote for it: a role which changes and develops in relation to the story. Shakespeare did not have this problem; he could present his setting in different ways at different moments in a few lines of verse:

> Alack! the night comes on, and the bleak winds
> Do sorely ruffle; for many miles about
> There's scarce a bush.

Chekhov, as we shall see, gives his setting life and flexibility in spite of the visible elements on-stage, not by means of the poetry of words but by means of his characters' changing sense of it.

When the curtain rises we see the setting simply as the country at the sentimental hour of sunset. Epikhodov is playing his guitar and other hangers-on of the estate are loafing, as is their habit, before supper. The dialogue which starts after a brief pause focuses attention upon individuals in the group: Charlotta, the governess, boasting of her culture and complaining that no one understands her; the silly maid Dunyasha, who is infatuated with Yasha, Lyubov's valet. The scene, as reflected by these characters, is a satirical period-piece like the "Stag at Eve" or "The Maiden's Prayer"; and when the group falls silent and begins to drift away (having heard Lyubov, Gaev, and Lopakhin approaching along the path) Chekhov expects us to smile at the sentimental clichés which the place and the hour have produced.

But Lyubov's party brings with it a very different atmosphere: of irritation, frustration, and fear. It is here we learn that Lopakhin cannot persuade Lyubov and Gaev to put their affairs in order; that Gaev has been making futile gestures toward getting a job and borrowing money; that Lyubov is worried about the estate, about her daughters, and about her lover, who has now fallen ill in Paris. Lopakhin, in a huff, offers to leave; but Lyubov will not let him go—"It's more cheerful with you here," she says; and this group in its turn falls silent. In the distance we hear the music of the Jewish orchestra—when Chekhov wishes us to raise our eyes from the people in the foreground to their wider setting, he often uses music as a signal and an inducement. This time the musical entrance of the setting into our consciousness is more urgent and sinister than it was before: we see not so much the peace of evening as the silhouette of the dynamic industrial town on the horizon, and the approach of darkness. After a little more desultory conversation, there is another pause, this time without music, and the foreboding aspect of the scene in silence is more intense.

In this silence Firs, the ancient servant, hurries on with Gaev's coat, to protect him from the evening chill, and we briefly see the scene through Firs's eyes. He remembers the estate before the emancipation of the serfs, when it was the scene of a way of life which made sense to him; and now we become aware of the frail relics of this life: the old gravestones and the chapel "fallen out of the perpendicular."

In sharpest contrast with this vision come the young voices of Anya, Varya, and Trofimov, who are approaching along the path. The middle-aged and the old in the foreground are pathetically grateful for this note of youth, of strength, and of hope; and presently they are listening happily (though without agreement or belief) to Trofimov's aspirations, his creed of social progress, and his conviction that their generation is no longer important to the life of Russia. When the group falls silent again, they are all disposed to contentment with the moment; and when Epikhodov's guitar is heard, and we look up, we feel the country and the evening under the aspect of hope—as offering freedom from the responsibilities and conflicts of the estate itself:

(Epikhodov passes by at the back, playing his guitar.)
Lyubov (Lost in thought). Epikhodov is coming—
Anya (Lost in thought). Epikhodov is coming.
Gaev. The sun has set, ladies and gentlemen.
Trofimov. Yes.
Gaev (Not loud and as if he were declaiming). Oh, Nature, wonderful, you
  gleam with eternal radiance, beautiful and indifferent, you, whom we call
  Mother, combine in yourself both life and death, you give life and take it
  away.
Varya (Beseechingly). Uncle!

Gaev's false, rhetorical note ends the harmony, brings us back to the
present and to the awareness of change on the horizon, and produces a
sort of empty stalemate—a silent pause with worry and fear in it.

All sit absorbed in their thoughts. There is only the silence. Firs is heard
muttering to himself softly. Suddenly a distant sound is heard, as if from the
sky, like the sound of a snapped string, dying away, mournful.

This mysterious sound is used like Epikhodov's strumming to remind
us of the wider scene, but (though distant) it is sharp, almost a warning
signal, and all the characters listen and peer toward the dim edges of
the horizon. In their attitudes and guesses Chekhov reflects, in rapid
succession, the contradictory aspects of the scene which have been developed at more length before us:

Lyubov. What's that?
Lopakhin. I don't know. Somewhere far off in a mine shaft a bucket fell. But
  somewhere very far off.
Gaev. And it may be some bird—like a heron.
Trofimov. Or an owl—
Lyubov (Shivering). It's unpleasant, somehow. (A pause.)
Firs. Before the disaster it was like that. The owl hooted and the samovar
  hummed without stopping, both.
Gaev. Before what disaster?
Firs. Before the emancipation.
  (A pause.)
Lyubov. You know, my friends, let's go. . . .

Lyubov feels the need to retreat, but the retreat is turned into flight
when "the wayfarer" suddenly appears on the path asking for money.
Lyubov in her bewilderment, her sympathy, and her bad conscience,
gives him gold. The party breaks up, each in his own way thwarted and
demoralized.

Anya and Trofimov are left onstage; and, to conclude his theatrical
poem of the suffering of change, Chekov reflects the setting in them:

Anya (A pause). It's wonderful here today!

Trofimov. Yes, the weather is marvelous.

Anya. What have you done to me, Petya, why don't I love the cherry orchard any longer the way I used to? I loved it too tenderly; it seemed to me there was not a better place on earth than our orchard.

Trofimov. All Russia is our garden. The earth is immense and beautiful. . . .

The sun has set, the moon is rising with its chill and its ancient animal excitement, and the estate is dissolved in the darkness as Nineveh is dissolved in a pile of rubble with vegetation creeping over it. Chekhov wishes to show the cherry orchard as "gone"; but for this purpose he employs not only the literal time-scheme (sunset to moonrise) but, as reflectors, Anya and Trofimov, for whom the present in any form is already gone and only the bodiless future is real. Anya's young love for Trofimov's intellectual enthusiasm (like Juliet's "all as boundless as the sea") has freed her from her actual childhood home, made her feel "at home in the world" anywhere. Trofimov's abstract aspirations give him a chillier and more artificial, but equally complete, detachment not only from the estate itself (he disapproves of it on theoretical grounds) but from Anya (he thinks it would be vulgar to be in love with her). We hear the worried Varya calling for Anya in the distance; Anya and Trofimov run down to the river to discuss the socialistic *Paradiso Terrestre*; and with these complementary images of the human scene, and this subtle chord of feeling, Chekhov ends the act.

The "scene" is only one element in the composition of Act II, but it illustrates the nature of Chekhov's poetry of the theater. It is very clear, I think, that Chekhov is not trying to present us with a rationalization of social change *à la* Marx, or even with a subtler rationalization *à la* Shaw. On the other hand, he is not seeking, like Wagner, to seduce us into one passion. He shows us a moment of change in society, and he shows us a "pathos"; but the elements of his composition are always taken as objectively real. He offers us various rationalizations, various images, and various feelings, which cannot be reduced either to one emotion or to one idea: they indicate an action and a scene which is "there" before the rational formulations, or the emotionally charged attitudes, of any of the characters.

The surrounding scene of *The Cherry Orchard* corresponds to the significant stage of human life which Sophocles' choruses reveal, and to the empty wilderness beyond Ibsen's little parlor. We miss, in Chekhov's scene, any fixed points of human significance, and that is why, compared with Sophocles, he seems limited and partial—a bit too pathetic even for our bewildered times. But, precisely because he subtly and elaborately develops the moments of pathos with their sad insights, he sees much more in the little scene of modern realism than Ibsen does. Ibsen's snow-peaks strike us as rather hysterical; but the "stage of Europe" which we divine behind the cherry orchard is confirmed by a thousand impressions derived from other sources. We may recognize its main elements in a cocktail party in Connecticut or Westchester: someone's lawn full of voluble people; a dry white clapboard church (instead of an Orthodox chapel) just visible across a field; time passing, and the muffled roar of a four-lane highway under the hill—or we may be reminded of it in the final section of *The Wasteland*, with its twittering voices, its old grave-stones and deserted chapel, and its dim crowd on the horizon foreboding change. It is because Chekhov says so little that he reveals so much, providing a concrete basis for many conflicting rationalizations of con-temporary social change: by accepting the immediacy and unintelligi-bility of modern realism so completely, he in some ways transcends its limitations, and prepares the way for subsequent developments in the modern theater.

Chekhov's Histrionic Art: An End and a Beginning

Purgatorio, CANTO VIII—[2]

> Era già l'ora che volge il disio
>   ai naviganti e intenerisce il core,
>   lo dì ch'han detto ai dolci amici addio;
> e che lo nuovo peregrin d'amore
>   punge, se ode squilla di lontano,
>   che paia il giorno pianger che si more.

The poetry of modern realistic drama is to be found in those inarticulate moments when the human creature is shown responding directly to his immediate situation. Such are the many moments—composed, inter-related, echoing each other—when the waiting and loafing characters in Act II get a fresh sense (one after the other, and each in his own way) of their situation on the doomed estate. It is because of the exactitude with which Chekhov perceives and imitates these tiny responses, that he can make them echo each other, and convey, when taken together, a single action with the scope, the general significance or suggestiveness, of poetry.

---

[2] It was now the hour that turns back the desire of those who sail the seas and melts their heart, that day when they have said to their sweet friends adieu, and that pierces the new pilgrim with love, if from afar he hears the chimes which seem to mourn for the dying day.

Chekhov, like other great dramatists, has what might be called an ear for action, comparable to the trained musician's ear for musical sound.

The action which Chekhov thus imitates in his second act (that of lending ear, in a moment of freedom from practical pressures, to impending change) echoes, in its turn, a number of other poets: Laforgue's "poetry of waiting-rooms" comes to mind, as well as other works stemming from the period of hush before the First World War. The poets are to some extent talking about the same thing, and their works, like voices in a continuing colloquy, help to explain each other: hence the justification and the purpose of seeking comparisons. The eighth canto of the *Purgatorio* is widely separated from *The Cherry Orchard* in space and time, but these two poems unmistakably echo and confirm each other. Thinking of them together, one can begin to place Chekhov's curiously nonverbal dramaturgy and understand the purpose and the value of his reduction of the art to histrionic terms, as well as the more obvious limitations which he thereby accepts. For Dante accepts similar limitations at this point but locates the mode of action he shows here at a certain point in his vast scheme.

The explicit coordinates whereby Dante places the action of Canto VIII might alone suffice to give one a clue to the comparison with *The Cherry Orchard*: we are in the Valley of Negligent Rulers who, lacking light, unwillingly suffer their irresponsibility, just as Lyubov and Gaev do. The *antepurgatorio* is behind us, and purgatory proper, with its hoped-for work, thought, and moral effort, is somewhere ahead, beyond the night which is now approaching. It is the end of the day; and as we wait, watch, and listen, evening moves slowly over our heads, from sunset to darkness to moonrise. Looking more closely at this canto, one can see that Dante the Pilgrim and the Negligent Rulers he meets are listening and looking as Chekhov's characters are in Act II: the action is the same; in both, a childish and uninstructed responsiveness, an unpremeditated obedience to what is actual, informs the suffering of change. Dante the author, for his elaborate and completely conscious reasons, works here with the primitive histrionic sensibility; he composes with elements sensuously or sympathetically, but not rationally or verbally, defined. The rhythms, the pauses, and the sound effects he employs are strikingly similar to Chekhov's. And so he shows himself—Dante "the new Pilgrim"—meeting this mode of awareness for the first time: as delicately and ignorantly as Gaev when he feels all of a sudden the extent of evening, and before he falsifies this perception with his embarrassing apostrophe to Nature.

If Dante allows himself as artist and as protagonist only the primitive sensibility of the child, the naïf, the natural saint, at this point in the ascent, it is because, like Chekhov, he is presenting a threshold or moment of change in human experience. He wants to show the unbounded potentialities of the psyche before or between the moments when it is morally and intellectually realized. In Canto VIII the pilgrim is both a child and a child who is changing; later moments of transition are different. Here he is virtually (but for the Grace of God) lost; all the dangers are present. Yet he remains uncommitted and therefore open to finding himself again and more truly. In all of this the parallel to Chekhov is close. But because Dante sees this moment as a moment only in the ascent, Canto VIII is also composed in ways in which Act II of *The Cherry Orchard* is not—ways which the reader of the *Purgatorio* will not understand until he looks back from the top of the mountain. Then he will see the homesickness which informs Canto VIII in a new light, and all of the concrete elements, the snake in the grass, the winged figures that roost at the edge of the valley like night-hawks, will be intelligible to the mind and, without losing their concreteness, take their place in a more general frame. Dante's fiction is laid in the scene beyond the grave, where every human action has its relation to ultimate reality, even though that relation becomes explicit only gradually. But Chekhov's characters are seen in the flesh and in their very secular emotional entanglements: in the contemporary world as anyone can see it—nothing visible beyond the earth's horizon, with its signs of social change. The fatality of the *Zeitgeist* is the ultimate reality in the theater of modern realism; the anagoge is lacking. And though Ibsen and Chekhov are aware of both history and moral effort, they do not know what to make of them—perhaps they reveal only illusory perspectives, "masquerades which time resumes." If Chekhov echoes Dante, it is not because of what he ultimately understood but because of the accuracy with which he saw and imitated that moment of action.

If one thinks of the generation to which Anya and Trofimov were supposed to belong, it is clear that the new motives and reasons which they were to find, after their inspired evening together, were not such as to turn all Russia, or all the world, into a garden. The potentialities which Chekhov presented at that moment of change were not to be realized in the wars and revolutions which followed: what actually followed was rather that separation and destruction, that scattering and destinationless trekking, which he also sensed as possible. But, in the cultivation of the dramatic art after Chekhov, renewals, the realization of hidden potentialities, did follow. In Chekhov's histrionic art, the "desire is turned back" to its very root, to the immediate response, to the movements of the psyche before they are limited, defined, and realized in reasoned purpose. Thus Chekhov revealed hidden potentialities, if not in the life of the time, at least in ways of seeing and showing human life; if not in society, at least in the dramatic art. The first and most generally recognized result of these labors was to bring modern realism to its final perfection in the productions of the Moscow Art Theater and in those who learned from it. But the end of modern realism was also a return to very ancient sources; and in our time the fertilizing effect of Chekhov's humble objectivity may be traced in a number of dramatic forms which cannot be called modern realism at all.

The acting technique of the Moscow Art Theater is so closely connected, in its final development, with Chekhov's dramaturgy, that it would be hard to say which gave the more important clues. Stanislavsky and Nemirovich-Danchenko from one point of view, and Chekhov from another, approached the same conception: both were searching for an attitude and a method that would be less hidebound, truer to experience, than the cliché-responses of the commercial theater. The Moscow Art Theater taught the performer to make that direct and total response which is the root of poetry in the widest sense: they cultivated the histrionic sensibility in order to free the actor to realize, in his art, the situations and actions which the playwright had imagined. Chekhov's plays demand this accuracy and imaginative freedom from the performer; and the Moscow Art Theater's productions of his works were a demonstration of the perfection, the reticent poetry, of modern realism. Modern realism of this kind is still alive in the work of many artists who have been more or less directly influenced either by Chekhov or by the Moscow Art Theater. In our country, for instance, there is Clifford Odets; in France, Vildrac and Bernard, and the realistic cinema, of which *Symphonie Pastorale* is an example.

But this cultivation of the histrionic sensibility, bringing modern realism to its end and its perfection, also provided fresh access to many other dramatic forms. The Moscow technique, when properly developed and critically understood, enables the producer and performer to find the life in any theatrical form; before the revolution the Moscow Art Theater had thus revivified *Hamlet, Carmen,* the interludes of Cervantes, neoclassic comedies of several kinds, and many other works which were not realistic in the modern sense at all. A closely related acting technique underlay Reinhardt's virtuosity; and Copeau, in the Vieux Colombier, used it to renew not only the art of acting but, by that means, the art of playwriting also. . . .

After periods when great drama is written, great performers usually appear to carry on the life of the theater for a few more generations. Such were the Siddonses and Macreadys who kept the great Shakespearian roles alive after Shakespeare's theater was gone, and such, at a further stage of degeneration, were the mimes of the Commedia dell'Arte, improving on the themes of Terence and Plautus when the theater had lost most of its meaning. The progress of modern realism from Ibsen to Chekhov looks in some respects like a withering and degeneration of this kind: Chekhov does not demand the intellectual scope, the ultimate meanings, which Ibsen demanded, and to some critics Chekhov does not look like a real dramatist but merely an overdeveloped mime, a stage virtuoso. But the theater of modern realism did not afford what Ibsen demanded, and Chekhov is much the more perfect master of its little scene. If Chekhov drastically reduced the dramatic art, he did so in full consciousness, and in obedience both to artistic scruples and to a strict sense of reality. He reduced the dramatic art to its ancient root, from which new growths are possible.

Intonation and Rhythm
in Chekhov's Plays

by Nils Åke Nilsson

"This was an important step in my work for the theater. I had my own scenic aims. . . . The play had no hero; the main parts were intended for character actors. More hazardous still was the fact that the love intrigue played a completely subordinate part; it hardly even existed. Finally there was not a single outward effect—no shots, no fainting fits, no hysteria, no slap, no trick or, as it was then called, *deus ex machina.* . . . I wanted to find an interest in the scenic form itself and capture the secret of comedy by simple means." [1]

These words are about a Russian play from the end of the last century, and if one does not already know who wrote them one might be tempted to guess at Chekhov. At the end of the 1880s and during the 1890s he worked on the drama, trying to find new forms, dissatisfied as he was with the stereotyped patterns dominating Russian drama at that time. It was not Chekhov who wrote the above words, however, but Vladimir Nemirovich-Danchenko, Stanislavsky's co-worker and co-producer at the Moscow Art Theater, who was then also far from unknown as a dramatist.

The play he talks about was called *A New Project* (*Novoe delo*) and was performed in 1890 at the Maly Theater in Moscow. Even if the author's views on his play are of later date and perhaps a little colored by historical perspective, *A New Project* differed very considerably from the domestic plays which were performed on the Russian stage about 1890. A play without love, without any exciting plot, with the interest wholly centered on the psychological characterization of the main figures,

"Intonation and Rhythm in Chekhov's Plays" by Nils Åke Nilsson. From *Anton Čechov: 1860-1960. Some Essays*, ed. T. Eekman (Leiden: E. J. Brill, 1960), pp. 168-180. Copyright © 1961 by E. J. Brill, Leiden, Netherlands. Reprinted (with slight stylistic changes) by permission of the author and E. J. Brill.

[1] V. I. Nemirovich-Danchenko, *Iz proshlogo* (Leningrad, 1936), p. 37.

with very laconic exchanges written in simple everyday language—this was certainly something new.

Chekhov followed Nemirovich-Danchenko's authorship with interest. "It seems to me," he wrote A. N. Pleshcheev, November 27, 1889, "that this Nemirovich is a very likable man and that gradually he will develop into a real dramatist. In any case he writes better and better every year." To him, Nemirovich-Danchenko's plays were one of several signs that new dramatic forms were slowly working their way forward on the Russian stage. The opposition to the conventionality of the theater and the drama which had been felt since the beginning of the 1880s gradually began to bring practical results.

It seems clear to me that one must look on the novelty of Chekhov's plays not only against the background of Turgenev's, as is always done nowadays. It is often considered that Chekhov, in his opposition to the set forms of the times, aligned himself with Turgenev's dramatic experiments. In this way one is able to find a certain continuity in the development of the Russian drama and Chekhov's plays do not stand so isolated as at first glance it might be supposed. Nemirovich-Danchenko had already felt that there was a certain similarity here,[2] as Meyerhold was also to do later.[3] It is known that Chekhov saw at least one performance of Turgenev's plays; his opinion was, however, negative: he thought them old-fashioned. (Letter to Olga Knipper, March 19, 1903.)

It seems that certain outer similarities have prompted too close a parallel. But these similarities can be explained in part by the fact that Turgenev's dramatic art, like Chekhov's, has its roots in an opposition to the prevailing conventionality of the theater of his times, the result of which was a search for new, simpler, more natural means of expression. And further, those qualities in Turgenev which are considered to presage Chekhov are that his plot is simple and realistic, his characters are everyday people, their actions natural, the dialogues smooth and colloquial but at the same time full of hidden dramatic tension.[4] Just these qualities, however, may be found in some few of those playwrights contemporary with Chekhov who understood, as he did, that a renewal was necessary. It is therefore not surprising that they are evident in Nemirovich-Danchenko's play cited above. It is thus quite clear that one must regard Chekhov's plays also against a background of these tendencies—weak as they may be—toward new forms which are to be found in several playwrights now quite forgotten who were active just those years around 1890. Of course I by no means wish to say that they give

[2] M. Stroeva, *Chekhov i Khudozhestvennyj teatr* (Moscow, 1955), p. 156.
[3] V. Mejerkhol'd, *O teatre* (St. Petersburg, 1912), p. 112.
[4] *Teatr* (1954), 7, p. 41.

a complete explanation of certain original innovations in Chekhov's dramatic technique which belong to him alone, but they can give a certain background to some of them. This is a question which still awaits deeper investigation.[5]

There is one special thing in Nemirovich-Danchenko's play that I should like to dwell on here. One of the main characters, A. Kalguev, says at one stage: "When someone speaks to me I hardly understand the words he utters at all. To be quite honest the words don't exist for me. I disown them completely. They never show me what the human soul in reality wants. But the sounds—they affect me. Do you follow me? The sounds of the voice. Like a prophet, I am always able to discern in them whether a man is happy at heart or not." [6]

The author demonstrates his thesis in different ways in the play. When Stolbtsov, the main character, explains at one point that he is really satisfied with his life and that there is no reason for him to work at the new project he had spoken so much of, his tone of voice belies the fact, and one of the characters does point this out. Then when Stolbtsov is promised money to start on his project he becomes so joyful that he wanders around humming a tune, and without words those present gradually understand that he has succeeded and is to be congratulated.

This idea that the intonation, the voice often better than the words, can unveil what is happening inside a person is of course no new discovery in Russian literature. The man who had propounded this thesis earlier with much emphasis was Leo Tolstoy, as is well known. It is constantly expressed in his novels. Speaking of Natasha in *War and Peace,* for example, he says that "she could not write because she found it impossible in writing to express even a thousandth part of what she was used to expressing with her voice, her smile, and her gaze." The same contrast between the communicative content of the words and the emotionally charged delivery of them which Nemirovich-Danchenko uses in his play had already been made use of by Tolstoy, in the following example from *War and Peace:* "'What? What? How dare you!' said Telyamin. But the words sounded like a piteous, despairing cry, begging for forgiveness. As soon as Rostov heard their sound an enormous stone of doubt fell from his breast." [7]

[5] There is some material on this subject in a paper by V. B. Khalizov, "Russkaja dramaturgija nakanune 'Ivanova' i 'Chajki,'" in: *Nauchnye doklady vysshej shkoly. Filologicheskie nauki* (1959), I, p. 20ff. See also N. P. Ljul'ko, "A. P. Chekhov i russkij teatr 80-90kh godov XIX v.," in *Vestnik Leningradskogo universiteta* (1955), 6, p. 82.

[6] V. I. Nemirovich-Danchenko, *Povesti i p'esy* (Moscow, 1958), p. 359.

[7] See V. Vinogradov, "O jazyke Tolstogo (50-60e gody)," in *Literaturnoe nasledstvo,* 35/36, p. 196ff.

This technique, new for the novel, of describing what is going on inside a person originated with Tolstoy in a demand for greater realism. What he was against was that the novel expressed feelings solely in words. The characters gave long descriptions of how they thought and felt. In reality, Tolstoy asserted, they did not. People intimate their feelings to each other less by the words themselves than by mime, the gestures and movements that accompany the words, and—of no less importance—by the intonation itself.

Similar demands for greater realism in the reproduction of human feelings must sooner or later be made for the stage. We have seen how one of the main characters in Nemirovich-Danchenko's play rejects the value of words as evidence of what a man thinks and feels. He sets the voice in place of the words. Chekhov goes further on this path. For him there is also a demand for realism in background: on stage everything must be "as in real life," as he never tires of stressing.

But on the other hand, modern drama—as Chekhov himself often points out—shifts the interest more and more from the main action to the inner man, from outward intrigue to psychological conflict. How to combine scenic realism with "the drama of souls"? How is the realistic playwright to reproduce feeling, the innermost thoughts of man on the stage? How much can words express? How far can he use everyday words without their losing their dramatic tension and—on the other hand— how far can he "dramatize" words without their ceasing to appear natural?

"No, not that. It was not that I wanted to say" (*ne to, ne to*), Chekhov's characters are often forced to say. They cannot find the right words for their thoughts and feelings, noticing suddenly that the words they are using do not express what they are really thinking. In the third act of *Uncle Vanya*, Sonya tries to explain to her father how difficult a time she and Uncle Vanya have had, but the words do not suffice: "That was not what I wanted to say (*ja govorju ne to, ne to ja govorju*), but you must understand us, Papa." "I am a gull. No, not that," Nina reiterates in conversation with Trigorin in the final scene of *The Seagull*. In the third act of *Uncle Vanya*, Elena Andreevna thinks of Sonya and her love for Astrov: "He is not in love with her—that is clear, but why should he not be able to marry her? She is not beautiful, but for a country practitioner, of his age, she would make an excellent wife. She is intelligent, so good and pure. . . . No, it is not that, not that" (*Net, eto ne to, ne to*). Her words do not express her inner thoughts: she is herself interested in Astrov. "Why am I saying these words?" Masha exclaims in despair in the first act of *The Three Sisters,* as she abstractedly repeats a line from a poem by Pushkin.

Like Tolstoy, Chekhov had to find other means of expressing feelings and thoughts outside of words. The most important of these were to be: first of all the voice; then different sounds (from the night-watchman's hammering, from guitar playing to the snapping string in *The Cherry Orchard*); associatively charged objects (from the symbolic seagull to Natasha's belt in *The Three Sisters*); the pauses, used very frequently and with great variation; silent scenes (the last scene in *Uncle Vanya* where Maria Vasilevna sits writing and Marina knits stockings; the last scene in *The Three Sisters,* where Kulygin and Andrei appear in the background during the three sisters' monologue as a reminder of commonplace life); and lastly the language itself, the structure of the sentences.

These devices are not used only to create a background atmosphere on the stage. The aim is also to communicate to the audience things which concern the characters or the setting or the action, things which the realistic drama according to Chekhov neither could nor should express in words.

Research in Chekhov's dramatic technique ought to tackle this system of devices as a whole and study it in its opposition to or cooperation with the dramatic diction. No other dramatic writer, I think, is so interesting from this special point of view as Chekhov. Lack of space will not allow of it here; I shall only attempt to make some remarks on an aspect of this system which as far as I know has received rather little attention: intonation and its rhythm.

For Chekhov, intonation was one of the realistic playwright's most important aids. In a letter to Olga Knipper dated January 2, 1900, he wrote: "I have written to Meyerhold and recommended that he not exaggerate when he represents a nervous person. The great majority of people are nervous, the majority suffer, only a very few feel a sharp pain, but where, outdoors or indoors, do you see people running about, hopping and holding their heads with their hands? Suffering must be shown as it is shown in life, i.e., not with feet and hands but with tone of voice and eyes, not with gesticulation but with grace. The subtler emotions characteristic of cultured people must also be given subtle outward expression. Conditions on the stage do not allow of this, you will say, but no conditions justify a lie."

This was advice given to an actor on how to express emotions on the stage. Yet it was also advice to the playwright. If an actor's voice was going to be of such great importance, then it was essential for the author to explain precisely how the lines were to be spoken. It is a fact that no playwright before Chekhov, and hardly anyone after him either, lays such great importance on directions for intonation. His four great plays overflow with them, culminating in his last play, *The Cherry Orchard.* In this play one can find about 175 directions on how the lines are to be spoken. It is important to note here that these directions are by no means stereotyped or trivial. On the contrary, they are notable for an abundance of variation; in actual fact each rarely occurs more than once. It is thus possible to find some eighty different directions for speaking. They are often complicated, sometimes being composed of wholly opposing parts, for instance: "cheerfully, in tears," "happily, agitated," "angrily and mockingly," "impatiently, with tears."

It is also possible to see that certain characters or scenes in Chekhov's plays are thought out acoustically, that a certain tone of voice or certain sounds are a dominating and characteristic element of them. When *Uncle Vanya* was to be performed at the Moscow Art Theater, Chekhov wrote to Stanislavsky about the last scene: "He [Astrov] whistles, you know . . . whistles. Uncle Vanya is crying but Astrov whistles." [8] Stanislavsky understood what Chekhov wanted to say with this laconic note. Here he found something characteristic of Dr. Astrov, who, fighting his own despair, is trying to appear unmoved. He thus included this detail in the first act as well. As soon as Astrov appears he starts whistling; it becomes a sort of leitmotif which characterizes an important part of him much more clearly than any words.

Chekhov wrote to Olga Knipper October 25, 1903, about Ranevskaya in *The Cherry Orchard*: "It is not difficult to play Ranevskaya; only one has to find the right key from the very beginning; one has to find a smile and way of laughing, one must be able to dress." Just as whistling is something characteristic for Astrov, so is the laugh something important for the picture of Ranevskaya. With his words Chekhov wanted to point out her limitations, [she is] an emotionally static person who lives through the sale of the property and the cherry orchard without being affected. Her unchanged laugh and smile tell her story more clearly than words.

Against this background of careful directions for intonation one understands better why Chekhov sometimes so energetically maintained that it was necessary to follow the author's directions on the stage, that the author really ought to have more to say on the stage than even the producer. On one occasion he was thus able to say that "I really do believe that no play can be set up by even the most talented producer

[8] K. S. Stanislavskij, *Sobranie sochinenij,* I (Moscow, 1954), p. 232.

without the author's personal guidance and directions. . . . There are different interpretations, but the author has the right to demand that his play be performed and the parts played wholly according to his own interpretation. . . . It is necessary that the particular atmosphere intended by the author be created." [9]

These intonational directions show how important the emotional key was for Chekhov, but they also show one more important thing: the rhythm of the emotional key. The Chekhov mood was, and perhaps often still is, interpreted as a dominating, all-pervading atmosphere of elegy and despair, an interpretation which threatens to make Chekhov's plays boring and monotonous. But what Chekhov did want was to give an illusion of life on the stage, and life was for him both laughter and tears, both hope and despair, both longing and triviality. It is certainly true that the emotional scale Chekhov works with is of no very broad register. The poles do not lie very far from each other. But in the middle register he uses, Chekhov has been able to capture very subtle nuances—our hasty review of intonation in *The Cherry Orchard* above clearly shows this.

In this middle register he works with perpetual changes and contrasts. It is as if he were keen that no one key become too dominant or last too long. There must be change and rhythm if his plays are really to give a picture of everyday life. His striving toward this end is most obvious in *The Cherry Orchard*. Here Chekhov marks it very clearly, underlines it, presumably because he thought that insufficient attention had been paid to it in his previous plays. As I said before, there are not many intonational directions in *The Cherry Orchard* that appear more than once. The only ones that occur more often are those that intimate that a line is to be spoken "happily" and "laughingly" or "sorrowfully" and "in tears." In the play there are some fifteen of each type, which in its own way thus shows how he tries to keep a balance between the contrasting keys.

Some of Chekhov's most usual contrasts juxtapose a lyrical or elated with a banal, everyday atmosphere, a melancholy and serious with a comic atmosphere, a lively and active with a calm and pensive atmosphere. It is characteristic for Chekhov that these keys not only succeed each other but are also to be found in balance in the same scene.

It is often said that there are many "indifferent" lines in Chekhov's plays. Apart from the self-characterizing monologues so typical of him, monologues whose syntactical construction—often without directions from the author—intimates their lyrical key, there are long passages with markedly colloquial lines. But these are only indifferent in that the semantic content of the words is at this point transferred to the background. Instead it is the way the words are spoken that carries the meaning, and the voice expresses what a person thinks or feels.

These indifferent remarks, I think, give the most obvious examples of how intonation and rhythm work in Chekhov's plays. I will use some of them here to clarify what I mean.

There are several types of indifferent remarks in Chekhov's plays. Let us begin with Gaev's billiard terms in *The Cherry Orchard*. The real meaning of the words has no relevance in the context where they are used. Gaev resorts to them on occasions when he is disturbed or embarrassed and does not know what to say. Chekhov always gives clear directions for intonation. The words are either to be spoken "in a disconcerted way," or "in deep thought," or "despondently."

Thus the semantic content is of no interest here; what matters is the intonation: it reveals the emotional state of mind behind the words. Chekhov works this type of "indifferent" words to the limit in *The Three Sisters* where Masha and Vershinin hold their strange dialogue:

> *Masha.* Tram-tam-tam . . .
> *Vershinin.* Tam-tam . . .
> *Masha.* Tra-ra-ta . . .
> *Vershinin.* Tra-ta-ta . . .

And the second time:

> *Vershinin.* Tram-tam-tam.
> *Masha.* Tram-tam.

The third time, Vershinin's voice is heard offstage: "Tram-tam-tam." And Masha answers him with a "Tra-ta-ta."

It is understandable that a dialogue such as this would puzzle the actors: what was its function in the context, what intonation was one to use here? Olga Knipper wrote to Chekhov and asked about the passage. Chekhov replied in a letter of November 20, 1901: "Vershinin speaks his 'Tram-tam-tam' as a question and you as an answer, and you think it is such an original joke that you speak this 'tam-tam' with a smile."

It is clear that these lines together form a dialogue of mutual understanding between Masha and Vershinin, a sort of love duet without words. One is reminded of the well-known scene in *Anna Karenina* where Levin and Kitty declare their love for each other without words, using only letters of the alphabet which they are able to interpret with the peculiar intuition of lovers.

And here is another type of "indifferent" exchange: in the second act of *The Cherry Orchard,* Epikhodov crosses backstage playing on his guitar.

Lyubov Andreevna (Pensively). Epikhodov is coming.
Anya (Pensively). Epikhodov is coming.

Lyubov Andreevna thus states that she hears and sees her bookkeeper pass by. It is a statement, i.e., the semantic content of the words is not completely to be disregarded as in the above examples. But it is no normal statement; if that were the case, Chekhov would not have noted that the line was to be said "pensively." It must therefore have a different contextual function. If this function is to be looked for in the semantic content of the words, a possible interpretation to these lines may be given with reference to the earlier conversation between Trofimov and Lopakhin, when Lopakhin said that giants would be necessary to solve the problems in Russia. Now when Epikhodov appears on the scene perhaps it occurs to Lyubov Andreevna and Anya that there are no giants to be found in Russia, but only such tragicomic figures as Epikhodov, "thousand and one misfortunes," as he is called.

But I think it is of no use here to stress the semantic content of these words by trying to find some hidden meaning behind them. The scene is conditioned first of all by the rhythm in the emotional key. After the serious conversation between Trofimov and Lopakhin the appearance of Epikhodov comes in marked contrast, as a change in the emotional key. It communicates something of the comic and trivial—concepts connected with the figure of Epikhodov; and further, after the lively, active conversation, a contrast of rest: Lyubov Andreevna's and Anya's pensive, abstracted lines.

In this connection it is worth remembering some words which Chekhov wrote to Olga Knipper, January 2, 1901, while rehearsals for *The Three Sisters* were in progress. "Do not look sad in any of the acts," he wrote. "Angry, certainly, but not sad. People who have long borne grief inside them and have become used to it only whistle a little and often become lost in thought. So you too must now and again lose yourself in thought on the stage." Most of Chekhov's characters are certainly such people who have long borne a grief or a longing within them. They often shut themselves off from the outside world for a moment, letting some indifferent words communicate their abstracted state of mind.

There is another similar passage in *The Three Sisters.* Chebutykin, who usually sits reading the paper, noting down the various curiosities he finds there, suddenly reads aloud: "Balzac was married in Berdichev."

And Irina meditatively repeats his words as she plays patience: "Balzac was married in Berdichev."

Chebutykin's words follow on a conversation between Vershinin and Tusenbach where Vershinin propounds his favorite theory that life in two or three hundred years will be better and happier but that the generations living now have no right to think of happiness. Chebutykin's words come when the discussion has reached a dead end and Tusenbach says that "it is difficult to argue with you both."

Some scholars have chosen to give Irina's repetition of Chebutykin's words a special meaning. That Balzac, a great poet, marries in Berdichev, a little village in the country which no one might have heard of before, perhaps starts Irina thinking that happiness is possibly to be found where one least expects it. Perhaps their Moscow dream, their great dream of finding happiness in the city, is only an illusion? It may be that happiness is also to be found in the small town where they now live?

I am very doubtful about this interpretation. If Chekhov had wished to include this idea in his play it would have needed further support, and one can hardly say that the thought is developed in other passages in *The Three Sisters*. In fact this scene is a direct parallel to the scene in *The Cherry Orchard* which we have already looked at. It is above all an example of the rhythm which Chekhov works with in intonation and emotional key. After the serious conversation between Vershinin and Tusenbach, Chebutykin's trivial line follows as a marked contrast, a return to everyday life. And afterwards, a moment of rest and meditation: Irina's abstracted, dreamy repetition of Chebutykin's indifferent words.

In the last act of *Uncle Vanya*, Astrov goes over to a map of Africa hanging on the wall and says a few words about how terribly hot it must be in Africa just then, to which Voynitsky replies: "Yes, I suppose so." This remark about Africa is like the one we have just spoken of; its effect is also abrupt, unexpected, without any visible function in the context. As with other indifferent lines, a hidden meaning has been sought in it.

Stanislavsky, who played Astrov in the first performance at the Moscow Art Theater, for instance, gave it a definite emotional content, let his voice give meaning to the words. Olga Knipper told of this: "How much bitterness and experience of life he put into this phrase. And how he pronounced these words with a sort of bravura, challenging almost." [10] It appears as if one ought to understand by Olga Knipper's remark that

[10] *O Stanislavskom* (Moscow, 1948), p. 266.

Astrov, with his words, brought out a sort of contrast to Russian life where everything is indifferent, dull, and apathetic; in other countries, far away, there is heat, there is something that burns and consumes.

Yet it is characteristic that the words may be interpreted in many other ways. A Soviet scholar, V. Yermilov, for instance, writes thus: "Astrov is ready to leave; his carriage is waiting for him at the door. And this remark about Africa conclusively transports everything that has happened here a moment before far, far away: it is as though Africa symbolized the immeasurable distance separating the heroes in the play from the dramas in which they so recently participated. . . . After the remark on Africa everything that has taken place on the estate becomes conclusively just as distant as Africa." [11]

As Chekhov himself said: "There are different interpretations. . . ." But if one is to judge by the author's own words, this was not at all his intention with the remark. In a letter to Olga Knipper September 30, 1899, he wrote about this scene: "You write that Astrov in this scene turns to Elena as a passionate lover, clutches for emotion as a drowning man clutches for a straw. But this is wrong, absolutely wrong. Astrov likes Elena; she appeals to him strongly because of her beauty, but in the last act he knows already that nothing will come of it, that Elena is going away from him forever—and he speaks to her in this scene in the same tone as he speaks of the heat in Africa, and he kisses her simply like this, because he has nothing else to do."

Thus we see that according to Chekhov himself there is no use seeking a hidden meaning behind these words. What matters here is the intonation; the words merely form a backdrop for Astrov's resigned tone of voice.

Another illuminating example of how Chekhov tries to create rhythmic variation in the emotional key is to be found in the scene between Lyubov Andreevna and Trofimov in Act III of *The Cherry Orchard,* a disturbed scene full of emotion which is unexpectedly and abruptly turned into something comic when Trofimov, rushing in agitation from Lyubov Andreevna, falls downstairs with a crash. Here, as in several of the earlier examples, a contrasting note comes in afterward, breaking the previous serious atmosphere of the scene. Chekhov is also capable of the opposite. In Act III of *The Cherry Orchard* Lopakhin has his great scene, a dramatic entrance and monologue similar to the climax which drama, before Chekhov, usually worked up to in the third or fourth act. When Lopakhin does make his expected and prepared entrance, however, it is by no means in the same effective way as it would have been

[11] V. Ermilov, *Dramaturgija Chekhova* (Moscow, 1948), p. 114.

made with one of Chekhov's predecessors. Varya thinks it is Epikhodov
coming back. He had just been teasing her and she waits at the door
with a stick and smites Lopakhin when he comes in. The new owner of
the cherry orchard thus makes rather a ridiculous entrance. It is clear
that Chekhov inserted this mode of entry to contrast with the coming
monologue, that it might not be too "dramatic" in the old meaning of
the word.

But Chekhov also works with rhythmic variations in the middle of a
monologue or a scene. An obvious example of this is to be found at the
beginning of *The Three Sisters*. It is Olga's and Irina's lyrical scene
which recalls the atmosphere of the house as it was a year ago at their
father's death; it is interrupted in the middle by a conversation between
Solyony, Chebutykin, and Tusenbach in the background. Only a few
words are heard: "Chebutykin: 'Damned silly (*Cherta s dva*).' Tusenbach: 'Utter nonsense, of course.' " It is clear that Solyony has said
something to make them indignant. These short exchanges occur just in
the middle of the lyrical conversation between the sisters. It is obvious
that they are intended to break the lyrical atmosphere, by introducing
a more trivial mood to prevent it from becoming too monotonous.

The final monologue of the three sisters is also constructed in a similar way. Right at the very end Masha's husband appears, in company
with Andrei, pushing a baby carriage at the same time as Chebutykin is
humming his everlasting "Ta-ra-ra-boom-de-ay, nothing matters." Against
the lyrical atmosphere and the poetic structure of the sentences, Chekhov
inserts the mute appearance of Andrei and Kulygin in contrast, as a
reminder of everyday life (compare Epikhodov's appearance in *The
Cherry Orchard*) and of Chebutykin's philosophy of hopelessness. He
is anxious that the lyrical intonation shall not become too dominant in
the monologue and thus brings in contrasting tones.

It is characteristic of today's Chekhov scholars that they look for new
meanings in the "indifferent" remarks. "It is said that Chekhov taught
us scenic simplicity, but his words are not simple," Nemirovich-Danchenko said during rehearsals for *The Three Sisters* in 1939.[12] His words
seem to have left their mark on the modern scenic interpretation of
Chekhov's play in the Soviet Union and on Chekhov research as well.
It is, of course, quite right to say that Chekhov's simple words are not
simple in that they are not inserted at random; there is always a reason
for them in the context. But I think that one may often go too far in
seeking hidden meanings behind the "indifferent" lines. I do not believe
that Chekhov tried to fill his plays with secret connotations which must

[12] M. Stroeva, *Chekhov i Khudozhestvennyj teatr*, p. 270.

be pieced together like a jigsaw puzzle. The most obvious reason for the indifferent remarks is always the rhythm, the variation in the intonation, in the emotional key. Certainly in their context these remarks also often evoke certain associations, but these associations are always of a general character. I consider it dubious to narrow them down by indicating one of them as being that which Chekhov intended.

. . . The inadequacy of words was a problem of the times. In comparison we can refer to Meyerhold and his attempts to solve this problem on the stage. At one point Meyerhold quotes Wagner as an example. He says that for Wagner recitative lines were not enough to express a singer's inner feelings, so he brought in the orchestra to help; the orchestra could express the unutterable. It is the same thing in a play: "The word is not a sufficiently strong means of revealing the inner dialogue." [13]

Thus, here the intonation becomes as valuable an accessory for Meyerhold as for Chekhov, yet he makes use of it in quite a different way. In his opposition to the declamatory style of the old theater, Meyerhold wishes to liberate the actor's voice from every trace of pathos and vibrato. He goes even further: he wants a cold, clear diction. But in it there is also to be a "mysterious tremble" which can better hint at what goes on inside a person than the bursts of temperament of the old actors.

"In the rhythm of the monotonously uttered words, behind the outer spoken dialogue, one feels an inner, hidden dialogue of sensation and impression which cannot be expressed by the words," as a reviewer described his impressions of Meyerhold's performance of Ibsen's *Hedda Gabler* in 1906. "The playgoer may forget the words that Hedda and Lövborg say to each other, but he must not forget the evocativeness of them.[14]

Meyerhold did not produce Chekhov in the same radical manner.[15] But he certainly had a different interpretation of his plays from the Moscow Art Theater. After the first performance of *The Cherry Orchard*, he wrote a letter to Chekhov in which he criticized Stanislavsky. It is interesting to note that here, too, he was looking for the key to the play in precisely its rhythmical–acoustic character. He compared it to a symphony by Tchaikovsky—a comparison many were to make after him. But he had in mind not so much its melancholy mood as its abstract,

---

[13] *Teatr. Kniga o novom teatre* (St. Petersburg, 1908), p. 166.

[14] V. Mejerkhol'd, *O teatre*, p. 190. But apart from the diction, Meyerhold also laid great stress on an actor's movements. Gesture, pose, gaze, and silence were of great importance for him. The producer was to work out a plan for the actor's movements on the stage where every change had to have a definite function and meaning and, together with light and the stage set, help to express what the words could not.

[15] *Literaturnoe nasledstvo*, 68 (1960), 430-434.

musical structure; he especially pointed out the rhythmical contrasts in Act III. "The producer," he concluded, "must first of all understand it [the play] with his hearing." [16]

[16] S. D. Balukhatyj and N. V. Petrov, *Dramaturgija Chekhova* (Kharkov, 1935), p. 120.

The Duality of Chekhov

by John Gassner

Two diametrically opposed interpretations of Chekhov have appeared in the English-speaking world, and they have been proclaimed with special fervor in the world of the theater. The first dominant view, while conceding his talent for vaudeville humor in a number of short stage pieces, lauded an artist of half-lights, a laureate of well-marinated futility, and a master of tragic sensibility even if his work failed to conform to classic standards of tragedy. This view came to be challenged with considerable vigor in England and America after World War II, particularly in the academic world. Without any ideological impetus, such as one could expect in Eastern Europe, to favor a new image of Chekhov as the prophet of a new society, there arose a tendency to discard the old image in favor of a tinsel view of Chekhov as a paragon of breezy extroversion. Young academicians were particularly eager to divest him of the atmosphere of gloom and soulfulness ("Slavic soulfulness," at that!) which he had accumulated in Western criticism and stage productions. Moreover, so many journalistic sources gave their support to proponents of this view that it became the prevailing one whether or not it was applicable to any particular work in whole or in part.

It must become evident, though, upon reflection, that this view has its inadequacies, if not indeed dangers—inadequacies even with respect to a brief humorous story such as the often-printed "A Work of Art," in which a physician is embarrassed in his provincial milieu by the gift of a nude statuette, let alone with respect to the great plays upon which rests much of Chekhov's reputation in the West. The advocates of a blithely extrovert interpretation or the image of a Chekhov purified of "Chekhovianism" are constrained to omit or at least play down too many facets, not to mention nuances, of his work to make it conform to a simplistic definition of comedy; the work thus becomes too thin and

"The Duality of Chekhov," by John Gassner. An early version of this essay was delivered in 1960 as an address at Brooklyn College on the occasion of the centenary celebration of Chekhov's birth. Copyright © 1967 by Prentice-Hall, Inc. Reprinted by permission of the author.

elementary, and would therefore have to be rated as little more than clever second-rate histrionics. The proponents of this recently "discovered" image have not known what to make of their extroverted Chekhov, just as their predecessors didn't quite know what to make of their introverted one. For the former, it seems sufficient that Chekhov, according to his biographer, David Magarshak, claimed that he wrote "comedies" and that in his original Moscow Art Theater stage productions Stanislavsky distorted the plays. For the latter, it was sufficient that Stanislavsky, who was after all known to be the scion of a wealthy merchant family and a gentleman of the Russian *ancien régime,* laved the plays in a tragical atmosphere until they could be read as rueful epitaphs for a vanishing upper class.

The latter view (though not without comic touches—or what the British weather forecasters call "bright intervals") has prevailed in England, where there has been a decaying upper class now for more than half a century. And British playwrights have long been prone to turn their "country houses" into "Heartbreak Houses," although hardly with the buoyancy of Bernard Shaw, the author of *Heartbreak House,* who felt no sentimental attachment to country houses or their upper-class occupants. In the United States we lacked the country houses that would afford a class basis for mournful Chekhovianism and therefore fared less well with it. Thus the Broadway director Joshua Logan had to go to the deep South for a Chekhovian country house in his *Cherry Orchard* adaptation, *The Wisteria Tree,* and even this sensible recourse did not quite secure Chekhovian introversion against Broadway's cosmopolitan (or merely deracinated) diffidence.

What the old tendency in Chekhovian production failed to perceive (the Lunt–Theater Guild production of *The Seagull* in the 1930s may be considered a happy exception) was that Chekhov himself was not dispirited even if a good many of his characters are, and that even the latter are not altogether willing to wallow in hopelessness. If this old-guard view of Chekhov had been entirely tenable, it would have been easy to advance claims for him as one of the progenitors of the Theater of the Absurd, and it is perhaps significant that no such claims have been advanced. What the "new-generation" view of the extrovert–Chekhov has failed to take into account is precisely the large area of stalemate against which Chekhov rebelled, and the fact that what he exposed in his plays plainly existed in turn-of-the-century provincial life. It was pervasive and oppressive enough, in fact, to arouse his scorn and indignation. It comprised a world abundantly present in his plays and stories, for a good writer does not launch an attack on something that lacks reality and he also does not tilt against anything to which he has failed to give existence as an artist. And Chekhov could not have done what he did if he had been a wholly detached naturalist, an intellectual snob, a blithely sneering sophisticate, or a superficial propagandist thundering against a crumbling *ancien régime*. It is absurd to assume that he had no empathy with his stalemated characters, no share in the sensibility that makes them so alive and appealing, as it would be to claim that he felt no ambivalence in portraying them sensitively or even sympathetically.

It is ambivalence translated into art (and that means into *artistic reality*) that distinguishes the writer even in laughter from the nonartist and that separates the poet from the poetaster. Chekhov's sensibility for stalemate as well as his attack on it is an important element in his artistry, and Stanislavsky was enough of an artist to discern it in the plays he brought to the stage. To this undertaking, of course, Stanislavsky also brought his own sensibility, as did the Moscow Art Theater actors, and there is reason to believe that before the Bolshevik revolution the Moscow Art Theater could not have entertained absolute hostility to the life represented by its greatest playwright. Surely Stanislavsky and his associates could not have been naïve enough to think that the closing scenes of *The Seagull, Uncle Vanya, The Three Sisters,* and *The Cherry Orchard* were "funny." Surely they could not be insensible to the presence of heartbreak in whatever affirmativeness is explicit or discoverable in the plays.

Most important of all, however, is the fact that both our old-generation and new-generation viewpoints have tended to fail on the very same ground. They have been almost equally remiss in overlooking the *positive* element in his work, which has its basis not simply in the natural buoyancy of his character, but in his *positivist* outlook as a physician and as a "man of the people" to whom "soul-sickness" seems largely self-indulgence and suffering seems essentially the result of individual and societal bumbling. Chekhov was surely the most positivist and least Dostoevskian of the Russian literary masters. The *old* generation of Chekhov admirers in the English-speaking theater tended to ignore or glide over this fact. The *new* generation, which became articulate after World War II, has tended to overlook the same fact in the very process of raising paeans to him as a writer of comedies. To publicize him without substantial qualification as a humorist is an insult to his engaged intelligence and passionateness.

Chekhov is passionate in both his scorn and his sympathy even when he displays a cool surface of detachment, a surface of naturalistic objectivity. This is often only his literary façade, so to speak. If anyone undertakes to appraise Chekhov seriously, he will, it is true, find much humor in the major works of fiction and drama. Chekhov may be a comic master, though hardly that alone (only ignorance of such works as "The Peasants" and "Ward No. 6" could allow such an unqualified generalization); he is far from being one of those clever jesters for whom a jest of any consequence is not, in Shaw's famous words, "an earnest in the womb of time." Only when this is realized can the critic do justice to Chekhov as a major figure of the literary world. Only then, too, can a theatrical production of a major Chekhov play find the necessary mean between its farcicality and tragicality.

The same kind of writer appears in the mature artistry of both his stories and his plays, and the style is intrinsically the *man* in both despite the more formal demands of the dramatic medium. Chekhov places wonderfully alive characters in the center of his work whether he gives them independence in a character sketch such as "The Darling" or the full but dependent reality of a dramatically involved person. If he relates them to their environment, he does not diminish them as individuals even when the milieu oppresses them, as it does in *Uncle Vanya* and *The Three Sisters*. The dissonances of social reality do not drown out the resonant singularity of the human voice. It is agreed that Chekhov supplants the external action of commonplace fiction and drama with *inner* action, thus producing the so-called plotless work we associate importantly with modern literature and theater. In reducing the role of plot, however, he does not diminish—he actually enlarges and intensifies—character revelation.

Chekhov performed the extremely difficult feat of maintaining the reality of character and the reality of environment in delicate equilibrium. Chekhov is a naturalist who did not content himself with observing surfaces but created in depth and consequently escaped the aridity of most naturalistic writing. And if, like other naturalists, he provided many a slice of life in his stories and plays, each slice was alive, whereas the naturalist's *"tranche de vie"* too often possesses everything but abounding life.

Chekhov, moreover, wrote with the simplicity of a person who is constitutionally incapable of imposing on anyone. He was that rare literary naturalist who wrote *naturally*. It is not only that his writing flowed easily but that he managed to write masterly stories and a number of major plays in which the characters behave and speak as if they were unaware of having been snared in the net of literature. They seem immersed in the stream of their own life. They feel for themselves, think their own thoughts, and dream their own dreams; so much so, in fact, that they seem to fly off from the center of the action and contribute to a play a centrifugal action (or, on occasion, *inaction*[1]) of their own. Although he wrote neither verse nor purple prose, his mature writing, full of delicate shadings of characterization and emotion, has the effect of poetry. In his chief work, moreover, the "poetry" is of such complex design that his writing has been described as virtually contrapuntal.

And one more technical point must be mentioned: It has often been noted that Chekhov is a great humorist yet also a profoundly moving writer. What this amounts to in terms of artistry is that his writing simply possesses a rich texture, that it exists on several levels of sensibility at the same time, and that his often limpid simplicity masks considerable complexity. Chekhov is especially modern in this one respect: that his mature work belongs, in the main, to a mixed genre. Whereas in past ages comedy and tragedy tended to exist separately, they tend to blend in modern writing. In his work, comedy may infiltrate tragedy, and tragedy may infiltrate comedy, producing controversy on the part of those who like to busy themselves with the fine points of literary classification. Chekhov is the master of the double mode, of what for want of a better term we may call tragicomedy or simply "drama." He was so effective in this genre partly because his various attitudes and moods blended so naturally. He was so effective also because he had such high spirits that disenchantment or depression could not often overcome him as it evidently did in such stories as "The Peasants" and "Ward No. 6."

A romantic half-truth has designated Chekhov as the Jeremiah of soul-bankruptcy. We can perhaps best approach this contention by noting that there have indeed been two major modes of modernism, as there have been *two* Chekhovs in literary tradition. It seems as if modernity has been divided between a modernism of *Thanatos* and a modernism of *Eros*. Chekhov belongs to the *positive* mode of modernism in spite of the widespread tendency to associate him with moribund, negativistic modernity. We have barely begun to do justice, whether in criticism or stage production, to one of the most buoyantly vital of European writers. Chekhov appears to have possessed "the even-tempered soul" Matthew Arnold attributed to Sophocles, although that soul moved through life modestly and never teetered on "high tragic" stilts to survey the landscape of our muddied existence. He was equable with a twinkle and sometimes with a sob, but he was equable. Yet he was not *so* equable

---

[1] A fine example of dramatic *inaction* in Chekhovian dramaturgy is the normally hyperactive merchant Lopakhin's unsuccessful wooing scene in *The Cherry Orchard*.

that he was devoid of passion and a critical faculty. He was critical of
the old regime in Russia, of the general lack of progress in that country,
of its dispirited intelligentsia and its ignorant peasantry; and he deplored
the inhumanity of the law, including the barbaric penal system in
Siberia. Chekhov did not allow himself to be overpowered by the ener-
vation he attributed to provincial gentry. As Gorky observed, Chekhov
"was always himself inwardly free." And he did not believe that anyone
was doomed to triviality if he did not doom *himself*. Stanislavsky, who
has been blamed for filling Chekhov's plays with gloom, also felt that
affirmativeness and made a point of it in his autobiography. And Chekhov himself made a point of it even if he disdained the obvious and
the unironic in his stories and plays. He believed, as he once declared
with unwonted didacticism, that each man must work for the good of
mankind despite his private misfortunes, and this idea is indeed the
plangent refrain, though not unmixed with irony, of *The Three Sisters*,
the darkest of the plays. He himself had known suffering and privation,
but he also brought characteristically, much resolve and energy to his
difficult family situation. "In my childhood," he once wrote, "I had no
childhood"; and he assumed the burden of supporting his parents and
brothers with his writing at an early age even while he was studying
medicine. As Lillian Hellman puts it in her introduction to a collection
of his letters, Chekhov "became the father of his family and remained
the father the rest of his life."

Throughout his life he possessed that sense of responsibility and
outward direction that produces major writers who belong to all humanity rather than to the minor fellowship of writers engaged in the
pursuit of purely private sensibility. "Writers," he wrote to his editor
Suvorin, "who are immortal or just plain good . . . have one very important trait in common: they are going somewhere and they call us
with them." Passiveness, despite his frequent concern with characters
who suffer stalemate, was the one fault he could not tolerate in a writer,
declaring that "he who wants nothing, hopes for nothing, and fears
nothing cannot be an artist." It is for that reason as well as because of
his social sympathies and medical training that he also rejected the indifference to science common among turn-of-the-century art-for-art's-sake
coteries. "Science and letters," he declared, "should go hand in hand.
Anatomy and *belles lettres* have the same enemy—the devil."

It can be said truly that much of his work is a marvelous combination
of compassion and buoyant intelligence; he noted the darkness of the
Russian milieu but also found many flecks of light in the darkness.
Stanislavsky noted how intensely Chekhov's submerged characters reject

total defeat, how "they dream, they rebel, and they reach out for what they want." Two significant lines originally in *The Seagull* reveal Chekhov's impatience with weakling intellectualism. When the comic schoolmaster Medvedenko declares that "The earth is round," Dr. Dorn asks him, "Why do you say it with so little conviction?"

Characters with whom Chekhov is in obvious sympathy often carry Chekhov's favorite work theme, based upon the belief that salvation for the individual or at least balm for his suffering lies in creativity. Nina, in *The Seagull,* is going to make a good actress of herself even after the failure of her love-affair with the novelist Trigorin; and while Uta Hagen played the role in the attractive Theater Guild production of the 1930s, there could be no doubt that Nina would become one. "If only one could live the remnant of one's life in some new way," cries Uncle Vanya and adds, "we must make haste and work, make haste and do something." Irina, in *The Three Sisters,* cries out at the end, "I will give all my life to those to whom it may be of use," and her fiancé, the Baron, pathetically rejoices at the prospect of exchanging his aristocratic profession of arms for useful employment. "Something formidable is threatening us," he says. "The strong cleansing storm is gathering . . . it will soon sweep our world clean of laziness, indifference, prejudice against work, and wretched boredom." Regardless of Chekhov's dissatisfaction with the early Moscow Art Theater productions of his plays, Stanislavsky came to appreciate the fact that Chekhov's characters possessed a high degree of resilience. In *My Life in Art,* Stanislavsky denied that they were moribund: "Like Chekhov, [they] seek life, joy, laughter, courage . . . [they try] to overcome the hard and unbearable impasses into which life has plunged them."

Chekhov himself continued his exertions as long as his health permitted; he practiced medicine among the peasants and on one famous occasion took an arduous trip to the Siberian peninsula of Sakhalin for the purpose of investigating Russia's prison camps. Outstanding in his mind were the two necessities: social reform and the application of scientific knowledge to human suffering. "God's earth is good," he once wrote with characteristic simplicity after his travels. "It is only we on it who are bad. Instead of knowledge, there is insolence and boundless conceit; instead of labor, idleness and caddishness; there is no justice, the understanding of honor does not go beyond the honor of the uniform! . . . the important thing is that we must be just and all the rest will follow from this." He was equally plain-spoken on the subject of science. "Surgery alone," he once declared, "has accomplished so much that the very thought of it is frightening. The period of twenty years ago appears just pitiful to anyone studying medicine nowadays. . . . If I were presented the choice of one of the two, the 'ideals' of the sixties or the worst community hospital of the present time, I wouldn't hesitate a moment in choosing the latter." He reminds us in this respect of another great devotee of art whose roots lay in the nineteenth century —Ibsen's English champion and translator, William Archer—who expressed his gratitude for the scientists who discovered anesthetics, "balsam anodyne," who did more for man than religion did in reducing the amount of pain in the world. Chekhov spoke plainly on this subject when he wrote "I am not in the same camp with literary men who take a skeptical attitude toward science."

The activism of social reform and science, moreover, made it possible for Chekhov to pursue a naturalistic style of literature—more apparent in his fiction than in his plays—which constitutes the other side of his richly nuanced and atmospheric art. He could face reality without being coarsened by it, and he knew that he could. Scorning moral censorship, he wrote that "there are people who can be corrupted even by children's literature," and that on the contrary, there are people "like good jurists and physicians who become purer the more they acquaint themselves with the sordidness of life." A responsible artist must conquer his squeamishness, must soil his imagination with the grime of life." We also meet Chekhov in a characteristic posture when we find him maintaining that a man of letters should be as objective as a chemist for whom "there is nothing unclean on the earth," that a writer has to realize "that dungheaps play a very respectable role in a landscape."

Too often in our century, modernism has been almost programatically identified with morbidity, negativism, and nihilism. Modernism, especially after the first and second world wars, became infatuated with this negative attitude in a variety of briefly fashionable temper tantrums, from dada-ism and expressionism to dramatic "absurdism," on the one hand, and with a mystique, on the other hand, ranging from the cult of the spirit absolute to the cult of the flesh absolute. Chekhov the man and the writer, on the contrary, belongs to the clear and broad, if by no means untroubled, stream of progressive modernism, to the modernism of hope rather than despair, and of activism rather than supine passiveness.

For Chekhov, who suffered from tuberculosis during half his lifetime and who died at the age of forty-four, the vivacity of health was not an easy possession. His health of spirit was hard-won and heroically maintained. Sympathy combined with skepticism helped him to maintain his balance under tension. He was a master of irony, and irony was in his case a sensible defense against excessive expectation on the part of one who believed in the possibility of progress. When his characters (such as Colonel Vershinin in *The Three Sisters*) spout optimism unbounded, it is plain that they are *troubled*. They do not speak the sentiments of their author, who remains more or less ironically aloof, although by no means hostile or indifferent toward them. It is plain that he did not share their protestations of deferred hope without a substantial discount.

Chekhov, to sum up, transcended the superficiality that often adheres to optimistic literature and at the same time escaped the morbidity that besets pessimistic profundity; and he kept a characteristic balance in other important respects. He stood virtually alone among the modern literary masters after 1890 in being complex without some mystique and subtle without obscurity. He was, so to speak, Olympian and yet also thoroughly companionable. It is chiefly by bearing these polarities in mind, and remembering especially the plain yet somehow elusive fact that there was ever sympathy in his comedy and some degree of comedy in his sympathy, that we may hope to bring his plays authentically to the stage.

The Chekhovian Sense of Life
From the Journal of Charles du Bos

July 22, 1922

For more than a week now I have wanted to set down the very
pleasant impression I had of the first volume of our Chekhov in Denis
Roche's translation. . . . The last two stories (masterpieces in Chekhov's
most condensed manner) give me the impression Chekhov always does
of coming straight from life. I would almost say that everyone else, however objective (with the one exception of Tolstoy), appears beside him
to give us not so much life itself as a judgment, albeit cleverly dis-
guised, or at the very least an idea, an attitude toward life. At most—
and we make the suggestion because of all we have learned elsewhere
about Chekhov, through his correspondence and Gorky's reminiscences
—we seem to hear Chekhov sigh with infinite gentleness and the kind
melancholy smile of which Gorky writes: "That's the way it is." Yes,
exactly—that's the way it is, but without emphasis, without increment
of any kind—never the "See how precisely that's the way it is" of the
best Frenchmen, or the "Am I not rather intelligent to have discovered
that that's the way it is?" of a Samuel Butler. . . . I said to Z. that
Chekhov's miracle is the tenderness that wells up from this unvaryingly
hopeless depth. Chekhov has no hope, but there are those who, unlike
[J. Middleton] Murry and me, cannot see something rightly bracing in
this hopelessness which they call despair. The shade of meaning lies
just there: a desperate being is a positive one. Chekhov's grandeur is
that he could remain negative (because he did not feel that he possessed
faith or reason enough to go on to any kind of positiveness) and nevertheless could give forth such a gathering of strength—quiet and always
as though at ease. (This is apt: bring it in with my idea of the strong

man, whose strength is applied only to the depicting of the weak.)[1]. . .

I leafed through *Sodom and Gomorrah,* as I often do in moments of severe depression and nervous exhaustion (and I must say that if I always turn to Proust in such moments it is on account of both the endless intellectual entertainment and the slow galvanization that comes from it), and thereon, I must admit, *I am simply bristling with reservations.*[2] After close self-examination, I do not believe I am prejudiced, but when the annihilation of the whole moral world is carried to that extent [as we find it in *Sodom and Gomorrah*], the universe becomes for me, as I have said, a smooth, varnished canvas, a little slippery, on which one slides indefinitely toward something—one doesn't know exactly what. And no doubt . . . there is a great deal to be said in favor of what I call his scientific indecency. It is perfectly clear, of course, that one can consider every variation on the caresses given to a young girl from the same point of view as one can bacteria in a culture; one can, but what's the point if it disgusts me? Something in me resists it. And all this comes back to the remarkable disproportion in Proust between understanding and character. His understanding has its equal only among the greatest; his character is not only—as he says somewhere of the character of men of genius—"loaded with faults," but slightly rotten with vices. Now a time always comes when a fault of character takes insidious vengeance on the understanding itself, and if *Sodom* is uneven, I would be inclined to believe it is because of that. . . .

Z., who in this matter would tend to go still further than I, quite correctly contrasted the case of Chekhov with that of Proust, and said more or less as follows: "Where would you find a transcription of life more complete, more precise, more pitiless, if you will, than in Chekhov without at the same time there being even a hint of anything vile?" Basically, she and I are agreed that *in the last resource all falls back* on the way you feel. More and more this criterion appears to me as the only truly *safe* one, even if it is not susceptible of proof (and that it is not seems to me here precisely to speak in its favor). For example (and here one must choose only moderns because up to the nineteenth century a certain propriety prevented one from saying everything), take a Constant, a Stendhal, a Dostoevsky, or a Chekhov—you get the impression that there is no vileness that one cannot wallow in provided one is fortified by purity of feeling. . . .

[1] Charles du Bos had in mind writing a book on Chekhov. This idea was never realized. [ED.]

[2] The *Journal* was written in French. Nevertheless, Du Bos often lapsed into English (he was bilingual), sometimes for extended passages. In this translation the original English is italicized in order to distinguish it from the English translation. [ED.]

May 24, 1923

I have just read to Z. in the really excellent translation of Denis Roche the beginning of "A Boring Story," and we agree that perhaps nothing Chekhov has written is more beautiful. . . . The very special feeling of being overwhelmed that you experience when you read almost any part of his works comes from the fact that, each time you pick them up again, you think you know what the word "life" means; and you see that you did not know. It would be most essential for me to show in my study what Chekhov teaches us to feel in this word because nobody gives us a better opportunity to feel it. *He has got even more essentially what has always struck me—with such a difference in the accentuation—as fundamental in Browning; I visualize them both as people who,* faced with all the clever and apparently solid structures of theory that we all finally more or less work out, tear away the superstructure of illusions instead and then come and tell us: "Yes, all that is very fine, but *don't you see that you have overlooked what is anterior to all that, what underlies* it all. Browning, Chekhov, Tolstoy, each in his own way, always appear to be saying to you: *first of all there is human nature, life, perennial feelings and moods; after that you may amuse yourself with difference of space and time, with nationalities, etc., but if you are really face to face with yourself you see that it will come to the same and that you are met just by the same cravings and difficulties [as] anybody else.* That is why, more than anyone, men like Browning and Chekhov would be needed in France today, where we are proceeding to forget what we have in common with others and to introduce signs of difference in a puerile way. . . .

April 24, 1924

. . . Basically, *this morning I seem to see quite clearly—and for the first time perhaps so clearly—that for me the three great human solutions that remain open could be figured under the names: Shelley, [George] Eliot, Chekhov—Shelley, that is* to revive the excellent formula of Mauclair on Watteau: "The gesture of the indifferent being who sets the world aside with a desperate gentleness." Flight, escape (not for some ulterior enjoyment, *and that is the limit of Gide,* but for uniting, and sustaining that unity from here below unceasingly, *with the highest, with the only [thing] worthwhile)—Eliot, that is the going entirely into the one channel of moral sympathy, the dedicating oneself without a single reservation to the sufferings of others and in particular to the voiceless suffering of daily life of which she alone has felt and described in* Middlemarch *the full poignancy—Chekhov, that is the respect of self including the respect of one's own indifference, the refusal of over-dramatizing, of ever looking on life as if it only were a problem, and that clean-cut—as fine as a faultless medal of the mind—intellectual honesty.*

May 2, 1924

. . . I must find the point of view from which the whole of Chekhov —and not this or that particular aspect—may be grasped. I will think it over again in the days ahead but it is obvious to me that he allows himself to be interpreted *in the round* only with relation to the idea of *decency,* of self-respect. I had thought of opening the six lectures on the shocking note: "One must respect even one's own indifference"; but this —*if perhaps in itself the very best*—contains a problem for entirely uninformed listeners in that it sets them at the outset on a path which might provide a wrong perspective; placing the stress on what is really the last link in a chain of logic, it might inculcate in them the picture of a Chekhov who is above all indifferent. No, indifference must enter in at the right time, but it is self-respect that must come first. Ah, this "to be decent" which in French can only be rendered with relation either toward prudery or toward sexuality. The *was ziemt* of Goethe is halfway between the *be decent* of Chekhov and our idea (now to be sure almost archaic) of propriety [*bienséance*]. But that's it—propriety is so much more social than self-respect; with the French the social always comes first, whereas Chekhov places so much stress on respect for others only in relation precisely to self-respect: for a French moralist, even of the seventeenth century, this is not at all the same shade of meaning. In both cases [the Chekhovian *be decent* and the French *bienséance*] the practical result is the same, but from the French point of view the underlying assumption is external, whereas from Chekhov's point of view it is internal—a *cleanliness* of the individual which extends to everything. (The *was ziemt* of Goethe corresponds to our idea of the fitting, almost with an aesthetic shade of meaning; it is not far from the very French theory of rules, almost literary rules.)

Decency ever so closely allies in the case of Chekhov to the notion of personal freedom. What he always insists upon [is] that each of us should squeeze the slave out of [ourselves] and become ever so gradually (he considers that it takes years to achieve the process) a free man. Of course, Chekhov himself makes much of the fact that, as a son and grandson of serfs, he felt this development to be indispensable to him—

a special case perhaps—but as one must observe after Murry's fine article about Gerhardi's book,[8] it is not in any way a question of a development necessitated by social status; and perhaps in Chekhov there was a remnant of idealism with respect to those whose families had never been serfs; but no, it is much more likely an example of his own exquisite form of modesty (no one has a more refined modesty than Chekhov) which assumes that one is perhaps oneself *liable to disadvantages that others may ignore.* And here it will be appropriate to cite, from Murry's article, the sections that deal with this process of liberation. The whole preface should be organized around two ideas: *decency and personal freedom,* and then at the end [one should] bring in the complex of indifference, the first hint that Chekhov could ever accept the possibility of a denial of the intellect; it would be a first hint, also, of this marvelous, this unique lay character of his very being—a character which should reemerge triumphantly at the end of the six lectures. *For what essentially I want to show in my Chekhov is what man can attain without religion and, more subtly still, without any form* of spiritual heroics. . . .

May 7, 1924

. . . On my way to Gide's house . . . I was rereading the beginning of [Chekhov's] "The Duel." At first this reading reminded me that I must not let myself be led astray by Chekhov the man to the detriment of Chekhov the artist, and especially that I must never lose sight of the fact that, however difficult it may be, *I want in his case to take up the hackneyed word*—life—*and try to convey why he only gives me the impression of having rendered it shorn from all additional intrusion.* . . . But this particular morning what struck me as always—beyond this smooth gliding of life which in Chekhov's mirror never lets itself be caught unawares—[was] *the way in which each of his characters, which we know Chekhov the man could not but despise*—because of his point of view—*always carries conviction, while we listen to him.* No one has ever been so consistent or profound as Chekhov in grasping the knot of complications, one hopelessly tangled and amounting *to impossibilities which make the human being drift.* Chekhov's characters are like those last autumn leaves fleeing before the force of the west wind which Shelley paints for us in his *Ode. They drift; and where he is unique is*

---

[8] W. Gerhardi, *Anton Chekhov: A Critical Study* (London, 1923). The article in question appears under the title "Anton Tchehov" in John Middleton Murry's *Discoveries. Essays in Literary Criticism* (London, 1924), pp. 83-107. The essay is dated Nov. 1923. [ED.]

that he conveys to us that they cannot do otherwise and, at the same time, without ever stating it, makes us feel that at a given moment, at the start, they might have been different. He seems always to imply— and at the same time: "It is no longer their fault—and yet it is their fault that it should no longer be their fault." "The Duel" is perhaps one of the works where one best perceives this *undercurrent of quiet, implicit teaching.*

May 19, 1924

As concerns Hardy I just chanced the other evening upon some of the Wessex Poems and was struck anew by that faculty—which is Hardy in the highest degree—to make, so to say, the whole cosmic agency stand behind the most casual occurrence; and then, that all-pervading sadness of Hardy which resembles no other, which is like the drop by drop of certain serums. "Neutral Tones," the title of one of his poems: *how that expression does fit the whole significance of his work. All in all he is the nearest to the Chekhov point of view; and just where the difference does lie will constitute a very nice point of discrimination in my opening lecture on Hardy. The resemblance, of course, lies essentially in the refusal of all denial of the intellect; the difference in the way in which the cosmic point of view—to which both always remain faithful —shows in Hardy more than in Chekhov: I mean, remains nearer the surface to be perhaps too readily apprehended.* Marcel told me that rereading *The Return of the Native* made him feel a little uncomfortable and when I had explained what I have just said he thought that perhaps his discomfort had something to do with that. With *Hardy one sees too much the groundwork—I mean the underlying view of the universe.*

As for Chekhov, he never permits himself to let it be seen. And pursuing this idea, I was saying, Saturday, that in connection with him I should withhold the expression, "slice of life," distorted by the unfortunate use the French naturalists made of it, and show that this inexpressible feeling of vitality conveyed by Chekhov rests in the very slow still flowing of life itself on which—like dead leaves on a pond (to take up again Bergson's excellent phrase about superficial states of the "I") —the characters float; and I added that rereading Chekhov's "Agafya" *I had seen a little further* into the deep reasons for the lack of resolution and even for the abrupt and at first disturbing breaks in Chekhov's stories; *it seems to me now that Chekhov stops when what might remain to be said could not be at the same time new and true. (There is in*

Chekhov the very subtlest adjustment between truth and novelty. He respects his reader—in the very same way in which he respects his neighbor—and is never inclined to detain him with anything that the reader can make out or imagine for himself.)

For example, the subject of "Agafya" is in essence the irresistible attraction that draws the village women to *the typical loafer, the man who has decided not to work with his hands, to keep himself free;* the man to whom it doesn't matter whether or not he is entrusted with a warden's post, ordinarily reserved for an old man, and who is so much more irresistible to women in that he is entirely indifferent to them. Every night one of them comes to join him in the forest and brings him some delicacy for which he overwhelms her with sarcasm. The night that Agafya joins him, he starts off by not bothering with her at all and sets off to shoot birds. When at last *he gives her what she wants, completely drowsy and benumbed she cannot find in her[self] any longer the strength to get home as usual before her husband's return.* The story ends when her husband calls her, and when she—drunk with fatalism at that moment —gets up to reply. And the significant thing to us is that, according to every canon of composition, the story ought not to stop here, we ought to be present at the encounter of man and wife, whatever the outcome; but precisely for Chekhov, we ought not, because, whatever the outcome, *it has been done a thousand times: from Chekhov's point of view, not only is it no longer interesting, but it is positively insulting to saddle the reader once more with what he already knows. He writes his story exclusively to show the relation between that exceptional type of man and the women who undergo his attraction: that is the subject; he has done it full justice;* now [if the story continued] we would come into the realm of the family, and it is at this threshold that Chekhov stops. Not that he is ever in any way *a votary of novelty for novelty's sake: no man ever treated the banal as such with a more liberal mastery than Chekhov, whenever the banal belongs intrinsically to the groundwork of his story. But always—and most particularly in his very short stories of the Agafya type—he wants some special angle of the real to be conveyed and then he does away with cheap padding.*

Of course, *this leaves unexplained the Chekhov transposition of life: in what precisely does the said transposition consist? to my mind at least, Chekhov offers no more difficult problem, and I am still far from having solved it for myself. His art seems to have for its object that the reader should perceive no transposition at all; and this is probably the point where Tolstoy and he come into closest contact. The difference of accent could be perhaps best insinuated* by the ballroom image which I used

for Tolstoy and that of half-stagnant water which would suit Chekhov
—I interpret the two, naturally, in relation to their method of depicting
life. It is likely that the contrast between Chekhov's slice of life and a
French slice of life (let us say, for convenience's sake, that of Maupassant)
rests in the fact that the French naturalists believed that to depict the
appearance, the surface of existence, consisted in keeping to those surface phenomena in such a way that very soon they are apt to become
mechanical. Chekhov's originality is that he shows the depths at the
very instant when the surface reflects them. . . .

June 19, 1924

. . . By a subtle subterfuge that is quite my own, it might be possible
to maintain that it is precisely where you find maladjustment to life
that life itself can best cast its fleeting, shimmering spell. (This notebook
fragment must come in here: "He rushed forth in pursuit of L.; he
wanted to catch up with her, and it seemed that it was life he wanted
to catch, that life which one can neither call back into being, nor reach,
nor capture just as one cannot catch his own shadow.") We can draw
much from this text . . . can show how to Chekhov's characters, to
Chekhov himself and to us all, life—except in moments of intense driving creativity—does not appear at all as a welling-up from within, as a
process developing inside; but as a light captured by a glance; a light
that is lost to sight and that reappears, sometimes, just as one had
despaired of it; a light *that beckons, entices,* and at the same time de-
ceives because it is always out of reach. There is a great deal in the
remark of Irina [*The Three Sisters*]: "You say life is beautiful. Yes, but
what if it only seems so!" A phrase true for all those to whom life is
something that *can* be (instead of something that ought to be) created:
you reach out your hand, you get to the point of believing that it is
closing on the prize, and what you have in your hand no longer glistens,
seems to have been instantly and all at once struck dead. Perhaps the
category of real living excludes just this illusion of life in itself. But on
the other hand—and this is one of the most moving sources of Chekhov's art—those for whom life is like a bird calling from a branch
become fantastically flexible—both when they take up again and again
some thrilling but deceptive vital impulse or other and when, the moment its falsity is revealed, they tumble to the depths of the weariest
hopelessness. The poetry of Chekhov's people—and how poetic they are!
—has to do with their very fragility; they are all at the same time brittle
and resilient.

January 17, 1925

[Charles du Bos is greatly interested in following up a particular notion, one which he raises in a discussion of the English novelist Hardy] . . . the idea of an essentially depressed person who at the same time has a tonic effect on others—in any case on me. In spite of apparent similarities [Hardy's] situation is quite different from Chekhov's. In Chekhov's case, it is not Chekhov himself who is depressed—or at least if he has in him a potential vein of depression, his fine and clear balance outweighs it—it is his characters who are depressed, which is a different matter; and this would more readily explain how his works can have a bracing effect (if not because of the characters' vitality, at least because of the will to vitality in the author who stands behind them). But again . . . Chekhov seems at this point to be bracing only to me; as for most others—I got the view of Jacques Rivière one day—reading Chekhov drives them to despair. Hardy, though, is himself depressed, the depressed type, and he communicates to his characters, and instills in them, his own depression—at least insofar as they have it. There, it must be said, is one of Hardy's vulnerable points, an area in which, besides, he has no objectivity at all—and here Chekhov surpasses him. . . .

March 31, 1926

. . . [Boris de] Schloezer . . . is not at all the ideal translator for Chekhov; to tell the truth, the ideal translator does not seem to exist for French: the problems of translating Chekhov are the most subtly evanescent possible. All Chekhov—I mean his whole mode of expression—rests in this flow of water, in this neutral malleability, which are the very characteristics of life itself. The translator is never given the opportunity for a hand-to-hand struggle with the exact difficulty of a text—a struggle in which he may be defeated, but where he at least knows what he confronts. With Chekhov the difficulty is everywhere and nowhere: no localization. Fortunately, there is scarcely a genius for whom an imperfect translation matters less (he is close to Tolstoy in this respect, too): I do not know a greater art which is more independent of all formal elements; it is as if language here were a vital process prior to all differentiation into this or that particular language. I would almost go so far as to say that what did not satisfy me in Schloezer's translation [of "A Boring Story"] serves the main object here, I mean adds to the unbearableness of his masterpiece, to its exhausting monotony; I said to Schloezer that nobody has ever equaled Chekhov for instilling in each of his characters the exact dose of Chekhovian essence which each can receive without his autonomy, his independence in relation to the author, being threatened at all; on the contrary, it is increased thereby. The hero of "A Boring Story"—we know from one of Chekhov's letters that basically Chekhov did not favor him—is treated so fairly that one never loses sight of the points where he is in the right. Yes, an unbearable masterpiece which, if I were a writer of stories or a novelist, would be disheartening to me—I mean, would make every effort useless. One cannot compete with it.

September 24, 1926

I remember that Saturday the 4th stamped with the very seal of solitude. That morning after I had displayed to the lecture audience the humanism of Chekhov—which met with unreserved approval—I tried to show them that area of my being which Chekhov does not satisfy: that solitary area of self-examination where doubt about the real personality of one's interlocutor swings between hope and a despair which is nevertheless revivifying. Are we dealing with a god or simply with a projection of one's innermost being? I remember that day as if the effort of communicating had in the end only intensified my isolation and had hurled me back on myself.

In fact, everybody came to speak to me about my exposition of Chekhov (and came to speak to me about it with that mixture of haste and relief that you feel when you have something to talk about so you can be silent about something that ought not to have happened anyway). But almost nobody (but Yura, Walter, and Jacques) alluded to the most personal part of what I said. It is always the same: the Russians excepted—and I am almost dangerously Russian in this respect!—nobody likes, or, I must add, can even tolerate the least bit of intimacy.

April 22, 1927

Here I also stumble on one of the most peculiar contradictions of my nature; what could be more peculiar in fact than this conjunction of the impossibility of abandoning myself without remorse, without second thoughts, to life and nothing more, and on the other hand the impossibility of accepting truth under other forms than those of life itself? I myself do not hold the key to this contradiction. It is altogether so central and so vast that it can only extend beyond the influence that Chekhov has over me; and nevertheless, this influence plays a role in it.

It may be that though [I am] theoretically quite clear on the perfectly time-bound character of the Chekhovian scientific approach—nobody knows just what Chekhov would think today, except that certainly he would no longer maintain just any kind of scientific approach (this has become unthinkable for anybody, including all honest scholars)—all the same the emotional state accompanying this scientific approach has undoubtedly saturated me; I have absorbed it much more than I realized; and it must have been this absorption that created in me the equation: life = truth.

Fragments from Reminiscences

by Maxim Gorky

Once he invited me to visit him at Kuchuk-Koy, a village where he had a small plot of land and a little white two-story house. There, as he showed me his "estate," he held forth animatedly: "If I had a lot of money, I would build a sanatorium here for ailing village schoolteachers. You know—I would build a truly light-filled building—very bright with big windows and high ceilings. I would have a fine library, various musical instruments, an apiary, a kitchen garden, an orchard; there could be lectures in agronomy, meteorology—a teacher must know everything, old fellow, everything!"

Then all at once he was silent, coughed a little, glanced at me out of the corner of his eye, and smiled that gentle, tender smile of his which always drew you to him irresistibly and made you pay special attention to what he was saying.

Does it bore you to listen to my dream? But I love to talk about it. If you only knew how much the Russian village needs a good, wise, educated teacher! We in Russia must create the right conditions for him and we must do it quickly, if we are aware that without widespread popular education the state will collapse like a house made of poorly baked bricks! A teacher must be an artist, an artificer, passionately involved in his work—but ours is an unskilled worker, a poorly educated person who goes to the village to teach children with the same enthusiasm he would feel if he were going into exile. He is hungry, crushed, intimidated by the possibility of losing a piece of bread. But in actuality he should be the leading figure in the village and be able to answer all the peasant's questions; the peasant should acknowledge in him a force worthy of attention and respect; and nobody should dare to shout at him—to humiliate him, as everyone does here: the village policeman, the wealthy shopkeeper, the priest, the district police official, the school guardian, the town head, and that petty official who goes under the name of inspector of schools, though he doesn't concern himself with

"Fragments from Reminiscences" by Maxim Gorky. From *O literature* (Moscow, 1953), pp. 32-42. Translated from the Russian by Leslie Jackson and Robert Louis Jackson. Gorky's reminiscences of Chekhov were first published in 1905.

improving the educational setup but only with fulfilling exactly the district regulations. Now isn't it absurd to pay a pittance to a man who is called upon to educate the people—do you understand—to educate the people! It is intolerable that this man should go about in rags, shiver with cold in damp, drafty schools, be poisoned with coal gas, catch cold, and by the time he is thirty contract laryngitis, rheumatism, tuberculosis. Now what a disgrace this is for us! Our teacher lives for eight or nine months of the year like a hermit without anyone to say a word to; in his solitude he grows dull—without books, without any diversions. And if he invites friends over to his house they accuse him of being unreliable—a stupid word with which crafty people frighten fools! All this is disgusting—a kind of mockery of a man who is doing vital, terribly important work. You know—when I see a teacher, I feel ill at ease before him—both because of his shyness and because he is badly dressed; it seems to me that I myself am somehow responsible for his misery—I mean it!

He fell silent, thought a bit, and, with a hopeless gesture, quietly said: "What an absurd, clumsy country our Russia is!"

The shadow of a deep melancholy fell across his wonderful eyes; the delicate wrinkles around them gave depth to his glance. He looked about and said with self-mockery: "Well, I have drummed up a whole editorial from a liberal newspaper for you. Come on, I'll give you tea because you were so patient."

This was typical of him: he would speak warmly, seriously, and simply, then suddenly would turn and laugh at himself and at what he was saying. You feel in that mild, melancholy smile the gentle skepticism of a man who knows the price of words, the price of dreams; yet that smile is imbued with a sweet modesty, a sensitive delicacy.

Quietly and without a word we went to the house. That day was clear, and hot; you could hear the sound of the waves that sparkled in the bright sunlight. At the foot of the hill, some satisfied dog whined cajolingly. Chekhov slipped his arm through mine and coughing a little, said: "It is shameful and sad, but true: there are a great many people who envy dogs."

But immediately, with a laugh, he added: "Every word I utter today is feeble. It means I am growing old!"

Time and again I would hear him say, "You know, a teacher came here—ill, married—can you possibly help him? I have fixed him up for the time being."

Or: "Listen, Gorky. There's a teacher here who wants to meet you. He can't go out, he's ill. Will you go to see him? All right?"

Or: "Some woman teachers are asking to have books sent."

Sometimes I ran into that "teacher" at his house: usually the teacher, flushed, aware of his awkwardness, sat on the edge of a chair and sought out words by the sweat of his brow, trying to speak smoothly and more like a "cultured" man, or with the excessive familiarity of a painfully shy person, making every effort not to appear foolish in the eyes of a writer and showering Anton Pavlovich with a hail of questions which had scarcely entered his head until that moment.

Anton Pavlovich listened attentively to the incoherent speech; a smile gleamed in his melancholy eyes; the fine lines on his temples quivered, and now in his deep, soft, measured, and even voice he himself began to utter simple, clear words, close to life, words which somehow immediately seemed to make his visitor more simple; the teacher left off trying to be clever, and as a result became right away more clever and interesting.

I remember one teacher. He was tall and thin with a yellow hungry face and a long aquiline nose sloping sadly toward his chin. He sat opposite Anton Pavlovich and staring at him fixedly with his black eyes, said in a gloomy bass: "These impressions of existence over the course of the academic year produce such a psychic conglomerate as to suppress absolutely any possibility of an objective orientation to the world about. Of course, the world is none other than our idea of it. . . ."

At this point he launched into the realm of philosophy and began to stride about it like a drunkard on ice.

"But tell me," Chekhov asked tenderly in a low voice, "who is it in your district that beats children?"

The teacher leaped up from his chair and waved his arms indignantly: "What do you mean? I? Never! Beat?"

And he snorted in an offended sort of way.

"Don't get excited," continued Anton Pavlovich, with a soothing smile. "Surely you don't think I am talking about you? But I remember—it was in the papers—in your very district, there was a beating."

The teacher sat down, mopped his perspiring brow, and sighing, much relieved, chattered away in his rumbling bass. "Right! There was one case. It was Makarov. You know—it was no surprise. It was brutal, but it's understandable. He is married, has four children; his wife is ill; he himself is, too—with consumption; his salary is twenty rubles; the school is a cellar; and the teacher has one room. Under such conditions, you would drub an angel of God without any cause, but the pupils, believe me, are far from angels!"

And the man, who had just been staggering Chekhov mercilessly with his whole store of words of wisdom, suddenly, ominously, shook his aquiline nose and began to speak simple words—heavy, just like stones—throwing vivid light on the cursed, terrible truth of that life which the Russian village lives.

When he said goodbye, the teacher grasped with both hands his host's small dry hand with the slender fingers and shaking it, said: "I came to see you as if I were going to the authorities, with fear and trembling, puffed out like a turkey-cock. I wanted to show you that, as they say, there are no hayseeds in my hair, and, you see now, I'm leaving a good, dear person who understands everything. That's a great thing—to understand everything! Thank you! I'm leaving. I'm carrying away a fine, good thought: great men are simpler, more perceptive, and closer in spirit to the ordinary fellow than all those narrow people among whom we live. Goodbye! I will never forget you."

His nose quivered, his lips parted in a kindly smile, and he added: "But in all frankness, scoundrels are also unfortunate people—the devil with them!"

When he went out, Anton Pavlovich looked after him, smiled, and said, "Good fellow. He hasn't long to teach."

"Why?"

"Because they'll persecute him. They'll fire him."

Pensive, he added quietly and softly, "In Russia an honest man is something like a chimneysweep that nannies frighten little children with—"

It seems to me that with Anton Pavlovich, everybody unwittingly felt an inner longing to be simpler, more truthful, to be more himself. More than once I saw how people cast off their motley attire of bookish phrases, fashionable expressions, and all the rest of the cheap patchwork with which the Russian adorns himself in his desire to play the European, as the savage does with shells and fishes' teeth. Anton Pavlovich did not like fishes' teeth and cocks' feathers. Everything motley, jangling, and strange that man puts on for empty vanity embarrassed him and I noticed that whenever he was confronted with a person in an elaborate getup he was overcome by a desire to rid him of all that oppressive and unnecessary trumpery, which distorted the person's real features and his living soul. Anton Chekhov lived out his whole life by the standards of his own soul; he was always himself, always inwardly free, and never was concerned with what other people expected of Anton Chekhov, or what other, cruder people demanded of him. He did not like conversations on "lofty" subjects—conversations with which the dear Russian man so busily consoles himself, forgetting that it is ludicrous and not at all amusing to discourse about velvet suits in the future when right now, you don't even have decent trousers. Wonderfully simple himself, he loved everything simple, real, and unaffected, and he had his own unique way of making other people simple.

Once three elegantly dressed ladies came to see him; they filled his room with the rustle of silk skirts and the smell of strong perfumes. Settling themselves ceremoniously near their host, they pretended to be very much interested in politics and began to "raise questions."

"Anton Pavlovich! How do you think the war will end?"

Anton Pavlovich cleared his throat, pondered, and softly answered in a serious, friendly voice, "Probably—with peace."

"Well, naturally! But who will win? The Greeks or the Turks?"

"It seems to me, whoever is stronger."

"But who, in your opinion, is stronger?" countered the ladies.

"Those who are better nourished and better educated."

"Ah, how clever!" One lady cried out.

"And whom do you like best—the Greeks or the Turks?" asked another.

Anton Pavlovich looked at her genially and answered with a gentle, kindly smile: "I like—marmalade. And how about you?"

"Very much!" one lady burst out animatedly.

"Oh, it is so fragrant!" another vigorously affirmed.

And all three started talking in a lively way, demonstrating on the marmalade question a fine, sparkling erudition and a subtle knowledge of the subject. Clearly they were perfectly satisfied not to have to strain themselves and pretend to be seriously interested in the Turks and the Greeks, to whom until then they had given not a single thought.

When they left, they merrily promised Anton Pavlovich: "We'll send you some marmalade!"

"You had quite a chat!" I remarked when they had gone.

Anton Pavlovich smiled quietly and said: "Everyone should speak his own language . . ."

Another time I met at his house a nice young public prosecutor. He stood in front of Chekhov and shaking his curly head, said smartly, "In the story 'The Conspirator,' Anton Pavlovich, you set before me a highly complex question. If I recognize in Denis Grigoriev an evil will acting consciously, I must without reservations put him in jail, as the interests of society demand. But he is a savage; he was not conscious of the criminality of his deed; I feel sorry for him! But if I relate to him as to a person acting without reasoning and if I give way to a feeling of compassion, how can I guarantee society that Denis will not again unscrew a bolt on the rails and cause an accident? That is the question! What is to be done then?"

He was silent, leaned back, and stared searchingly into the eyes of Anton Pavlovich. His court uniform jacket was quite new and the buttons on his chest glistened just as self-confidently and stupidly as the eyes in the shiny little face of the young judicial zealot.

"If I were a judge," said Anton Pavlovich seriously, "I would acquit Denis—"

"On what grounds?"

"I would say to him, 'You, Denis, have not yet ripened into the conscious criminal type, be off and—ripen!"

The jurist laughed but immediately took up his solemn mien and went on: "No, esteemed Anton Pavlovich—the question I put to you may be decided only in the interests of society, the life and property of which I am called upon to protect. Denis is a savage, yes, but he is a criminal—that is the truth!"

"Do you like the phonograph?" Anton Pavlovich asked sweetly all of a sudden.

"O yes! Very much! A wonderful invention!" the youth answered with animation.

"But I for one can't stand phonographs!" Anton Pavlovich confessed glumly.

"Why?"

"Well, they talk and sing but never feel anything. And everything emerges from them in caricature, dead—and do you like photography?"

It seemed that the lawyer was a passionate devotee of photography; he began at once to talk about it with enthusiasm, not at all interested in the phonograph, in spite of his resemblance to that "amazing invention" so aptly and truthfully characterized by Chekhov. Once more I saw peering out of the uniform a lively and rather amusing little man, who still behaved in life like a playful puppy snuffing about.

When he had escorted the young man to the door, Anton Pavlovich said gloomily, "There you have the kind of pimple that sits on the seat of justice disposing of people's fates."

And after a moment of silence, he added, "Attorneys love fishing, especially for little fish."

He was a master of the art of finding banality everywhere and showing it up . . . an art within reach only of those who make the highest demands on life, one that grows only out of the most passionate desire to see people simple, beautiful, and in concord. Banality always found in him a stern and discerning judge.

Someone told in his presence about the publisher of a popular newspaper—a man who was always discoursing about the need to be loving and kind toward people; he told how this man once gratuitously insulted a railway conductor and in general was very rude to people dependent on him.

"Well, what do you expect?" said Anton Pavlovich with a gloomy laugh. "After all, he's an aristocrat, an educated man—he even studied at the seminary! His father wore bast shoes but he wears shiny boots."

And the way he spoke made the "aristocrat" seem suddenly insignificant and comical.

"A very talented man," he said about one journalist. "He always writes so nobly, so humanely . . . lemonadely; but he calls his wife a fool right in front of people. His servants' rooms are damp and his housemaids always suffer from rheumatism."

"Do you like N. N., Anton Pavlovich?"

"Yes, very much. He's a nice man," Anton Pavlovich affirms with a cough. "He knows everything. He reads a great deal. He's still reading three of my books. He's fuzzy-headed; today he tells you that you are a wonderful person and tomorrow he tells someone that you took some silk socks from the husband of your mistress—black ones with blue stripes."

Someone was complaining in his presence about the dullness and heaviness of the "serious" sections in the fat monthly magazines.

"Now don't you read those articles," Anton Pavlovich advised firmly. "That is inside literature—the literature of friends. Mr. Red, Mr. Black, and Mr. White put it together. One writes the article, another takes exception to it, and the third reconciles the contradictions of the other two. Just as if they were playing whist with a dummy. And none of them asks himself what use is all this to the reader."

Once a certain stout lady came. She was healthy, attractive, and well dressed and she began to speak in a "Chekhovian way." "Life is dreary, Anton Pavlovich. Everything is so gray—people, the sky, the sea, even the flowers seem gray to me. I have no desires—there is anguish in my soul. Just as if I had some illness—"

"It *is* an illness," said Anton Pavlovich with conviction. "It is an illness. In Latin it is called *morbus imitatus*."

The lady, fortunately, seemed not to know any Latin or perhaps concealed her knowledge.

"Critics are like gadflies that keep horses from ploughing," he said, smiling his wise smile. "A horse works with all his muscles tense like the strings on a bass viol, and a horsefly sits on his rump, tickling him and buzzing. He has to make his skin quiver and swish his tail. What is the fly buzzing about? He hardly knows. He just has a restless disposition and wants to make his presence felt, as if to say, I also live on the earth! Don't you see, I can even buzz, I can buzz about everything! I have been reading criticism about my stories for twenty-five years and I do not remember a single suggestion worth anything, not one good piece of advice. Only once Skabichevsky made an impression on me; he wrote that I will die drunk under a hedge—"

A delicate mockery always played about his melancholy gray eyes, but at times these eyes would grow cold, piercing, and hard; at such moments his melodious voice sounded harsher and then it seemed to me that this unpretentious, gentle man, if he had to, could stand up strongly and firmly against a hostile force and not give way before it. But now and then I seemed to sense in his attitude toward people a touch of some sort of hopelessness, almost of cold, quiet despair.

"What a strange being is the Russian man!" he said once. "He is like a sieve; nothing stays in him very long. In his youth he greedily fills up on everything that comes his way; but after the age of thirty all that's left is some sort of gray rubbish. To live well, to live as a human being, one must work! Work with passion, with faith. And we Russians can't do it. An architect builds two or three decent houses, then sits down to play cards and plays all the rest of his life or is always at the theater hanging around backstage. A doctor, if he has a practice, no longer keeps up with scientific developments, reads nothing but a medical journal, and at forty is seriously convinced that all illnesses are catarrhal in origin. I never met a single civil servant who understood the least little bit about the meaning of his work: usually he sits in the capital or in a provincial town, makes up regulations, and sends them to Zmiev and Smorgon to be carried out. But as to whose freedom of movement these papers restrict in Zmiev and Smorgon—the civil servant thinks as little about that as an atheist does of the torments of hell. Once a lawyer gets the reputation for being a successful defense attorney, he stops worrying about justice and defends only property rights, plays the horses, eats oysters, and passes himself off as a subtle connoisseur of all the arts. The actor plays two or three roles passably well and thereupon stops studying further roles but wears a top hat and thinks he is a genius. Russia is a land of greedy, lazy people; they eat and drink dreadfully much, love to sleep in the daytime, and snore in their sleep. They marry for the sake of order in the home and take a mistress for social prestige.

They have a dog's psychology: beat them and they squeal piteously and hide in their kennels; fondle them—they turn over on their backs with their little paws in the air and wag their little tails—"

These words rang with an anguished and cold contempt. But while he scorned, he pitied, and when it happened that someone was abused in his presence, Anton Pavlovich immediately took his part: "Come now! After all, he's an old man. He's seventy—"

Or, "He's young yet; he does it out of ignorance—"

And when he talked that way I saw not a trace of smugness on his face.

In a young person, banality seems only funny and petty but after a while it envelops a man; it saturates his brain and blood with its gray shadow like poison and coal gas fumes and he becomes like an old signboard corroded with rust; as if something were written there—but what? You can't make it out.

Even in his earliest stories, Anton Pavlovich could already make out in the dreary sea of banality its somber absurdities with their tragic overtones. One need only read through his "humorous" stories attentively to convince oneself how much of the cruel and repulsive the author sorrowfully observed and, with a feeling of shame, concealed behind his droll words and situations.

He was in a way chastely modest; he never allowed himself to say to people loudly and openly: "Now, try to behave more decently," in the vain hope that they themselves would guess the urgent need for behaving decently. He hated everything banal and filthy; he described the abominations of life in the noble language of the poet, with the gentle smile of the humorist; and you hardly notice behind the outward beauty of his stories their inner meaning full of ·bitter reproach.

The very respectable public, when they read "Daughter of Albion," laugh and hardly see in that story the most vile mockery of a satiated gentleman, of a lonely being, a stranger to all and everything. And in every one of the humorous stories of Anton Pavlovich I hear the quiet, deep sigh of a pure, genuinely human spirit, the hopeless sigh of compassion for people who are unable to respect their own human worth and unresistingly submit to brute force, live like slaves, and believe in nothing but the need to gulp down as much greasy cabbage soup as possible and feel nothing but terror lest someone powerful and brazen should beat them.

Nobody understood so clearly and keenly as Anton Chekhov the tragedy of life's banalities; nobody before him could with such merciless truthtelling depict for people the shameful and painful picture of their life in the dreary chaos of petty bourgeois prosiness.

His enemy was banality; all his life he fought against it; he ridiculed it and portrayed it with a keen impassive pen; he could find the rot of banality even where at first glance everything seemed quite in order, even in splendid shape . . . and banality took revenge on him with a very nasty trick when it placed his corpse—the corpse of a poet—in a railway car for the transport of "oysters."

The yellowish-green stain of that car seems to me precisely the vast, triumphant smile of banality at its weary enemy while the hypocritical melancholy of the countless "reminiscences" in the daily papers conceal, I sense, the cold odorous breathing of all that banality, secretly gratified at the death of its enemy.

When you read the stories of Anton Chekhov, you feel just as if it were a melancholy day in late autumn when the air is so transparent you see sharply outlined in it bare trees, cramped little houses, and gray people. Everything is so strange—lonely, helpless, and still. The deepening blue distance is empty and, as it fades into the pale sky, breathes a dreary cold across the land, covered with frozen mud. The author's mind like an autumnal sun lights up with cruel clarity the scourged roads, the crooked streets, the cramped and filthy houses in which wretched little people are suffocating from boredom and laziness, flooding the house with their unintelligent, somnolent bustling. There anxiously, like a gray mouse, "the darling" scampers to and fro—she is a nice, gentle woman who loves so slavishly, so very much. You can even slap her in the face and she, meek slave that she is, will not even dare to groan aloud. Olga from *The Three Sisters* stands gloomily beside her; she also loves very much and unprotestingly submits to the whims of the depraved and banal wife of her lazy brother; before her eyes her sisters' lives are shattered; she weeps and cannot help anyone at all; in her heart there is not one vital, forceful word of protest against banality.

There is the lachrymose Ranevskaya and other former masters of *The Cherry Orchard*—egotistical, like children, and feeble, like old people. They are late in dying and they whine, seeing nothing around them, understanding nothing—parasites, without the strength to fix themselves to life again. The wretched little student Trofimov speaks eloquently about the need to work and—loafs and amuses himself out of boredom by stupid scoffing at Varya who is working indefatigably for the welfare of loafers.

Vershinin dreams of how fine life will be in three hundred years and goes on living without noticing that everything around him is decaying, that before his eyes, Solyony is prepared to kill poor Baron Tusenbach out of boredom and stupidity.

There file before us a long line of people—slaves to their love, their stupidity and laziness, their greed for the good things of this earth; there pass men who are slaves to a dark fear of life; they move along in clouded anxiety filling life with incoherent speeches about the future, feeling that there is no place for them in the present.

Sometimes in their gray mass, a shot rings out; some Ivanov or Treplev figured out what he had to do—and died.

Many of them dream gloriously about how good life will be after two hundred years, but one simple question never enters their heads: who will make it better if we do nothing but dream?

A great wise man, aware of everything, passed by this dull, gray crowd of feeble people, looked at the dreary inhabitants of his country. Then with a melancholy smile, in a tone of soft but profound reproach, with hopeless anguish on his face and in his heart, he said in his fine, honest voice:

"You live abominably, gentlemen!"

Chronology of Important Dates

1860	Born January 17 (Russian calendar) in Taganrog on the Azov Sea.
1879	Graduates from Taganrog high school. Moves to Moscow. Enters the School of Medicine of the University of Moscow.
1880	Publishes his first stories.
1884	Graduates from the University. Begins medical practice. Publishes first collection of stories.
1887	First performance of *Ivanov* in Moscow.
1890	Travels to and from the Island of Sakhalin off the coast of Siberia. Trips to Europe: 1891, 1894, 1897, 1898, 1904.
1896	First performance of *The Seagull* in St. Petersburg.
1898	Settles in Yalta after suffering pulmonary hemorrhage.
1901	First performance of *The Three Sisters*. Marries the actress Olga Knipper.
1903	Publishes last story, "The Betrothed."
1904	First performance of *The Cherry Orchard*. Goes to Badenweiler, Germany, where he dies July 2.

Notes on the Editor and Authors

ROBERT LOUIS JACKSON (born 1923), the editor, is Professor of Russian Literature at Yale University. He is the author of *Dostoevsky's Notes from the Underground in Russian Literature* and *Dostoevsky's Quest for Form: A Study of His Philosophy of Art.*

BORIS EICHENBAUM (1886-1959) was a distinguished Soviet critic and scholar. His many works include studies in the field of poetics, major works on Tolstoy, Lermontov, etc.

LEONID GROSSMAN (1888-1965) was a prominent Soviet critic and scholar. He wrote extensively in the field of Russian literature, and was a leading Dostoevsky scholar.

DMITRI CHIZHEVSKY (spelled also Čiževskij or Tschiževskij)—born 1894—is a distinguished Ukrainian scholar who is now Professor at Heidelberg. His books in Russian and German include studies of Hegel in Russia, a history of Old Russian Literature, etc. Professor Chizhevsky spent seven years at Harvard (1947-1954).

VSEVOLOD MEYERHOLD (1874-1942) was an outstanding Russian actor and theater director. He joined the troupe founded by Nemirovich-Danchenko and Stanislavsky in 1898. He left the Moscow Art Theater in 1903 and began directing his own troupe, gradually developing his own revolutionary approach to the theater.

A. P. SKAFTYMOV (born 1890) is a prominent Soviet scholar. His writings include studies in poetics, folklore, work on Dostoevsky, Tolstoy, etc.

G. BERDNIKOV is a Soviet scholar.

V. YERMILOV (1904-1965) was a well-known Soviet critic and scholar. He has written on Gogol, Dostoevsky, Chekhov, etc.

M. N. STROEVA (born 1916) is a Soviet scholar specializing in the history of Russian and Soviet theater.

S. D. BALUKHATY (1893-1945), a prominent Soviet scholar, was a member of the "formalist" school of literary criticism in the 1920's. He is noted particularly for his extensive writing and research on Chekhov and Gorky.

FRANCIS FERGUSSON (born 1904) is University Professor of English at Rutgers University. He is the author of *The Idea of a Theatre, Dante's Dream of the Mind,* and other works.

NILS ÅKE NILSSON (born 1917) is Professor of Slavic Languages and Literatures and Director of the Russian Institute at the University of Stockholm, Sweden. His books include *Die Apollonius-Erzählung in den slavischen Literaturen, Ibsen in Russland,* etc.

JOHN GASSNER (1903-1967), distinguished American critic and scholar, Sterling Professor of Playwriting and Dramatic Literature at Yale University, was drama critic for *Educational Theater Journal* and other periodicals. He was also head of the Play Department of the Theater Guild in New York. His books include *Masters of the Drama* and *Form and Idea in Modern Theater*.

CHARLES DU BOS (1883-1939) was a major French critic and scholar. He is the author of *Byron et le besoin de la fatalité, Mauriac et le problème du romancier catholique*, etc. His extensive *Journal* was published posthumously.

MAXIM GORKY (pseudonym of A. M. Peshkov, 1868-1936) was a Russian writer. He is the author of numerous novels, stories, and plays, an autobiography, various reminiscences, and a large body of critical writings.

Selected Bibliography

An extensive bibliography of articles and books on Chekhov exists in Russian. Numerous writings on him have appeared also in Europe, the United States, and elsewhere. The critical and biographical works listed below represent at best only an introduction to this body of works.

Bibliographical

RUSSIAN

Masanov, I. F. *Chekhoviana.* Part I. Moscow, 1929.

Polotskaja, E. A. *A. P. Chekhov. Rekomendatel'nyj ukazatel' literatury.* Moscow, 1955.

ENGLISH

Heifetz, Anna. *Chekhov in English: A List of Works By and About Him.* Edited and with a foreword by Avrahm Yarmolinsky. New York, 1947.

Yachniss, Rissa. *Chekhov in English: A Selected List of Works By and About Him, 1949-1960.* New York, 1960.

FRENCH

Laffitte, Sophie, *"Chekhov vo Frantsii,"* in *Literaturnoe nasledstvo.* Moscow, 1960. LXVIII, 705-746. [This essay, "Chekhov in France," includes (pp. 743-746) a bibliography of translations of Chekhov into French, a selected bibliography of Chekhov in French criticism, and a listing of performances of Chekhov plays in French theaters.]

History of Chekhov Criticism

Aleksandrov, B. I. "Chekhov v russkoj kritike," in *Seminarij po Chekhovu.* Moscow, 1957, pp. 40-95.

Balukhatyj, S. D. "Ot 'Trekh sester' k 'Vishnevomu sadu,'" *Literatura,* I (1931), 109-178.

Bogatyrev, Sh. "Chekhov v Chekhoslovakii," in *Literaturnoe nasledstvo.* Moscow, 1960. LXVIII, 747-776.

Jakóbiec, Marian. "Antoni Czechow i literatura polska," *Slavia Orientalis*, X, No. 3 (1961), 293-306.

Laffitte, Sophie, "Chekhov vo Frantsii," in *Literaturnoe nasledstvo*. Moscow, 1960. LXVIII, 705-746.

Lyskov, Ivan P. (ed). *A. P. Chekhov v ponimanii kritiki*. Moscow, 1905.

Meister, Charles Walter. "Chekhov's Reception in England and America," *American Slavic and East European Review*, XII (1953), 109-121.

Mirsky, D. S. "Chekhov and the English," *The Monthly Criterion*, No. 6 (1927), 292-309.

Semanova, M. *Chekhov i sovetskaja literatura: 1917-1935*. Moscow-Leningrad, 1966.

Shereshevskaja, M. A. "Anglijskie pisateli i kritiki o Chekhove," *Literaturnoe nasledstvo*. Moscow, 1960. LXVIII, 801-832.

Śliwowski, René, "Z problematyki receptcji Czechowa na Zachodzie," *Slavia Orientalis*, X, No. 3 (1961), 307-320.

Winner, Thomas G., "Chekhov v soedinennykh shtatakh Ameriki," *Literaturnoe nasledstvo*. Moscow, 1960. LXVIII, 777-800.

Critical and Biographical

Bakshy, A. *The Path of the Modern Russian Stage and Other Essays*. London, 1916.

Balukhatyj, S. D. *Chekhov-dramaturg*. Leningrad, 1936.

————. *Problemy dramaturgicheskogo analiza. Chekhov*. Leningrad, 1927.

Batjushkov, F. D. "Anton Pavlovich Chekhov," in *Istorija russkoj literatury XIX-veka*. Edited by D. N. Ovsjaniko-Kulikovskij. Moscow, 1911. V, 187-215.

Bentley, Eric, "Apologia," in Chekhov, *The Brute and Other Farces*. Edited by Eric Bentley. New York, 1958, pp. i-vii.

————. "Craftsmanship in *Uncle Vanya*," in *In Search of Theater*. New York, 1959, pp. 322-343.

Berdnikov, G. *Chekhov-dramaturg*. Moscow, 1957.

Bitsilli, P. "Tvorchestvo Chekhova. Opyt stilisticheskogo analiza," *Godishnik na Universiteta sv. Kliment Okhridski*, Sofija, *Istoriko-Filologicheski Fakultet*. Sofija, 1942. XXXVIII, 6.

Bruford, W. H. *Anton Chekhov*. New Haven, 1957.

Brustein, Robert. "Anton Chekhov," in *The Theatre of Revolt*. Boston-Toronto, 1964, pp. 137-179.

Chukovsky, K. *Chekhov the Man*. Translated by Pauline Rose. London, 1945.

Derman, A. *Anton Pavlovich Chekhov: kritiko-biograficheskij ocherk.* Moscow, 1939.

Eekman, T. (ed). *Anton Čechov: 1860-1960. Some Essays.* Leiden, 1960.

Ehrenburg, I. *Chekhov, Stendhal and Other Essays.* Translated by A. Bostock and Y. Kapp. London, 1962.

Elton, O. *Chekhov.* The Taylorian Lecture. Oxford, 1929.

Ermilov, V. *Chekhov: 1860-1904.* Moscow, 1949. [Republished in expanded form in 1954.]

———. *Dramaturgija Chekhova.* Moscow, 1948. [Republished in expanded form in 1954.]

Farrell, J. T. "On the Letters of Anton Chekhov," in *The League of Frightened Philistines and Other Papers.* New York, 1945.

Garnett, E. "Tchehov and His Art," *The Quarterly Review,* CCXXXVI (1921), 257-269.

Gerhardi, W. *Anton Chekhov: A Critical Study.* London, 1923.

Halm, Dr. Hans. *Anton Tschechows Kurzgeschichte und deren Vorläufer. Forschungen zur neueren Literaturgeschichte.* Weimar, 1933, LXVIII.

Hingley, R. *Chekhov: A Biographical and Critical Study.* London, 1950.

Kernan, Alvin, "Truth and Dramatic Mode in the Modern Theater: Chekhov, Pirandello, and Williams," *Modern Drama,* I (September, 1958), 101-114.

Kurdjumov, M. *Serdtse smjatennoe. O tvorchestve A. P. Chekhova.* Paris, 1934.

Lamm, Martin. *Ibsen och Čechov.* Oslo, 1947.

Laffitte, Sophie. *Tchekhov par lui-même.* Paris, 1955.

Lavrin, J. "Chekhov and Maupassant," in *Studies in European Literature.* London, 1929, pp. 156-192.

Lunacharskij, A. V. "Chem mozhet byt' A. P. Chekhov dlja nas?" *Pechat' i revoljutsija,* IV (1924), 19-34.

Magarshack, David. *Chekhov: A Life.* London and New York, 1952.

———. *Chekhov as a Dramatist.* New York, 1952.

Mann, Thomas. "Chekhov," in *Last Essays.* Translated by Richard and Clara Winston and Tania and James Stern. New York, 1959, pp. 178-203.

Matlaw, Ralph E. "Čechov and the Novel," in *Anton Čechov: 1860-1960. Some Essays.* Edited by T. Eekman. Leiden, 1960, pp. 148-167.

Merezhkovskij, D. S. "Chekhov i Gor'kij," in *Polnoe sobranie sochinenij.* St. Petersburg and Moscow, 1911, XI, 39-92.

Mikhajlovskij, N. K. "Ob otsakh i detjakh i o g. Chekhove," in *Literaturno-kriticheskie stat'i.* Moscow, 1957, pp. 594-607.

Murry, J. Middleton. "Thoughts on Tchekhov," in *Aspects of Literature*. London and New York, 1920, pp. 76-80.

Nag, M. "Ibsen, Čechov und Blok," *Scando-Slavica*, X (1964), 30-48.

Nemirovich-Danchenko, V. I. *My Life in the Russian Theatre*. Translated by John Cournos. Boston, 1936.

Némirovsky, Irine. *A Life of Chekhov*. Translated by Erik de Mauny. London, 1950.

Nilsson, Nils Åke. *Ibsen in Russland*. Stockholm, 1958.

Ovsjaniko-Kulikovskij, D. N. "Chekhov," in *Istorija russkoj intelligentsii*, III. *Sobranie sochinenij*. St. Petersburg, 1911. IX, 45-128.

Papernyj, Z. *A. P. Chekhov. Ocherk tvorchestva*. Moscow, 1960.

Roskin, A. *A. P. Chekhov. Stat'i i ocherki*. Moscow, 1959.

Schneider, E. "Katherine Mansfield and Chekhov," *Modern Language Notes*, L (1935), 394-397.

Shestov, L. "Tvorchestvo iz nichego," *Mosty*, V (1960), 121-150. [Translated by S. Koteliansky and J. M. Murry as "Anton Tchekhov (Creation from the Void)." Cf. Leon Shestov, *Chekhov and Other Essays*. New Introduction by Sidney Monas. Ann Arbor, 1966, pp. 3-60.]

Shklovskij, V. "A. P. Chekhov," in *Zametki o proze russkikh klassikov*. Moscow, 1953, pp. 289-322.

Simmons, Ernest J. *Chekhov: A Biography*. Boston and Toronto, 1962.

Skaftymov, A. P. *Stat'i o russkoj literature*, Saratov, 1958. [This collection of essays includes studies on *Ivanov* and *The Cherry Orchard*, "Ward Number 6," and "My Life."]

Sobolev, Ju. *Chekhov*. Moscow, 1930.

Stanislavsky, K. *My Life in Art*. Translated by J. J. Robbins. Boston, 1924.

Stroeva, M. N. *Chekhov i Khudozhestvennyj teatr*. Moscow, 1955.

Struve, G. "Chekhov i Grigorovich. Ikh lichnye i literaturnye otnoshenija," in *Anton Čechov: 1860-1960. Some Essays*. Edited by T. Eekman. Leiden, 1960, pp. 207-266.

————. "Chekhov in Communist Censorship," *Slavonic and East European Review*, XXXII (1955), 327-341.

————. "On Chekhov's Craftsmanship: The Anatomy of a Story," *Slavic Review*, XX (1961), 465-476.

Thomas, H. *Anton Chekhov—Physician and Literary Artist*. New Haven, 1922.

Toumanova-Andronikova, N. *Anton Chekhov: The Voice of Twilight Russia*. New York, 1937.

Valency, Maurice. *The Breaking String. The Plays of Anton Chekhov.* New York, 1966.

Winner, Thomas. *Chekhov and his Prose.* New York, 1966.

———. "Chekhov's *Seagull* and Shakespeare's *Hamlet:* A Study of a Dramatic Device," *The American Slavic and East European Review,* XV (Feb., 1956), 103-111.

Woolf, Virginia. "The Russian Point of View," in *The Common Reader.* London, 1925; New York, 1948.

Zaitsev, B. *Chekhov. Literaturnaja biografija.* New York, 1954.

TWENTIETH CENTURY VIEWS

European Authors